PENGUIN BOOKS

IN HARM'S WAY

'Compelling . . . This acid, self-effacing and tautly written book is a journalistic jewel. The notes I made as I read it confirm gems of either description or analysis on almost every page . . . His caustic appraisal of the medium's limitations must be read by all in our business . . . accurate, balanced and self-critical . . . It has humbled us all in the news business. I consider Martin Bell one of the greats'
– Nik Gowing in the *British Journalism Review*

'In its portrayal of the ordeal of Bosnia, and especially Sarajevo, this is a powerful book. It is also one which has much to say about the process of television news-gathering'
– Richard Crampton in *The Times Literary Supplement*

'[Bell's] story is that of a civilized and passionate man cast into situations fraught with danger and livid with mankind's bestialities . . . His sanity, clarity of vision and humanity are rare, especially coming from the savage world he inhabits and records for others'
– Martin Booth in the *Independent*

Martin Bell started as a trainee news assistant in the BBC Norwich newsroom. He joined the staff of BBC TV news in 1965, and his first foreign assignment (covering the overthrow of President Kwame Nkrumah of Ghana) was in 1966. Since then he has worked on assignments in eighty countries, including eleven wars: Vietnam; Middle East (1967 and 1973); Angola; Rhodesia; Biafra; Nicaragua; El Salvador; the Gulf; Croatia; and Bosnia. From 1978 to 1989 he was the BBC Washington correspondent.

Martin Bell was awarded an OBE in 1992. He was also voted Royal Television Society Reporter of the Year in 1977, and again in 1993 for his work in Bosnia.

IN HARM'S WAY

MARTIN BELL

PENGUIN BOOKS

PENGUIN BOOKS

Published by the Penguin Group
Penguin Books Ltd, 27 Wrights Lane, London w8 5tz, England
Penguin Books USA Inc., 375 Hudson Street, New York, New York 10014, USA
Penguin Books Australia Ltd, Ringwood, Victoria, Australia
Penguin Books Canada Ltd, 10 Alcorn Avenue, Toronto, Ontario, Canada m4v 3b2
Penguin Books (NZ) Ltd, 182–190 Wairau Road, Auckland 10, New Zealand

Penguin Books Ltd, Registered Offices: Harmondsworth, Middlesex, England

First published by Hamish Hamilton 1995
This revised edition published in Penguin Books 1996
1 3 5 7 9 10 8 6 4 2

For Melissa and Catherine

CONTENTS

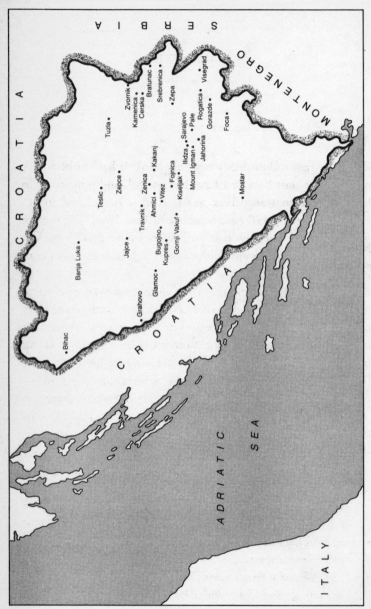

Map of Bosnia Herzegovina

PROLOGUE

This is my first and probably my only book. It has not been easy to write, not least because I have had to spell and punctuate for the first time in thirty-three years. Also it has caused me to reflect more than usual on the life that I have lived. For the last thirteen of those years I wrote nothing down on paper except in indecipherable notebooks, so the option of stringing old scripts together was not available to me.

It is a book about truth and television and war, and about living on one's nerves perhaps rather too long, and surviving in difficult times and dangerous places. It is also a book about bean soup and white suits and lucky charms. It is about a lot of things. The Bosnian war is less its subject than its connecting thread. I have written it because this war has mattered to me more than anything else I have lived through, and still does; and I felt the need to attempt a more permanent record of what happened and how we dealt with it than that which is available in a breathless minute and forty-two seconds on the evening news.

It is a book about journalism but not only for journalists. It is intended to interest real people.

I am solely responsible for the faults in the chapters that follow. If they have any merits as well, the credit for those belongs to the many friends with whom I have worked beyond the rim of the supposedly civilized world, and to the BBC which gave me the freedom not only to live this life but also to write about it. And then when I had done so, though I was sometimes critical of the hand that fed me, they never asked me to cancel out a line of it. Substantial changes have been made since the 1995 edition. That was about a war still in progress. This, we must pray, is about a war that has run its course and is at least in a state of long-term suspension. I have not felt the need to amend any of the judgements that I made. Rather, I believe that subsequent events have confirmed them.

But I did learn a lot from my brief encounter with authorship. I learned that the issues dealt with here mattered not only to me, but to the legion of people – many, many more than I expected – who cared enough to pick up the book and read it. (One even called me 'the Homer of the ninety-second broadcast'. I'm not sure what he meant by that, but it sounded distinctly gratifying.) I learned that my eccentricity baffled the booksellers. They didn't know whether to classify *In Harm's Way* as Biography, Politics, Military or Journalism. One of them even tried Travel. I learned that the subtitle translates into Portuguese as *Reflexoes de um Troglodita de Guerra*. I like being called a war zone troglodyte. I have always preferred the views of others, since I can never be surprised by my own.

My fondest moment was in the course of the book-promotion tour, when I took a flight from Dublin to Manchester. In the airport departure lounge I was spotted by a returning Mancunian. A look of extreme alarm passed over his features. 'Don't tell me,' he said – and at this point his voice dropped to a whisper, 'don't tell me there's a *war* in Manchester?' 'No,' I assured him. 'Or if there is, it's only between the booksellers.'

My thanks are especially due to Kate Jones of Hamish Hamilton for her guidance through the shoals and pitfalls of publishing; to Sasa Schmidtbauer for his courage and logistical skills; to George Steiner for his inspiration a long time ago; to Bernardo Stella and Peter O'Toole for their more recent encouragement; and to Hélène and Liz, whose friendship I shall treasure for all the days of my life.

MARTIN BELL, May 1996

I

MARCHING AS TO WAR

As the most junior soldier in the British army, Private 23398941 Bell M., I reported to Gibraltar barracks in Bury St Edmunds on 18 June 1957. It was at that time the regimental headquarters and training depot of the Suffolk Regiment, in the days when there still was a Suffolk Regiment. It was built like a fortress in Victorian red brick, and indeed for all practical purposes it was a fortress. It kept the soldiers in and the rest of the world out with walls as high as a prison's, and for all practical purposes it was a prison too. But I had no choice but to turn up for this particular rendezvous with destiny. For those were still the years of National Service.

My platoon sergeant, 'Mac' Sennett, was one of those larger-than-life characters, loud and proud, without whom the army would cease to function. Then as now it was run by its non-commissioned officers. Upon the arrival of yet another intake of unschooled recruits his first task was to instil into us a sense of our good fortune in happening to belong to the finest regiment the army had ever known. Others might be more fashionable, ours was the best. His way of doing this was to shout abuse at us. 'Private Bell,' he would exclaim, on spotting some perceived misdemeanour in my turnout or bearing, probably both, 'you are a horrible little man. What are you?'

'A horrible little man, Sergeant,' I dutifully replied, since one's faults are usually more obvious to others, and he didn't seem open to persuasion. And so he went on down the line of Suffolk's finest.

For one who was to hang out so much with soldiers from so many armies in so many wars, my own career in uniform was short and inglorious. I spent two years with the Suffolks, mostly on Internal Security duties, which was how the army classified its mission in trying to deal with the EOKA insurgency (I was one of those who failed to capture Colonel Grivas) and in putting down countervailing riots by Turkish Cypriots in Nicosia. Riots were our regimental specialty. They were to us as polo was to the cavalry or Arctic warfare to the Marines. The casualties in the riots of 1958 were not insignificant, and few of them were ours. Yet we were one of the more docile and disciplined county regiments. The Scots and Irish were exiled to the Troodos mountains. And so innocent of the politics was I, that I never for a moment inquired why we were there, or doing what we were doing.

The training depot also provided me with the first of life's hurdles to fall at. This was the dreaded WOSB, the War Office Selection Board, the process used by the army to separate its sheep from its goats. Our intake included an unusually high number of recruits identified by the regular staff as 'college boys' – to be singled out for double punishment, extra fatigues and possible selection as officers. This led to a daunting leadership and initiative test in the grounds of a decaying country house in Wiltshire. We were divided into competing teams and given impossible tasks, for instance crossing an imaginary river using an assembly of poles, planks and ropes. I failed the test emphatically – on the grounds, I was told, of being too aggressive. (For 'aggressive' read 'insecure': I knew I was out of my league.)

Years later one of my favourite brigadiers, Robin Searby of the 9th/12th Lancers, was posted from duty in Bosnia to Westbury in Wiltshire, to preside over the Regular Commissions

Board, and precisely the ordeal that I had failed in the place where I had failed it. (It hadn't changed: this was a system that knew an 'other rank' when it saw one.) He kindly looked out my records from thirty-seven years back and sent them to me.

Unusually this candidate was invited to sit his intelligence tests twice. The first sitting disclosed an intellect that could best be described as adequate. An enlightened educational adviser was suspicious of the precision of the first result and ordered a resit. On the second paper clear evidence of the powerful intellect of which we are all aware shone through.

(Brigadiers use sarcasm as one of their principal weapons – they learn it on the sarcasm course at Staff College.)

According to the record, the deputy president of the board was wavering. But the president was adamant: 'He directed that the candidate's application was unsuccessful.' Brigadier Robin concluded, 'Was the nation robbed of the services of a great general?' Hardly, I think: not even the services of an adequate second lieutenant. For two years I laboured in the intelligence section of the First Battalion, moving pins on maps and rising slowly through the ranks, but doing little to endear myself to the officer class that I had so signally failed to join.

'The trouble with you, Corporal Bell,' said Captain Pat Hopper, the Signals Officer, 'is that you think too much.' This was because I had amended one of his signals to improve the grammar. It was an unanswerable charge. I did then, and still do. The Intelligence Officer, Lieutenant (later Brigadier) Charles Barnes, put it more sweepingly: 'Why,' he asked, 'am I always blessed with idiots in my section?'

The duties were not arduous and spare time was plentiful. To make use of it, I became secretary of the Corporals' Mess and editor of the regimental magazine, *Castle and Key*. The first of these positions gave me a grandstand view of the drinking habits of the British soldier (a defending officer at a court martial described the absorption of nineteen pints at one sitting as 'normal social drinking'). The second provided me with a platform for opinions about army life which, expressed otherwise, would have led me straight to the guardroom under close escort. Looking back on the file, I realize that the selection board fiasco was not forgotten. Rank still rankled. The following anonymous offering was entitled 'Chain Reaction':

> The Major General cut himself while shaving,
> And cursed the Brigadier, who madly raving,
> Then cast the most chastising and infernal
> Aspersions on the morals of the Colonel,
> Who passed them to the Major; and he, rapt in
> The darkest thoughts, relayed them to the Captain,
> Who rocketed the Subaltern, who rose
> To loose all hell among the NCOs,
> Who in their wrath and mad acerbity
> Picked on one last poor buckshee private – me.

The army in those days was still under Indian influence, and indeed had Indian camp-followers, but I am not sure that the word 'buckshee' is still understood today. In this context it means the last and most expendable character at the end of the chain of command. I am convinced that the process still happens.

Yet I learned. I learned so much that, against all probabilities and predictions, I am proud to have done my time in the Twelfth of Foot. I even acquired a tape of the regimental quick march and played it on Radio Two at Christmas 1993 along with 'The Love Songs of Willie Nelson' in what my foreign editor assured me was a selection of the most tasteless music he had ever heard. I counted that as a real achievement. I wear the regiment's tie and attend some of its reunions. This is not simply because in this company I am one of the youngest old soldiers (it was amalgamated out of existence with a lesser-known outfit from Norfolk shortly after I left). It is also because of what Sergeant Sennett taught me all those years ago, on hazy summer afternoons in a field overlooking the Bury St Edmunds to Newmarket railway line. Some of it, about the naming of parts and judging of distances and identification of bushy-topped trees, has long since vanished from all but the vaguest memory. Nor have I been called on again to strip and reassemble a bren gun, or name its parts. But the fieldcraft stays with me still – about lines of fire and the uses of dead ground and the art of staying alive in dangerous places. I use it just about every day of my working life in Bosnia. I am convinced that it has helped to save my life and the lives of those I work with. For which much thanks to Sergeant Sennett, who could galvanize the barracks and sound reveille with the unaided power of the human voice. It was actually worth being shouted at.

These days the BBC has devised its own form of National Service. It offers a Hostile Environments Course, run by ex-soldiers, to teach fieldcraft and other survival skills to its camera teams and reporters. I excused myself on the grounds that I had already done mine – the theory with the Suffolk Regiment and the practice on various battlefields over the long years.

I left the army in June 1959 without regrets, except that I had been briefly and improbably promoted to the rank of acting sergeant, and I had wished to keep as souvenirs the red sash and swagger stick that went with it. Not many national servicemen got to be sergeants outside the Education Corps, and it was my single accomplishment in life to date, although I noticed that no one else was much impressed. I had no idea what the future held in store for me, except that it would begin with three years at King's College, Cambridge. (If I had been smart enough to do the studying first, I could have avoided the soldiering altogether.)

7

Of two things I was absolutely sure. One was that nothing I had learned in the army would ever be of the slightest use to me. The other was that I would never again be called on to wear its uniform. I was quite wrong on both counts.

There cannot be many people who get out of uniform at the age of twenty and back into it thirty-two years later, but that was what happened to me. They were different uniforms, of course. The old and scratchy battledress of 'Dad's Army' had long since been replaced by more practical combat fatigues. My possible eligibility for these had to do with Saddam Hussein's invasion of Kuwait in August 1990. I calculated that there would clearly be an opening there for old-fashioned war correspondents, and I volunteered for the job at the same time as it came looking for me. It somehow seemed the natural thing to do – my last hurrah as a war reporter. So it was that in October 1990 I headed north on the highway from Dhahran into the Saudi desert, in search of one of the lost tribes of the British army. At least that was how I thought of them. I already suspected that my fate would depend on theirs.

What I found in their encampment was an hierarchical society in which power passed from one generation to another through the same ruling families, as it had done for hundreds of years. The chief man took advice from the elders of the tribe, but when he spoke they listened and obeyed. They had a strong sense of tradition and reverence for their predecessors. Their codes of dress were strict and sometimes eccentric. They not only lived in tents but wore them: after sundown, the tribe's leaders sported strange green and gold tent-like hats, for no other reason than that they always had. Though they had a reputation as fearsome warriors, their conversation was generally pacific, about their pastimes of hunting and horse-riding. If they had ever touched strong drink before (and they sometimes spoke wistfully of it), they had none of it here. And much the same applied to their womenfolk, to whom they referred feelingly but with something of the same affection that they reserved for their horses. Neither wine nor women nor horses were with them here. This was my introduction to the British cavalry.

For the duration of the Gulf war – which was a short war with a long preamble – I was disconnected from civilian life and attached to the Queen's Royal Irish Hussars, whose predecessors had charged at Balaclava but who were now better equipped for survival with the latest Challenger tanks. They belonged to the army's Seventh Armoured Brigade, also known as the Desert Rats, part of the allied force arrayed against the Iraqis occupying Kuwait. Since they were preparing for what Baghdad had announced as the 'Mother of All Battles', I had expected to find them studying at least the Order of Battle of the Revolutionary Guards. They were immersed instead in back copies of *Horse and Hound* and *Field and Stream*.

They were professional soldiers, quite as tough as any infantry, but disguised as Irishmen of uncertain provenance, country gentlemen and various sorts of adventurer. Only the Londonderry accent of Arthur Currie, the Gunnery Officer, spoke plainly of where he came from. None came tougher, or gentler, than their commanding officer, Lieutenant-Colonel Arthur Denaro, a former secret soldier whose exploits in the SAS were spoken of in whispers. Their numbers included a Deceptions Officer, Robin Watt, who was actually the regimental artist, with a sideline in sketching the desert wildlife. And they had resolved the problem of their Irish identity: the Irish Tricolour and the Red Hand of Ulster flew side by side among them. I liked them at once. But they knew as little of us as we did of them, and the period of mutual astonishment lasted for a while.

Each of the two brigades, the Seventh and the Fourth, had a team of seven journalists attached to it. These were divided into three categories: the pencils, the snappers and the oily rags. The pencils were newspaper reporters, the snappers were photographers and the oily rags were television people; a TV reporter was a hybrid, part pencil and part oily rag. The veteran pencil, Phil Jacobson of *The Times*, narrowly saved me from being the oldest man on the field of battle, for even brigadiers come so much younger nowadays. We were issued with finely printed accreditation cards: 'Authority for a British War Correspondent Accompanying an Operational Force'. Mine had the serial number 001. The fiction held that we were *with* the army but not *of* it (which was supposed to be a significant distinction in the event of our being captured, though we somehow doubted if the Iraqis would see it that way). For all practical purposes we were soldiers without the means of self-defence. We were thrust into desert camouflage uniforms topped with a choice of steel helmets or sun hats. (Hats, floppy, ridiculous was the quasi-military way in which we described them, and only Kate Adie had the courage to wear one on camera – but then probably only she could have got away with it.)

We were under army command and discipline, we took battlefield first-aid courses, we were trained and equipped against chemical warfare, and we dug trenches. Did we ever dig trenches! We dug trenches until our picks broke and our hands blistered. We dug trenches until our news editors wondered why we weren't filing any more. We dug trenches and then fell into them, because we were ordered to observe a total blackout at night. Our chief minder, Major James Myles, an infantryman of great charm but matching zeal, assured us that this was the professional and soldierly thing to do. It would earn us the respect of our peers, he said. He also then fell into the trenches, and nearly missed the war on account of it. We dug trenches in the sand, and in the rock which lurked just under the sand, at every stop in that trackless desert from Saudi Arabia to Kuwait.

I had supposed that the era of trench warfare was over, but it was as if the new doctrines of rapid manoeuvre were for Staff College use only and did not apply to us peons in the desert. It gave the real soldiers great amusement to watch us, even more to photograph us for their family albums, with special focus on the discomfort of supposed television 'celebrities'. And they never failed to advise us on our shortcomings. The Royal Engineers, the world's leading experts in trenches and bunkers, and serious hoarders of mechanical diggers, talked a very good game indeed. One of them, surveying our attempt at a bomb shelter, said he would give us a nine point five for artistic impression but a rather lower mark for technical merit. I later forgave them in Bosnia, but only just, because of the dangers we shared.

At the time I suspected that these media response teams were no more than an ingenious scheme to raise the morale of the troops in the field and take their minds off the forthcoming war. We were the pick and shovel brigade, the Desert Storm cabaret act: we gave them something to laugh at and write home about. But what this was in fact, following the chaotic press arrangements of the Falklands campaign, was the army's new way of dealing with the press.

It was not the preferred way. The preferred way, at least of the old army (cavalry and Guards), was to summon the hacks to battlefield or barracks, inform them of the latest triumphs and achievements, and then send them packing back to their ink-stained lairs. But this was thought to be hardly appropriate in the world of the 1990s. The new way was not only to allow us full access under controlled conditions, with a travelling censorship system operating alongside, but to invite us to share the dangers and hardships of the front-line soldiers in such a way that we could hardly fail to identify with them. The process was called 'bonding', and – unusually for an army plan – it worked. Most plans do not survive their first brush with reality, but this was an exception. Or perhaps it was the Irish Hussars, and the Royal Scots Dragoon Guards and the Staffordshire Regiment with them, who made it an exception.

The plan was much criticized by those free spirits of journalism who operated outside the media response teams and who roamed the fringes of the battlefield gathering what they could. They believed that we had somehow defected from principled reporting and sold our souls for a mess of army combat rations. The most prominent of these, and the least restrained with his criticism, predicted a desert débâcle which never occurred. He wrote a lot about bodybags. Another denounced us as the tame press, 'Mythmakers of the Gulf war'. To hell with them both, I thought, and went on shovelling.

In fact they probably had a better time of it than we did, and not only because they dwelt in hotels and dug no trenches. In the war's long gestation period, which was an open season for creative and speculative journalism, they filed more than they knew. We, on the other hand, under canvas and censorship, knew more than we filed. Much more. We had the Desert Storm battle plan explained to us, all 120 pages of it, ten days before the first armoured units rolled across the Iraqi border. So did every front-line soldier: it was the way the modern army operated. But to have hinted at it, even had there been no censorship, would have endangered their lives as well as ours. Journalists are not good keepers of secrets, but only the desert knew ours.

We spent forty days and nights in that desert — there seemed to be some kind of resonance there. We filled our days with unusable briefings about the air war, and at night saw the distant flashes of falling bombs. Only one solitary Scud missile came back at us. We were assured that the opening ground bombardment would pack the explosive equivalent of 76,000 Scuds. We noted the language of euphemism in which this business was done: the Iraqis were never killed, but rather had their 'assets written down'. It must have been quite uncomfortable for them. Military people talk this nonsense to hide from themselves the reality of what they are doing. Intercepted radio traffic was more direct, and included desperate pleas from forward Iraqi units for anything with four wheels on it to come and rescue their wounded. Censorship blocked that too.

Because of the censorship, and the total ban on anything operational, we were driven back on endless colour stories about Our Boys in the Desert. It was as tabloid as I have ever been – the *Sun* would have been proud of me. But we had in our gang of seven a real master of the art, Colin Wills of the *Sunday Mirror*, and I doubt if he gave me a passing grade on any of it, except for the story of Pedro the Rat. Pedro was the genuine article, a real desert rat, a rat with good PR. He was the friend and mascot of a military policeman, Andy Martorell, and lived in his top pocket. They directed the traffic together, on the principle that two pairs of eyes were better than one. The story generated such a response from the British public, who seem rather to like it when their army goes to war, especially in the company of animals, that not only did the soldier receive fan mail afterwards, but so did the desert rat: a parcel of hamster food sent by a home-front admirer.

Looking back on it, I confess that this was hardly serious journalism, and we probably were manipulated in some measure into composing such military mood music, if only because it was all that was available to us. But it was harmless enough, it satisfied a real public curiosity about what life was like for soldiers waiting for war – there were 32,000 families at home with a strong personal interest in the outcome – and it had us in the right place at the right time when the war eventually began.

Most of all it taught some necessary lessons both for this war and others that followed. These lessons were learned in the highly unofficial Arthur Denaro War College, a roughly land-scaped patch of desert where the Irish Hussars held their regular study sessions, with their tanks and trucks parked around it. There was plenty of raw material for the inevitable sand-table, and a sign saying 'Bad Guys' was stuck into the map of Iraq. The curriculum was wide-ranging, from the plan of battle to the Iraqi defence belt and the role of the media in warfare. I was obliged to contribute a short speech, as the only one old enough to have served in Vietnam. I assured them that the American generals who now commanded them had been colonels in the Vietnam war, and had developed the current doctrine of over-whelming force from the incremental mistakes that had been made there. Whatever the *Independent* warned to the contrary, there was such a thing as the balance of forces, and it would not be a long-drawn-out war.

Most usefully, the desert academy taught me about fear and how to deal with it. These were lessons that applied as much to a reporter responsible for a TV news team of six or seven as to a colonel responsible for a regiment of 400: and I carried them over to the coming Balkan wars. 'None of us,' said Arthur Denaro, 'can really conceive what a modern armoured battle is going to be like. We have to be aware that people are going to freeze up in the gunner's seat and drivers will miss a gear.' He taught us that there was nothing un-British in feeling fear or talking about it. 'We are all going to be frightened. I'd be concerned if I had a guy who wasn't frightened. It's not fear that concerns me but how he is going to cope with it.'

I learned to cope with it by looking at the sunrise. It was a technique which I worked out in the Gulf and used again in Bosnia. As I always get up early, I would watch the sun rise and say to myself: today is the first day of the rest of my life, and I shall do whatever business I have to do, but I and those with me are going to conduct ourselves in such a way that we get to see that same sun set. So far we always have – with the shattering exception of a close and good friend who died in Bosnia. I was not with him at the time, and will never know whether it would have made any difference if I had been.

The prayer of Sir Jacob Astley before the battle of Edgehill in 1642 was also a useful standby: 'O Lord thou knowest how busy I must be this day, if I forget Thee, do not Thou forget me.'

In truth we were more apprehensive about the Gulf war than we needed to be. I even went so far as to write a farewell letter to my daughters and to their mother, in case the worst should happen. (I left it in a safe place, and threw it away hurriedly and rather ashamedly afterwards: I had clearly been too much under the influence of the bodybag theorists.) But fear can strike unexpectedly, and is no respecter of rank. At Arthur Denaro's last briefing, beside his tank 'Churchill' on the morning of the assault, I noticed that one of the officers was grey in the face and trembling badly; he bravely stayed with it – *that* was courage – but had difficulty functioning normally for the next hundred hectic hours.

I was lucky. I had with me the calming presence of cameraman Nigel Bateson, who also figured large in the Bosnian campaign (with his size, he could hardly figure small in anything). We were also well served by our travelling companions, Major 'Jumbo' Lloyd and Sergeant Andy Richardson, the Gunner and the Grenadier, with whom we shared the battery major's Warrior armoured personnel carrier, and went to war alongside the Irish Hussars. And it helped that the long wait was over and a fragment of history was happening around us, as British tanks rolled into action for the first time since the Second World War.

What we had not expected, but were delighted to discover, was that it was not that much of a war, even to the extent that for most of the way we could ride on top of our armour instead of hiding in it. That was a relief, for it is no small challenge to photograph a war through the postage-stamp-sized window at the back of a Warrior.

The omens were spectacularly forbidding. The sun was blacked out by smoke from a hundred burning oil wells, and the skies wept drops of oil. But darkness at noon was as close to Armageddon as we got. We crossed the Iraqis' breached defences with hardly a trace to be seen of their massed divisions, and were twenty miles into Iraq before making contact with the southernmost elements of their retreating army. Their resistance was sporadic and ineffective, and most of them wished only to surrender. To impress those who didn't, the brigade commander, Brigadier Patrick Cordingley, halted the advance at nightfall and called down the most intensive artillery bombardment in British history, made possible by the army's new multiple rocket launchers. It looked like a fireworks show from hell, its impact was deafening and it shook the desert floor beneath our feet. The brigadier was not at all convincing in his role as trained killer. 'Poor bastards,' he said, 'I can't help feeling sorry for them.'

Those who survived surrendered at first light. The squadrons of tanks swept past them, and past thousands like them, on an accelerated dash into Kuwait and across the Basra Road. The only casualties – alas, more severe in 4 Brigade – were from an erring American 'tank-buster' aircraft which tried to bust the wrong side's tanks. By then the Irish Hussars had hauled out their Union Jacks and were flying them from every turret, not as an expression of nationalism, but to give the Americans the help they needed to distinguish between friend and foe. Had they been able to listen closely they could also have heard the sound of Arthur Denaro's ancestral hunting horn. The advance across the desert was not the 'Mother of All Battles' that had been advertised, but more like a live-fire exercise with Iraqi extras.

It was then that my problems really began, for the climax of the war was the filing nightmare that every journalist dreads: so much to say and absolutely no means of saying it. Because of the speed of the advance our satellite dish never caught up with us, but was adrift for three days in the desert. On the fourth we borrowed a helicopter and found it. Colonel John King, the chief censor and commander of the forward transmission unit, which included the dish and was nowhere near as far forward as I needed it, held it where it was for a few hours while I pieced together a report for that evening's news. Kate Adie, travelling with it, was outstandingly supportive. Colleagues do sometimes help each other, even in journalism, and I shall be for ever grateful to her.

The result, though doubtless flawed, was a first-hand and reasonably vivid account of the British army in action. I don't know whether it was 'tame', but at least it was accurate and original and untouched by censorship; and it saw the war as the front-line soldiers saw it. But it was only just in time to rate as news rather than history. I learned the lesson and have tried to apply it since: look after the logistics and the tactics will look after themselves.

At that point our ambiguous special status, part privileged and part captive, ended. The media response teams were discharged from their duties and dispersed into the real world. In Kuwait City's battered airport I hitched a ride on the executive jet of Britain's Gulf war commander, General Sir Peter de la Billière, in the company of a group of newspaper editors who had been given a lightning tour of the field of battle; the army's idea of 'bonding' with the press seemed a great deal more comfortable among its upper echelons, but I had still learned more in my trenches. In Dhahran I took the longest bath of my life to wash off the accumulated grime of the desert sandstorms. I handed back the uniform and helmet and ridiculous floppy hat without regret. I would soldier no more.

I was quite convinced that this was the end of an already longish career as a war reporter. What I had no way of knowing was that it was, in a sense, just the beginning; and that what I had learned in uniform, on combat-related issues from fear to fieldcraft, would be put to vital use in the years ahead.

Of course it is not necessary to have been a soldier to be a war reporter – though I have known some for whom it was a substitute for the career they never had. (One of our number filed for Reuters and served as occasional watchkeeper with the Royal Scots Dragoon Guards.) We are, or should be, unrepentant civilians, but it helps to have a certain sympathy with soldiers – by which I mean real soldiers, not out-of-control militiamen or thugs in uniform. Real soldiers have a genuine and informed dislike of warfare; and that applies to the most battle-hardened of them regardless of rank, from General Norman Schwarzkopf of the United States army to Sergeant Andy Mason of the Desert Rats.

Andy was our combat photographer in the Gulf war. He was a paratrooper who had been promoted in the field in the Falklands campaign, and had served in some unquiet corners of Northern Ireland. We called him the tough and ruthless one, which sometimes came out as rough and toothless, because his various scrapes with adversity had left their mark. He later turned up implausibly under a blue helmet in Bosnia, but he was hardly a natural-born peacekeeper, and barely came through with his sergeant's stripes intact. In the Gulf war he was more widely quoted than any officer, because of his experience and availability (he worked from the tent next door). He knew the stuff we needed.

'Andy, which was the worst of your wars?' we asked.

'All wars are worst,' he answered.

2

PEACEKEEPERS' ACCOMPLICES

It was 10 April 1992, the end of the first week of Bosnia's war. I had made it through the road-blocks from Belgrade to Sarajevo, but was spinning wheels, hitting brick walls, getting nowhere. Usually you can pull the levers of experience and they point you one way or another, they show you paths round immovable obstacles – but not this time. Twenty-five years of reporting other wars weren't helping me with this one. I had not even got far enough forward for the fieldcraft to kick in. Sinister tales were seeping into the capital, especially from eastern Bosnia along the Drina valley, of genocide on a scale unknown in Europe for fifty years. The second hardest part was to separate truth from rumour. The hardest part was to get to the valley to do so in the first place.

In war reporting the last road-block is the one where luck runs out – that was a constant, from Vietnam to Bosnia. We hit our last road-block five miles from Zvornik, a town on the Drina that Serbs and Muslims used to share – and were still sharing, although expecting war, when we had passed through it two days earlier. There were four of us in the team: Katharina Geissler with the camera, Vladimir Marjanovic as interpreter, myself, and a German soundman who had already fallen silent as if shell-shocked, and whom I now realized it would have been kinder to leave behind – you never find these things out until too late. And the prospects were hardly inviting.

Drunk and dangerous and barely coherent, a Serb militiaman stood squarely across our road. If I die and go to hell, I expect him to be there at the gates to greet me. No, he assured us, we could not pass. He had orders, and even if he hadn't he would not allow it. We had no business to be there. We had no papers with the correct official stamp in Cyrillic script. We were Ustasha, Croatian Fascist spies. If we did not turn back we would be shot, and he left us in no doubt as to who would do the shooting. He unslung his rifle and fingered the safety-catch speculatively.

We beat a prudent retreat. At the local command post the resourceful Vladimir had better luck with the man's superior officer. Our mission was explained (there were reports, we said falsely, of massacres of Serbs – and these did occur soon afterwards), our credentials were examined, confidences were exchanged over coffee and slivovitz, and much was made of my personal relationship with Zeljko Raznjatovic, also known as Arkan, the leading freelance warlord of the neighbour-hood. (I had profiled his paramilitary 'Tigers' quite extensively in the previous war, when he led a campaign to liberate Serbs from ruined Croatian villages – at least, the villages were ruined by the time his Tigers had done with them. He was a man of great fluency, dynamism and surface charm: but he was also an alleged war criminal, and not known for taking prisoners.)

The Arkan connection unblocked the road and, at the second attempt, we were through. Soon enough we came upon the reason why the Serbs that day were a little shy of visitors. Three miles ahead a Muslim policeman signalled us urgently into a side road, and we caught up with the rearguard of a great and forced migration of whole communities of Muslims and some Croats. Here it was in its early stages. It later came to be known as ethnic cleansing.

This egregious euphemism was Bosnia's contribution to the

language of war. It covered a multitude of crimes from intimidation to murder. It took its origins from the training manuals of the old Yugoslav army, where advancing units were ordered to 'clean' or 'cleanse' – the word *ciscenje* means either – the area ahead of them of mines or obstacles or enemy. As the Serbs adopted it, all non-Serbs became their enemy, civilians as much as soldiers. The defenders fled. They were lightly armed, demoralized and no match for Mr Arkan's commandos.

At least 2,000 of the victims had just arrived and were camped in the next village. They had been evicted without warning. They had no possessions but what they could carry – and a mother with a babe in her arms could carry little else. There was no transport for them and no protection. Along mountain paths and mule tracks from the most remote settlements, some 20,000 of them were on the move that day, heading for safer territory towards Tuzla on a trail of tears. I shall remember it for the rest of my life as the day that Bosnia died – the old multi-ethnic and shared Bosnia, the Yugoslav Bosnia. The map was being redrawn before our eyes. There are times when journalism seems almost privileged, like having a front seat at the making of history. But this was less a privilege than a burden – that we could see all this happening, and yet could do nothing to prevent it.

The people didn't know that. They treated us like the saviours we certainly were not. They applauded us wildly as we passed among them. Since their ordeal began, which was by now quite widely known, they had seen nothing of the United Nations, the European Community monitors, the International Red Cross or any of the outside agencies usually so busy in ex-Yugoslavia. We were the first indication they had received that the world beyond their valleys either knew of their plight or cared. What they did not know – and neither at the time did we, though we were both to find out later – was that there would be a world of difference between knowing and caring, and indeed between caring and acting.

'Terrible things are happening,' said one, a schoolmaster, 'and have been happening for two days. It is a terror which has been made by the Serbs and is being made right now. You can even now hear some shells.' We could, and so could the straggling column of refugees which had come to a halt around us at a fork in the road. People flinched as the crump of artillery stirred the morning air. They appealed for our help. I felt as helpless as they did – and guilty besides, since I had a set of wheels which I was keeping for my purposes instead of using to help them. But with Vladimir's assistance I gave them the speech that they wanted to hear, and promised to tell the world.

We returned to Sarajevo after further adventures on the highway from Tuzla, threading our way through thousands of fleeing Muslims. It was the last time we were able to use that road, for the war was closing in on every village. I am not by temperament a campaigning sort of journalist. Reporting is what I do for a living: it is a job, not a *jihad*. But this was clearly more than just another news story – or for that matter just another war – and I knew I had a responsibility to those people beyond the mere professional business of describing what had become of them. To this was added already an element of doubt – that for all the reputed power of television, whatever I did would hardly make a dinar's worth of difference.

I was pacing the floor of our edit room at the Hotel Serbia near Sarajevo, for I am always unable to think straight sitting down, trying to do justice to what we had seen and to find the words for Katharina's remarkable pictures, when I saw a motor-cade with Serbian police out-riders drawing up at the hotel entrance beneath our balcony. It was clearly depositing an important personage. An important personage was just what the circumstances called for, so I dropped what I was doing and hurried down.

It was my first meeting with Colm Doyle, the Irish army major who was Lord Carrington's personal representative in Bosnia and the only diplomatic mediator on the ground with whom both sides would deal. Except that I did not so much meet him as harangue him, even as he was trying to check into the hotel, with a breathless account of the ethnic cleansing and a demand that he have it stopped. He was a bit taken aback by this outburst from a total stranger, and pointed out that he had only just arrived, but he would certainly do what he could. He took it up with the Bosnian Serb leadership the next day, including some of the detail that I had given him, and was met by the usual tactic of brazen denial. In the Balkans, as Misha Glenny has memorably pointed out, the only truth is a lie.

Colm was not new to Sarajevo. In the winter before the war began, when the Muslims were preparing for independence and the Serbs for war, he led the small team of European Community monitors who were trying to keep the peace between them. A man of inexhaustible patience and energy, he was recruited after the outbreak of war by Lord Carrington to be his eyes and ears on the ground and to broker local ceasefires wherever possible. It was an impossible task for these agreements were broken almost as soon as they were reached, and at one of the signing ceremonies at the airport everyone had to take cover under the table on which the ceasefire had been signed.

Both sides were set on a collision course at a terrible cost to their people, and the war had already taken on such a momentum that the most gifted of mediators would have been powerless to prevent it. But that did not mean that they should stop trying, or that we as journalists stood neutrally between those who wished to intensify the conflict and those who wished to end it. There were two chief peacemakers in the field and both became friends and allies. One was Colm Doyle for the European Community, the other was Lew MacKenzie for the United Nations.

Lewis MacKenzie of Princess Patricia's Canadian Light Infantry was at the time in the throes of promotion from brigadier to major-general. He had no way of knowing it but he was about to become a national hero and the most famous living Canadian – at least for the few months of celebrity which is all that television allows. He was one of the veterans of UN peacekeeping and indeed wrote the book on it.* He had served in eight previous missions from Egypt to Vietnam, and it was this experience which qualified him for his most difficult appointment of all: chief of staff to the UN Protection Force which was supposed to police the ceasefire in Croatia from a base in Sarajevo.

It was a position which came with two immediate drawbacks. One was that it was largely a desk job, in which he would have to handle the paperwork for the force commander, Lieutenant-General Satish Nambiar of India. General MacKenzie was a man of action whose idea of relaxation was to risk his neck on the motor-racing circuit; he was not a natural-born paper-shuffler. The other drawback was that within three weeks of his arrival in Bosnia a war broke out around him, the like of which even he had not seen before. The UN's new headquarters in the PTT building came under fire, its vehicles were targeted and its soldiers abducted at road-blocks. It was the only known case in military history where a headquarters staff received messages of sympathy and concern from the front-line troops in the field.

This was a sudden emergency for which the UN did not have even an inadequate mandate: it had no mandate at all. But as the casualties rose, and tens of thousands of desperate refugees

---

* *Peacekeeper*, by L. MacKenzie, Vancouver, Douglas & McIntyre, 1993.

came flooding across fluctuating lines of conflict, it could hardly do nothing either. The war was already beyond the reach of diplomacy, but the humanitarian crisis had to be dealt with by somebody. And along with Colm Doyle's mediation efforts the UN was, as General MacKenzie described it, 'the only game in town'. So he left his desk job behind, and moved with alacrity to become the commander of endangered convoys and broker of improbable ceasefires. His total operational force was rather like a stage army, trying to appear larger and more formidable than it actually was. It consisted only of the general himself, his Canadian ADC, Major Steve Gagnon, his resourceful Argentinian staff officer, Major Jorge De La Reta, and a handful of Swedish security guards and French drivers. Lew MacKenzie was the only general in the world commanding a mere platoon.

The war was unstoppable. On some days the fighting was so intense that the UN could only build up its bunkers and shelter in them until the storm passed. On other days it could move about the city and save lives. In the forty-eight hours of the 2nd and 3rd of May it did both. This turning point in the war and in the UN's mission began with an attack by government soldiers of the Territorial Defence Force (the Bosnian army was not yet formed) on the officers' club of the old Yugoslav army, whose troops were still quartered in Sarajevo. I knew there was serious trouble because we were being threatened, most unusually, by hoodlums on the government side – and because the trams had stopped. They were not to run again for nearly two years.

The Serbs retaliated with a fierce artillery and tank bombardment which set fire to the tramcars, ruined the City Hall, devastated the main shopping street and led to many civilian casualties – and also, incidentally, to a heated argument among the journalists caught up in it about whether it was better to stay where we were or to flee. As usual, I led the escape artists.

Also caught up in it, incredibly, were a group of more than a dozen Chinese tourists. They had come on a package holiday from Peking to admire the marvels of non-aligned Yugoslavia, and were staying at the Hotel Europa which was rather conspicuously aligned in the Serbs' target zone. Somehow no one had told them there was a war on. The hotel offered features which were not in their travel brochure: incoming tank fire and a running battle in the streets outside. If their guide, who was the only one among them who spoke English, had not been a chainsmoker before this ordeal, he certainly was one now. He spoke at three puffs to the sentence: 'We come Belgrade and ask how we get Sarajevo, and they say there the bus! We check into hotel and I see hole in window. I say maybe somebody shooting here. What a night! I spend whole night in toilet.'

Faridoun Hemani of the news agency WTN asked if he had a message for his family in China. 'Simple message. Don't come Yugoslavia.'

The Bosnian President, Alija Izetbegovic, would have done well to heed the Chinese advice. He had avoided the bombardment of his capital, having been away at a European Community negotiating session in Lisbon, but in escaping one hazard he landed right in the middle of another. For on his return to Sarajevo airport that night he was kidnapped by the Serbs, together with his bodyguard and his daughter Sabina who acted as his interpreter. The Serbs, who at that time still controlled the airport, wished to exchange him for their corps commander, General Kukanjac, who was trapped at his headquarters in Sarajevo and under siege. Now the UN was no longer marginalized: its services were in sudden demand, and General MacKenzie was asked to arrange the exchange.

It might have been possible if he had been able to deploy more troops, or more than the four armoured personnel carriers which were all that the UN had available. It might also have been possible if General Kukanjac had not then demanded not only his own evacuation, but also that of his entire headquarters staff of 400: as their commander, he could hardly leave them behind.

The president was being held at Lukavica barracks on the Serb-held side of the airport. To negotiate the deal, General MacKenzie had to talk his way through a crowd of angry demonstrators at the gates. 'We are here to get your sons back,' he said. 'We are here to help you. Let us in or your wounded will die.' He had supposed that they were Muslims clamouring for the return of their president. In fact they were Serbs wishing to have him strung up as a war criminal. But the absence of an interpreter probably helped, and his all-purpose plea got him through.

The agreement that General MacKenzie and Colm Doyle negotiated depended on both sides' good faith which was definitely not to be taken for granted, but it was the best that they could manage under the circumstances. The bodyguard remained in Lukavica as a hostage. President Izetbegovic and Sabina were taken under UN escort to General Kukanjac's headquarters in Sarajevo. There the larger convoy formed, to include twenty of Kukanjac's vehicles, as much equipment as they could carry, and all of his men. The plan was that the UN would lead this convoy back through the city, with the president's part of it peeling off towards his office, and the Serbs heading out for the safety of Lukavica.

But it was too tempting a target for the mainly Muslim Defence Force. They had held the barracks under siege for days, and now their quarry was escaping under UN protection. Four hundred yards down the narrow side road, they intercepted it. They wrenched open the door of an army ambulance and fired into it at point-blank range. At least seven of the headquarters staff were killed, including a colonel shot while he pleaded for the life of one of his soldiers. The two endangered leaders made it to safety – President Izetbegovic to the Presidency and General Kukanjac to the barracks at Lukavica. But most of the general's soldiers were not with him – some were dead and the rest were taken prisoner. He was later quite falsely accused of deserting his troops. In fact there was nothing he could have done about it. He was under UN escort, and the UN lacked the firepower to protect them.

The press – especially television – was a witness to all this except the violent and bloody denouement. We had been present with the demonstrators at the gates of Lukavica, we had been close to the troubled negotiations and accompanied the UN convoy to General Kukanjac's headquarters; there his chief of staff, Colonel Jarkevic, had given us a guided tour of the now ruined barracks, and expressed well-founded concern about the safety of his men. He himself was wounded in the ambush and was lucky to escape with his life.

The incident left a deep impression on me, partly because of my closeness to the negotiators. War reporting is not only a chronicling process, but a learning process, and knowledge illuminates new areas of ignorance: the more you know, the more you know that you don't know. Some of the lessons were particular to this case and some applied more generally.

Lesson number one was to stay with it. The reason why I was not a witness to the ambush was that it happened in the evening, and I had been compelled to break out to our base in Ilidza and file for the *Six O'Clock News*. There are many arguments for a rolling and continuous news service, but quality of reporting is not one of them. More means worse. The multiplication of deadlines takes us away from the real world, and drives us back into our offices and edit rooms. It is safer there, and we may find reasons to stay. There were days in Sarajevo when my radio colleague, who was already working for a rolling news service, had to broadcast as many as twenty-eight separate reports. Not only did he never leave the Holiday Inn, he hardly had time to pick up the phone and talk to the UN spokesman.

Lesson number two was that the department of preconceived notions was alive and well and living in distant newsrooms. The full story of the convoy incident took a little time to piece together – from Lew MacKenzie and Steve Gagnon, from survivors such as Colonel Jarkevic, from doctors in the military hospital and from what could be seen of the hijacked and blood-stained vehicles. It was a story – unusually – of government forces probably acting on their own initiative but attacking Serbs and killing them in cold blood. The war was then four weeks old, and had followed the well-established pattern of Serbs attacking Muslims. We had reported it like that because it had been like that. But now it seemed that both black hats and white hats were taking on shades of grey. In talking to London, I sensed some consumer resistance. 'Are you sure about this ambush? It's not on the wires yet.'

'It will be – and yes, I am sure about it.'

'The casualty figures seem a bit high.'

'The casualty figures *are* a bit high. I've talked to the doctors, I've seen the inside of the ambulance, General Kukanjac is hopping mad, and I know well enough what happened. Look, this is the Balkans. Perhaps it's not as simple as you would like it to be, but Serbs can be victims too.'

The third and most enduring lesson was that, in peacekeeping, we in the press were engaged in an entirely new relationship with the military – that is, the blue-helmeted military. Of course we had our differences with the UN – usually over interpretations of its mandate – but we were fundamentally its partners and not its antagonists. We shared its dangers and frustrations. We were to some extent responsible for its deployment in the first place. We wished it to succeed.

At the time we were travelling between Serb- and Muslim-held sections of the city in such a nondescript camera car that we flew a Union Jack on it as a badge of neutrality. In the evening we would celebrate our survival by holding a flag-lowering ceremony to the music of Elgar's *Pomp and Circumstance* – once it even drew a salute from a passing Serb colonel. In the midst of the mayhem a show of Britishness seemed somehow reassuring. Lew MacKenzie and Colm Doyle were welcome regular guests at these occasions – and not just because we wished to pump them for information about what was going on. A lot of the time they did not know what was going on; some of the time we did. But we saw it from different perspectives, and at the end of the day we gave each other a sort of 'reality check'.

It was a striking contrast to the media–military relationship that I was used to, even in the Gulf. Soldiers and journalists are not always like-minded people. 'Journalists,' said my grandmother, 'are a shady lot and seldom the sons of gentlemen.' (She should know, because she married one: Robert Bell was news editor of the London *Observer* in its heyday.) Most soldiers in their war-fighting function would probably agree. To them we still are a shady lot – undisciplined, unkempt and unpatriotic. They regard us with suspicion and astonishment, which we reciprocate. The issues that divide us range from casualty reporting to censorship to operational security. Our instinct is to publish and be damned, theirs is to censor and be safe.

But in peacekeeping it was different. The usual frictions and difficulties did not arise. The UN was running an open and transparent operation. It had no codes and no secrets except possibly its contingency plans for withdrawal. There were fourteen of them. It had no intelligence gathering except what it called military information (though that was actually intelligence by another name) and it needed more of that than it had. That was where the press could be of use. In most cases it was on the ground before the UN arrived, went to front lines where the UN had no access, and had long-established contacts with the warlords. The average UN field commander served for only six months; he was just getting to know his patch and its brigand-commanders when it was time for him to leave and be replaced by another. There was a time during the twilight of the UN's mandate when its Bosnia commander was on leave, his right-hand man was new to the job, and the UN's institutional memory was represented by a lieutenant-colonel who had served in Sarajevo for a mere two months. He knew about as much about Bosnia as I did about the tribe of Hussars to which he belonged (not my Irish ones but another sort – the landed gentry in uniform). Officers sped with bewildering frequency through an ever-revolving door. The warlords knew this weakness, and exploited it.

So, inevitably, in peacekeeping and subsequently peace enforce-ment, a flow of information occurred between the UN – and later IFOR – and the press. It worked both ways. We knew things they needed to know, both for informed decision-making and for their own safety. We had been there before they arrived, and would still be there when they left. Others may see this differ-ently, but for me it was not unprofessional behaviour or a breach of whatever codes were supposed to govern us to pass informa-tion to them. I had always wished to be declared redundant as a war correspondent and become a peace correspondent instead. And to help the UN was to serve the cause of peace.

Once in the course of the Muslim–Croat war of 1993, I acquired a map of the two sides' front-line positions near Vitez. It showed them in detail, ruin by ruin and trench by trench. I needed it for the safety of my own team working there, but I knew it would also be helpful to the UN since the fighting cut across one of the blue helmets' main supply routes. I had no qualms whatever in passing the map to them. (This helped us to break the ice with the Coldstream Guards, whose attitudes to the press – as to so much else – were not exactly born of the age we live in. They also benefited from viewing our front-line footage of the fighting raging around them. From that point on we enjoyed a more relaxed relationship with them – or at least with their No. 2 Company and with Majors Other Windsor-Clive and Bill Cubitt who commanded it.)

Journalism has often been a cover for espionage, and for all I know may still be. Spot-the-spy is a fascinating game to play among one's colleagues. Journalists are licensed to ask militarily sensitive questions in dodgy places. But in all my time no intelligence service has ever asked me to work for it – except once and very briefly, and I declined. However, when my war zone wanderings are over and if I ever have grandchildren, I know how I wish the conversation to go. 'Grandfather,' they will ask with their eyes aglow, 'were you ever a spy?'

'Why yes,' I shall answer, 'actually I was. Just once, I spied for peace.'

3

THE ROAD TO WAR

There was a sound which said, you are now entering Bosnia. In later months it could have been the machine-gun and mortar fire in any one of seventeen different war zones. In November 1991 it was the clanking of wooden sleepers on the great iron bridge which carried both road and rail traffic across the river Sava from Serbia. On the far side of the bridge, at that time, the hedgerows were bristling with signs urging peace in Bosnia. They had seen the war in Croatia and they knew what it boded. One of the signs said simply, 'No Vukovars here'. The Croatian river town had been under siege since the summer, and had fallen to the Serbs two days before. A Serb colonel told me, as a matter not just of record but of *pride*, that they had poured down 2,000,000 shells on it. By the time they had captured it they had levelled it. To the victor went the prize, and the prize was a pile of rubble, like some Stalingrad on the Danube.

Now, across the clanking bridge, I was in Bosnia for the first time, accompanying a convoy of Vukovar's survivors. They were women, children and old men – the young men had been removed to prisoner-of-war camps, or had disappeared – and they were taking the roundabout route, initially under Serb escort, to Croatia. Bosnia at that time was a sort of middle kingdom, still accessible to both sides in the Croatian war. And because a fragile if threatened peace prevailed there, the Bosnian town of Dvorovi was chosen as the handover point for Vukovar's survivors. (My interpreter Vladimir Marjanovic remarked feelingly that Dvorovi, my first Bosnian dateline, was the only one that I ever learned to pronounce to his satisfaction.)

It was not an exchange, for the Croats had no prisoners to hand back: they had just surrendered. Rather it was an early example of the practice later known as ethnic cleansing – the forcible removal of whole populations, under the gun, from land on which they had lived for hundreds of years. Then, as later, the international agencies were on hand as witnesses, guarantors and in some sense accomplices of these grim transactions. They took no pride in it, but saved lives by their presence.

A German European Community monitor who had been based in Bosnia for some weeks and had observed the storm gathering there, drew me aside. 'Do you know,' he said, 'that what we have seen in Croatia has been only the beginning? I am sure of this, that the war when it comes here will be much worse. And we have but a few weeks to stop it.'

He was right, of course. But in those early days hopes still rested in negotiation. Lord Carrington for the European Community and Cyrus Vance and Herb Okun for the United Nations were touring the Balkan capitals seeking the basis of a global settlement for all the republics of ex-Yugoslavia. If they failed, the war would spread from one republic to another, inevitably. Historically and geographically, Bosnia stood next in line.

Inevitably? The BBC, to put it mildly, does not encourage its reporters to trespass into areas of political speculation. But later, surrounded by the death and destruction of Bosnia's war, I had to ask myself whether it could not at some point have been prevented. A highly placed friend of mine, much closer to the detail and documents than I could ever be, described the sequence of diplomatic events as 'a catalogue of missed opportunities'. George Schultz, Ronald Reagan's Secretary of State, called the conduct of the allies over Bosnia 'pathetic and shameful'.

To this day I don't know the answer – civil wars are hard to start, and once started all but unstoppable. But I *do* know the issue which future historians, with access to the documents of our time, will analyse with particular rigour. That is the recognition of Slovenia and Croatia, agreed by the foreign ministers of the European Community at a meeting in Brussels in December 1991. Up to that point the common and principled position of the Twelve had been that a settlement for some of the republics had to await a settlement for all of them. The dangers of a separate deal for Slovenia and Croatia, though it was strongly argued by the German Foreign Minister Hans-Dietrich Genscher, were well known at the time.

The then Secretary-General of the United Nations, Javier Perez de Cuellar, in the final days of a distinguished term of office, wrote to the President of the Council of Ministers, Hans van den Broek of Holland, to convey the sense of foreboding expressed by Cyrus Vance after meeting many of the main players, including the Bosnian leadership. 'More than one of his high level interlocutors described the possible explosive consequences of such a development as being a "potential time bomb" . . . I am deeply worried that any early, selective recognition could widen the present conflict and fuel an explosive situation especially in Bosnia Herzegovina and also Macedonia . . . I believe therefore that uncoordinated actions should be avoided.'

Lord Carrington wrote to similar effect on 2 December, of the impact of selective recognition on the conference he chaired, the only existing machinery for a diplomatic settlement:

An early recognition of Croatia would undoubtedly mean the break-up of the conference . . . There is also a real danger, perhaps even a probability, that Bosnia Herzegovina would also ask for independence and recognition, which would be wholly unacceptable to the Serbs in that republic ... This might well be the spark that sets Bosnia Herzegovina alight.

His prophetic words were answered, not by Mr van den Broek to whom they were addressed, but by Mr Genscher in the apparent role of puppet-master. The German foreign minister objected that Lord Carrington's remarks were 'likely to encourage those forces in Yugoslavia which up to now have firmly opposed the conclusion of the peace process'. The Germans pressed their case strongly for reasons which had something to do with the politics of their governing coalition (the CDU's Bavarian partners coveted Mr Genscher's job). But they also had the unwitting help of the Serbs. With enemies like the Serbs, they didn't need friends. Both the fall of Vukovar and the bombardment of Dubrovnik showed the Croats to all the world as the victims of Serb aggression, and made it harder for the European Community to deny recognition.

The decision was taken on 16 December 1991. The Germans were not in a mood to be outvoted: it was an issue that mattered more to them than to anyone else round the table. As a friend, who observed their diplomacy from a privileged vantage point, described it, 'Bonn believed that the act of recognition would somehow be like waving a magic wand over the problem.' But at the first vote only the Belgians and Danes were with them; Mr van den Broek himself opposed them strenuously. Then something happened in the course of the ministerial dinner and before the final vote at two in the morning, which changed the minds of the reluctant Nine, Britain and France included. The Germans prevailed. Much later, with the benefit of two years' hindsight of the consequences, it was characterized by one of the mediators as 'a damn near criminal decision'. It opened the way to a fateful referendum on Bosnia, and the declaration of an independent republic against the wishes of one of its constituent peoples. It left Bosnia in a sort of limbo to be fought for, and in effect condemned 200,000 people to death.

If that seems too harsh a judgement – what else were the Serbs, given their history and paranoia, expected to do? And to the argument that their reaction could not have been predicted, the answer is that it could have been, and was. It was predicted both by Lord Carrington and by the Secretary-General of the United Nations in their prescient letters to the European Community's Council of Ministers. It was predicted by the Community's own monitors on the ground. And it was predicted by the British and German ambassadors in Belgrade, in messages which were discounted at the time, but will one day form part of the historical record. In the judgement of the American ambassador, 'War in Bosnia now became virtually inevitable.'

As to *why* these warnings were ignored, that too may be better left for historians to deal with. They will have the documents, while we for the present have only the word of mouth. But they may be struck by an interesting coincidence: the British concession to the Germans on the recognition of Croatia occurred at exactly the same time as the German concession to the British on the opt-out clauses of the Maastricht Treaty – an issue of much greater consequence to the British government. Was it Mr Major's charm that won the day, or was the coincidence in fact rather more than a coincidence? According to independent witnesses of the process there was, if not a formal agreement, at least an *understanding* of matching concessions. As a contact of mine put it, who had been engaged in the diplomacy from the start, 'It would require a great deal of naivety not to see the linkage between the two.'

Where exactly the truth lies in all this I am not sure. Mr Hurd is a humane and decent man, and a politician with a sense of history. He has shown himself from time to time to be, if not tormented, at least troubled by the moral dilemmas of the Bosnian war, and it seems unlikely that he would have agreed to such a trade-off unless its consequences had been in some way hidden from him, in the filtering process that sometimes occurs between diplomacy and politics. (It is not unknown for ambassadors and international negotiators to 'write for the spike'.) Otherwise, how could the fate of an entire nation and the lives of hundreds of thousands of people have carried so little weight against arguments of political expediency?

I don't know the reasons. I do know the results. I have lived with them every day of my working life in Bosnia. They are drawn in blood on the map of a broken republic. Most alarming of all, from my usual vantage point on the ground and close to these events, is the perception that with the end of the cold war history has gone into fast rewind: it is as if we are flashing back to 1914, only pausing along the way to fail to absorb the lessons of 1938.

Let others allege conspiracies where they find them. The problem at the political and diplomatic level has seemed to me to lie rather in *inattention*: that just as action has consequences, so does inaction. Maastricht mattered more than Mostar – it was as simple and brutal as that. And by the time the international community had agreed some modest package of measures to help the Bosnians on the government side or penalize their enemies, the condition of the patient had so deteriorated that a far more drastic intervention was needed. The same thing happened to UNPROFOR (United Nations Protection Force): by the time it was deployed its force structure and mandate were already obsolete.

It may not have helped that, within the Foreign Office, policy on Bosnia was to a large extent set by the United Nations Department: that is, it reflected Britain's interests within the United Nations, rather than those of the British people at large, still less those of the Bosnian people whose future was being decided.

There were two kinds of journalists in Bosnia: those, such as Maggie O'Kane of the *Guardian* and John Burns of the *New York Times*, who went on crusades, and whose commitment and eloquence I greatly admired, and those like me, who did not. It may have been the difference between print and broadcasting, but in television it was always the understated narrative, the accumulation of fact and image, that made the case more strongly than any argument.

In one instance, though, I did go off on a small crusade of my own. It was about the absence, for the first two years of the war, of any British diplomatic presence on the ground. This war, after all, was the most pressing issue of European diplomacy; it had damaged every institution that attempted to deal with it, from the European Community to the United Nations. It was threatening the special relationship with the United States, not to mention the new world order. And yet the British were among those not present in Sarajevo. So on the basis of what information, I wondered, was the government framing its policy on Bosnia? Surely not by reading the *Guardian* or watching the BBC?

Now the *Nine O'Clock News* is definitely not the right place for crusades – except perhaps in one memorable and special case by Michael Buerk on Ethiopia. But the semi-private and quasi-diplomatic setting of a Chatham House lecture in the summer of 1993 was well suited to the purpose. I put it as provocatively as possible, to get the audience's attention: 'If there is a value in diplomatic reporting on the ground – and there must be, else why these chanceries all over Europe? – one would expect to find some diplomatic presence in Sarajevo. Yes, it is danger-ous, but not impossibly so. The aid agencies work there. The

journalists work there. Two hundred and sixty thousand Sara-
jevans have endured it for more than a year. But the diplomats?
It is as if we were practising comfort station diplomacy. Brussels
and Lisbon, yes. But Sarajevo, no. We are supposed to have the
Rolls Royce of a diplomatic service. But in Bosnia it isn't even
a Trabant. That is, it isn't there. It doesn't go.'

I do not know for sure if this philippic had the required effect,
but my spies around the polished tables informed me that at
least it hit a tender spot on the diplomatic anatomy. Some
months later a mission was established in Sarajevo – a typical
half-measure, without an ambassador. It is a full embassy now,
although a fraction of the size of others from less consequential
capitals. It has been my general experience that British diplomats
engaged on the issue, who are intelligent men and women with
at least some sense of the realities on the ground, have had little
enthusiasm for the policy – even perhaps the policy vacuum –
which they were required to defend and promote. Yet unlike
their opposite numbers on the Bosnia desk of the State Department, such as George Kenny, none of them had resigned. I asked
one who wished to why he hadn't. His answer wasn't principled,
but frank. It was a matter, he said, of boarding-school
allowances.

In the end, inattention prevailed at every level. The Bosnian
war was described by the American Secretary of State Warren
Christopher as a 'problem from hell', which was a coded way of
saying that there was nothing that he or anyone else was able or
willing to do about it except to wish it away. And to a large
extent, the West averted its gaze.

The most powerful symbol of this was Douglas Hurd's first
visit to Sarajevo, in July 1992. The war and ethnic cleansing
were at their worst, Mr Hurd held the presidency of the Council
of Ministers, and the Bosnian government was looking for
tangible evidence that Europe understood the suffering of its

people and was finally willing to help. Also, and by chance, Mr Hurd came to Sarajevo on the day chosen by a local cellist, Vedran Smiljovic, who had once played the concert halls of Europe, to enlist the world's musicians in its defence. His plan was that on the stroke of midday musicians everywhere should stop what they were doing, get out their instruments and play Albinoni's *Adagio*, whose haunting notes, as Vedran played them, were the very anthem of the city's suffering. 'Let everyone,' he said, 'take his instrument in every place, maybe the metro, maybe an aeroplane, open your instrument and play Albinoni.'

It was twelve o'clock exactly, and Mr Hurd came out of the Presidency as if on cue. There was a violinist on one street corner, a trumpeter on another, and Vedran with his cello and in his full concert hall finery of faded white tie and tails at the scene of the bread queue massacre of May 1992 – at that time still the city's worst – all playing the *Adagio*. Mr Hurd, accompanied by the Bosnian president, was making a mandatory diplomatic pilgrimage to the shrine of the massacre site. With large and enthusiastic crowds around him, for these were still the early days of their ordeal, it was the perfect opportunity for him to reach out to them in the instinctive glad-handing way of politicians, and find out what *they* thought, how *they* lived, and what *they* needed from him.

But he did none of this. It was as if he saw and heard nothing, and was deaf to more than the *Adagio*. He strode silently to his motorcade. From there President Izetbegovic had planned a visit to the hospital, for which he believed that he had the foreign secretary's consent, so that Mr Hurd might see for himself some of the human costs of the war. The president led the way and turned right towards the hospital. Mr Hurd sped straight on to UN headquarters at the PTT building, and from there to the airport and home.

His staff at the time explained that there had been a misunderstanding. To the Bosnian government it was no misunderstanding, but another case of a politician who couldn't get out fast enough. Vice-president Ejup Ganic put it bitterly: 'They come and they go,' he said, 'and they know nothing.'

4

HOMES FROM HOME

For at least the first two years of the conflict, Lukavica barracks was the 'Last Chance Saloon' of Bosnian war reporting. It was there, on the Serb side of Sarajevo airport, that whoever had braved the hassle and hazards thus far had to make the decision about whether to go any further. There were compelling reasons not to.

Sarajevo was not exactly the promised land, but it was the sought-after dateline – and it lay little more than a mile away, across a runway that was a free-fire zone for the snipers of both sides. There were no good choices to be made, and indecision could be most dangerous of all, since Lukavica itself was both a target for the Muslims and a fire-base for the Serbs. Since outgoing fire attracts incoming fire (one of the lessons of war which I have been trying for years, and in vain, to impress on my German friend Ulli Klose of RTL), the barracks was not a safe place to ponder your options. But one thing you knew was that whatever you did, whether you turned back or pressed forward, self-reproach would surely keep you company: for you were acting either like a coward or like an idiot.

The day we came to Lukavica the war was just entering its third month – an especially dangerous place and a dangerous time. The fighting had spread to Dobrinja, the neighbouring suburb on the north side of the runway, which had been the Press Village for the 1984 Winter Olympics. (Journalists envy

43

sportscasters – at least, this one does – and I remember wondering where I had made the wrong career move; why couldn't I be Harry Carpenter or David Coleman, and get to see such places in the good times?)

Dobrinja was under bombardment and clouds of smoke. Ethnic cleansing was not yet a term in general currency, but the Serbs were using the barracks to send out expeditions to do just that, to purge the suburb of all but its Serb inhabitants. They did not hide this from us, indeed they were proud of it. They set out in the style of bands of heroes, flashing three-fingered salutes and waving their AK47s in the air, to save their people from all sorts of rumoured atrocities: which was exactly how this war began, in ignorance and hatred. They even invited us to accompany them, and it was an invitation I should probably have accepted, though whether we would have survived it I shall never know. But we had other risks to calculate, about crossing the airport runway.

We take these decisions more or less collectively (which is why in front-line television we have a better sort of army, without officers). Cameraman Nigel Bateson said that he was willing to try if I was. So did his soundman Rob Feast. I chimed in tamely that I was willing to try if they were. That left our interpreter Vladimir Marjanovic with something rather less than the casting vote. But this sophisticated Serb had been with us in the direst circumstances from Vukovar to Zvornik without showing even a flicker of apprehension. Perhaps he inherited his nonchalance from his grandfather, who had served with the Serbs' Royal Horse Guards in the face of risks and dangers that made ours seem trivial. Vladimir also voted to go forward.

The first days of any assignment in a war zone are the most dangerous. Knowledge is safety – or relative safety. (The only truly safe course of action is to stay at home.) And in this case we had no information about what lay ahead of us or around us.

We did not know the road or the risks, where the snipers were if there were snipers, or where the mines were if there were mines. The weather was getting murky, and we were heading into the darkness in a double sense.

'Fast as you like,' urged Nigel, which was his coded South African way of accusing me of driving too slowly and loitering in no man's land with intent to be shot at. But our unarmoured camera car was hardly the best in the fleet at the best of times; it had been sent to the Balkans to die, which it eventually did. It was overloaded and in anything but rally-driving form.

No one had been that way for days. Beware the road with the debris of battle still on it – war reporting is the only business where you welcome other traffic. Mercifully, in this uncharted territory where your first mistake could be your last, we found the right track past the ruins of Butmir, and crept across the airport runway in the gloom and the drizzle without attracting incoming fire. It was the longest ten minutes of my life. I thought dark and quite unjustified thoughts about the valour of my esteemed colleagues (Vladimir included) who had fled from the city in haste three weeks before, after coming under mortar fire which had damaged their transport, their morale and their editing machines. It was easy to be critical, and I unfairly accused them of panicking. It was their escape which had made our return necessary, for risks are like costs, which only increase by being passed from one to another.

At the airport terminal we were not alone. The United Nations had been through the same experience, out and in again. They too had fled under fire from Sarajevo in May – and then returned, better equipped, to try again in June. As with us, those making the attempt were not the ones who had departed, but an advance party of a company of the Royal 22nd Regiment, French Canadians from Quebec, whose title was anglicized as the 'Van Doos'. In the manner of front-line troops almost everywhere, they could not have been more welcoming. They were regrouping in the darkened and shattered terminal after a difficult journey from Daruvar in Croatia, and they invited us to spend the night with them. We were delighted to accept, as tracer fire lit the night outside and explosions rocked what remained of Dobrinja, just across the road.

Later, much later, the Canadians were to earn an unenviable reputation as the UN troops most easily intimidated, but that was the result of political indecision in Ottawa. It was certainly not reflected in the bearing of the Van Doos. When their mission was opposed, their commanding officer, Lieutenant-Colonel Michel Jones, got his men to Sarajevo by deploying them in battle formation against the Serbs, who duly gave way. Perhaps it was easier in the early days: certainly a show of force was more effective.

We still had to re-establish ourselves in the city. At this point I remembered the words of my old sergeant-major, from another army at another time. He claimed to know a lot about fools, since in his view so many served under him. 'A fool and his equipment,' he said, 'are easily separated.' And, 'Any fool can be uncomfortable.' Accordingly we hung on to our equipment and set about making ourselves comfortable.

It was at this point, having survived the airport road into New Sarajevo, that we ran into Faridoun Hemani, an old friend from the news agency WTN. He offered to drive us into the centre by way of the back road, which he claimed to know. When one of our more notorious radio correspondents dies at the wheel as he surely will (he has so far overturned one Land Rover and considerably dented two others), Faridoun will be left standing as the most dangerous man in the Balkans without a gun: an admirable friend and journalist, but a somewhat imperfect driver. On the twisting back road also known as the Ho Chi Minh Trail, which was like a narrow alley connecting the target zones of a Serb rifle range, he was demonstrating his skill at dodging the sniper fire when he collided with one of his own kind racing the other way.

'Well, bless my soul, you nearly killed us there,' said I, though Nigel Bateson remembers the conversation more colourfully. From that day on I have allowed no one to drive me in the city, on the sound French principle that one is never so well served as by oneself. The only exception has been our chief logistician and wagonmaster Alan Hayman, but he was once a sergeant-major in the Royal Electrical and Mechanical Engineers, and thus has special rights.

By now we were running out of time as well as luck, and money too. For the battered Vauxhall, which was still motoring though with one door hanging off, was not only our camera car but also our bank. To avoid being robbed at the Serb roadblocks, we had stashed away 10,000 German marks in an empty Coca Cola can in the pocket of the door that had just been rammed. We had to work with crowbar and tin opener to retrieve the can from the pocket and the money from the can. Only then could we set about the next task, which was to find places both to live and to work in. A chastened Faridoun suggested the hospital, where he had set up his headquarters. I thought this unduly pessimistic for us, though probably realistic for him. It was, besides, directly in the Serbs' line of fire.

Thanks to the courtesy of General MacKenzie, who was now installed as the UN's commander in Sarajevo, we found a nest of empty offices under the ramp leading to his main base at the PTT building. Our newly liberated cash enabled us to pay for them, as part of a complex rental agreement which also included a mysterious and welcome supply of fresh vegetables. The PTT building was not yet the Balkan Alcatraz that it later became, for this was when access was relatively easy, before the French arrived. (Later, they would search us twice on entering and once on leaving, and keep us out completely during their sacred two-hour lunch break.) But because it was UN headquarters it was already a target, so we protected ourselves against the incoming mortar fire with heavy steel plates four feet high. As a result short people were safer than tall people, but the plates supplied at least the illusion of safety. They too were paid for in large denominations of German marks stained with Coca Cola.

The following day our dauntless engineers, Tim Barrow and Harvey Watson, ran the gauntlet of the airport shooting gallery in still unarmoured vehicles to bring us the satellite dish. In next to no time, it seemed, we were not only operational on our own account, but hosting the world as well. American and French networks moved in with us, and various fiercely competitive Swedes and Greeks. (Anyone who thinks that our own Kate is forceful has not met Anna Boutros of the Antenna network, truly the warrior queen of Greek television; not since Margaret Thatcher had I met such a blend of charm and intimidation.) The new arrivals brought their satellite telephones with them. The dishes multiplied, and within a week the place came to look like a fortified mushroom farm. Through no intention of ours it became the unofficial international press club, and redefined the BBC as the 'Bunker Broadcasting Centre'.

On our first satellite transmission from the new headquarters we included some images of the fortifications, which touched off a torrent of questions from head office. It may seem ungrateful, but sometimes I felt we could use a management that cared a little less. It wasn't so much that they were trying to calm our fears as that we were trying to calm theirs. 'Those steel plates – can't you get some more and don't they come any larger?'

'No, those are all there were. And there's a lot of metal flying through the air but not much actually being made.'

'How safe are you?'

'Safe as we can make it – but you didn't send us here to cover a flower festival.'

'Anything we can do to help?'

'Nothing really – except perhaps fewer phone calls. Some things here we just have to work out for ourselves.'

One of these was to find a place to live. The obvious candidate was the Holiday Inn. It was the city's only modern hotel, and its ugliest building even before the war got at it, having been designed by an architect who had played too much as a child with yellow Lego. But it was out of commission at the time, since the war had actually started in it. It was a Serb hotel; Radovan Karadzic had his political headquarters there, held court in the lobby, and proclaimed his new republic in its conference room. When a peace rally outside was fired at in early April 1992, his opponents stormed the building and partly wrecked it. It was not yet back in business.

There were other options, though none of them safe. A friend lent us his home on the top floor of a cliff of old flats overlooking the Presidency. It had room for us all except the two engineers, who remained as General MacKenzie's guests at the PTT building. From our balcony Nigel's camera commanded a wide field of fire from the Old Town to New Sarajevo, including the districts being most fiercely fought for. We even had comforts: sometimes there was water and sometimes there was power, and very occasionally both.

Food was a problem. There was nothing for sale in the market but dandelion leaves, which I bought one day in a spirit of solidarity, but found to be truly uneatable. We had some tinned reserves with us which Nigel proceeded to turn into excellent meals, for he was as gifted with the stove as with the camera; his was a life with different kinds of pans in it. He would park his tripod on the balcony every evening, and aim the lens in the general direction of the Jewish cemetery. So it was that he recorded some of the war's most vivid images while at the same time cooking spaghetti and spinach soup. The spinach soup seemed as permanent a feature of our lives as the 5 a.m. bombardment by the Serbs. We went to bed with one and woke up with the other.

Three weeks later the Holiday Inn reopened its doors, and I took a room there not so much for the comfort (there was none) as for the gossip. I pride myself on having become something of a connoisseur of war hotels. Generally, as with the Continental Palace in Saigon and the Camino Real in San Salvador, their charm is that they defy their surroundings and provide a measure of calm and luxury in a turbulent world. The Holiday Inn offered neither. I loved it. It was and remains the ultimate war hotel, like living at ground zero. From there you didn't go out to the war, the war came in to you. Its southern frontage was shattered by shellfire and uninhabitable: every week the Serb gunners would open up new ventilation shafts which had not been in the original design. Corridors were carpeted with broken glass. The atrium could have served as the set of a doomsday movie: indeed, in an everyday sense it already did. Journalists gathered in the gloom to exchange their rumours, and the still uniformed waiters with nothing to serve, moved ashtrays silently among them.

The hotel had three entrances, all of which were in the Serbs' direct line of fire. The least unsafe was reckoned to be the winding ramp to the underground garage, which had to be tackled at speed. My dashing colleague Jeremy Bowen held the record with a racing descent, all tyres screeching, which won the admiration of all who observed it, except those travelling with him. Another friend, Slobodan the CNN interpreter, was less successful. Having been slightly wounded on the airport runway, he was hit for the second time in one day while heading for the safety of the hotel garage, and was only saved from death by his steel helmet. He left Sarajevo after that and did not return.

By now the war had been raging long enough that news of it had even reached America. It was starting to attract some very odd types: head-bangers, Walter Mittys and war tourists, designer-dressed as combat photographers and seeking to prove their courage to someone, usually themselves. Even the regulars included some real eccentrics. One of these was a radio reporter who, as if there were not dangers enough outside, insisted on abseiling down the well of the hotel atrium. His car carried a slogan urging the snipers of all sides not to waste their bullets on him, since he was immortal. He was also French, of course. But alas, the bullets did not bounce off him. Towards the end of 1994 he was badly wounded in the hand by cannon fire: a further cautionary lesson for us all.

Another registered eccentric, now the longest-serving journalist among us and even then to my mind the best, was Kurt Schork of Reuters. A slightly built American, bearded and burning-eyed, he was not at all in the usual image of the wire service reporter. Journalism was his third career. He started on Capitol Hill as administrative assistant to a radical Congressman from Massachusetts, became executive director of a New York mass transit system, and from there took off to freelance in Cambodia and Kurdistan. Reuters found him in Kurdistan, sent him to Sarajevo and kept him there. For someone with Kurt's contempt for comfort, it was the perfect posting. Once established, he did more than file his dispatches, which he did faster and better than anyone. He helped the helpless, rescued the wounded, and became the conscience-in-residence of the Sarajevo press corps. At a series of increasingly acrimonious press conferences, it was he who held the United Nations to its mandate, and demanded answers when it seemed to shrink from its mission. On the occasion when the UN tried to claim that the city was no longer under siege but only in a state of 'tactical encirclement', it had to withdraw this fiction under the fire-power of his anger and indignation. Though he later developed a close relationship with Lieutenant-General Michael Rose, and they even lectured together at the army's Staff College, he was a thorn in the side of the UN, and of the Serbs.

I met him first at Sarajevo, after a round of fruitless negoti-ations at the airport, in dialogue with the Serbs' military com-mander, General Ratko Mladic. It was a very short dialogue. Kurt led off with a question about their siege of Sarajevo. The general responded by lunging towards him and shaking him by the throat. Nikola Koljevic, the Serbs' vice-president, attempted to intervene and pleaded with me to do the same. 'Mr Martin,' he said, 'I think you should restrain your friend.'

'Professor Koljevic, I'll do my best. But do you think you can restrain *yours*?'

For Kurt the Bosnian war was and still is an epic struggle between good and evil. I meet more Serbs and see more shades of grey in it than he does, but I have never wavered in my admiration for him.

The other fixed star in our firmament, and every bit as much one-of-a-kind, was Christiane Amanpour of CNN. She was half Iranian and half British by birth, and spoke with the accents of Roedean or Cheltenham except when broadcasting, when her inflections tended to drift into mid-Atlantic: sometimes even into mid-Atlanta, for that was where CNN came from. She was both aggressive and agreeable – a rare combination, but not enough to impress the BBC which had turned her down for a job on *Breakfast News* when it started up. (I put that in the same category as a former news editor of mine who told David Frost that he had no future in television.) Our loss was CNN's gain. Christiane made a name for herself in the Gulf war, and came to Sarajevo with a reputation for courage and persistence, plus an infinite ability to talk live about any topic under the sun. We knew when she was 'winging it' – improvising precariously off the top of her head – and it was then she was at her most convincing. When interviewing their correspondents in the field, CNN anchor people had developed the irritating habit of asking them, 'Tom – or Dick or Harry – will you share your insights with us?' Christiane was one of the very few who actually had insights to share.

She was also, to my mind, suicidally brave. She never let her camera crew go anywhere she wouldn't – the first test of a serious TV reporter in a war zone. Against all the best advice I gave her, she ventured even into the government-held section of Dobrinja, the Sarajevo suburb which was at that time under a siege within a siege: there was no way into it except by a single road under constant Serb fire. She came through this journalistic equivalent of Russian roulette, but only by luck, judgement had nothing to do with it. I wouldn't say she ever settled down – she is not a settling down sort of person – but she did later become slightly more circumspect and start to pay a little attention to the art of staying alive, as a result of which she is mercifully still with us, as boisterous and charming as ever.

After three months in Sarajevo, we left our base in the PTT building and our friends at the Holiday Inn. It was a precipitate departure, and I felt at the time it was yet another panic attack: though I was hardly in a position to criticize, being in hospital in London recovering from precisely the kind of experience my colleagues were trying to avoid. But there were other reasons for moving besides the obvious one of dodging the ever increasing volume of shrapnel. We needed to find serviceable winter quarters within reach of the first British UN troops, who were on their way. The Cheshire Regiment had been stood by in August 1992, and would finally arrive in October.

We set up shop, for a third time, in the Hotel Kontinental at

Kiseljak, ten miles from the capital and in territory held by the Croats. It was not so much a hotel as a down-market boarding house, notable for its proprietor's bean soup and her attack dog Ricki, who guarded our satellite dish against all comers including ourselves.

Kiseljak was the nominal UN headquarters, though the UN commander, General Morillon, was nearly always elsewhere. It was also the place where the French troops struck a firm and principled blow against the UN's multinationalism by refusing to eat the meals engineered for them by the Danish cooks, who were indeed engineers by trade and had known very little about cooking, until thrown untrained into the culinary front line. So the UN troops had to improvise. The French seceded and established their own barbecue, and the British Chief of Staff, Brigadier Roddy Cordy-Simpson, came to us for the bean soup.

By then the weather was worsening and other stragglers from Sarajevo joined us, lodging in various ice palaces along the road from Kiseljak to Busovaca. They also visited us for the gossip, and for the soup. We never intended it that way, but wherever we went the BBC office became the local rumour control. And along with the British troops there came serious scribes from the weightier end of Fleet Street, or perhaps I should say Wapping, many with reminiscences of the recent Gulf war which they graciously sought to share with us. On one occasion the company included not only our own Kate Adie, but Robert Fox of the *Daily Telegraph* and Robert Fisk of the *Independent*. (Some tension persisted between these two, since one had once been arrested by the Turks in the mistaken belief he was the other.) I remember sitting back in awe as the certitudes flew and the decibel level rose. I was at the time either handing the operation over to Kate or taking it over from her, but it made no difference. When I handed it over, the usual roles would be reversed, and *she* would brief *me* on what had happened in

Bosnia during the five weeks I had been there. She once did the same in Saudi Arabia, on which our lack of inside knowledge was exactly equal. It's part of her essential charm: that's who she is.

The Hotel Kontinental did the business for us. It was warm, it was comfortable, and it gave us the home from home we needed during the first grim winter of the war. But we knew this couldn't last, and it didn't. Tensions were rising around Kiseljak between Muslims and Croats, who were digging in for the war they both expected. One of their trench lines was ominously close to our headquarters, and sniper fire occasionally whistled past it. There were other reasons to move. The Serbs were besieging the .Muslim-held eastern enclaves. Cerska and Kamenica had fallen, and if Srebrenica followed – which it eventually did – its 60,000 refugees would have no place of refuge but Tuzla. Accordingly, our faithful satellite dish was dispatched up there across the snow and the ice and deep-rutted mud of the worst road in Bosnia. It was the oldest dish in the business, the same one we had used in the Gulf war. By the time it came rattling down again three weeks later, its circuitry rebelled and refused to work. Once again, and for a third time, we had moved when we should have stayed put.

I was tired of second-guessing, and reached for the only link with the world outside, which was the British army's satellite phone in the press office at Vitez. The conversation was not encouraging. 'Good morning, this is Martin. I'm in Vitez.'

'Martin who?'

That one always got me going. I had worked for these people for thirty-two years and they still didn't know who I was. I explained through gritted teeth that I was not Martin Sixsmith, and there was hardly enough good news here for Martyn Lewis.

'Oh . . . how are you getting on?'

'Not too well. Look, I haven't got a satellite dish or a

cameraman or an editor or any editing machines or a producer or an interpreter or a roof over my head. I've just had my hair all but parted by a sniper and World War Three is going on around me. Now *will you please send me some help?*'

The reason for the dash to Vitez was that the war between Croats and Muslims had finally broken out, all around the British base. It wasn't exactly the best of times to go home-hunting. But by then we knew what to look for, and when our reinforcements arrived they found it: two still undamaged houses in the lane beside the camp. We worked in one and lived in the other, staying there for a year; and we all agreed that it was the best base we ever had. Complete with the civilizing presence of three cats, it was friendlier and somehow more appropriate than the finest hotel in the land (which was the Hyatt in Belgrade, and inaccessible anyway). The one slight drawback to our new home was that it stood 800 yards, and on some days less, from the nearest active front line. Despite being rather too often in the line of fire, we became the social centre for British soldiers as well as journalists; and we entertained them not only because we liked them, but because it was somehow reassuring to have a Warrior 'battle taxi' parked in the front garden. Later, when the fighting abated briefly in the summer, we even held barbecues featuring Bosnian roast lamb, British beer and the inescapable music of Willie Nelson.

It was the nearest the soldiers came to civilian life, and we learned more than we ever needed to know about the Cheshire Regiment, the Prince of Wales's Own Regiment of Yorkshire, the 9th/12th Lancers and the Light Dragoons. The ladies among us, who always exercised an influence out of proportion to their numbers, agreed on a division of responsibilities. The producer looked after the infantry, and the interpreters minded the cavalry. Everyone benefited. And sometimes the war seemed a world away, though it was just across the fields. Only the Coldstream

Guards held aloof for a while, for aloofness is one of the things that they do best. But even they were finally persuaded that we weren't going to sell their secrets to the *News of the World*.

Our hosts in Vitez were a gentle middle-aged couple, Mato and Ruska Taraba, who ran a small-holding and simply added us to it. Now they were tending a herd of BBC people as well as eleven goats. Like so many of their generation, they were Titoists. The old despot had done so much for them, not least in holding off Armageddon for forty years. They had his picture on the wall and his books on the shelves. It was his dream as well as theirs which was perishing in flames and fighting on the surrounding hillsides. Mato said, 'As far as we are concerned, it is a war of thieves.' And Ruska asked me, 'Mr Martin, why do you always walk when the others are running?'

'I always walk,' I told her, 'because I am getting on in years a bit, and you can as easily run into a bullet as away from one.'

Mato himself was neither walking nor running but working in his field at the back, when he was shot. A sniper's bullet hit him in the leg and severed an artery. Fortunately he was found before he had lost too much blood by our good friend and ally, Nicole Courtney of Reuters. Having been on the BBC's battle-field first-aid course at Aldershot, she was able to apply her field dressing expertly, and probably saved his life.

As it happened I had been intending to interview Mato that very day. The BBC, in pursuit of its Holy Grail of 'bimediality' – which in practice is no more than a common-sense job-sharing arrangement between radio and television – had asked me for a contribution from Vitez to the radio programme *Farming Today*. 'What about?' I asked.

'About farming in Bosnia,' they said.

'But there isn't any farming in Bosnia. A lot of the land is in the line of fire, and there's no diesel for tractors on the rest. It's being dug with spades.'

'Then do us a piece about that.'

So I did, and I put my heart into it. My one and only report ever for *Farming Today* was about the ex-agriculture of ex-Yugoslavia. I could not interview Mato because he was under the surgeon's knife but I did describe what had happened to him as a sad and simple story of a front-line farmer's life. It was obviously something that the programme's audience, listening in their peaceful corners of Britain, could relate to. I come from a farming family, and know that farmers like nothing better than to discuss their various woes and forthcoming ruin. Though Mato's problems were clearly of a different order, the programme received many messages for him expressing the concern of the farmers at home and wishing him a speedy recovery. When told of this he was deeply touched.

Though Mato and Ruska benefited economically from our stay, our departure was in fact rather better news for them, since it followed one of the few real ceasefires of the war, and the unlikely federation between Muslims and Croats, now allies rather than enemies. Even so, our two best friends in Vitez wished us to return. Their house was within the sound of gunfire, as the fighting continued between Muslims and Serbs for the high ground above Travnik. Ruska confessed to me later that during one of these cannonades she had turned to her husband and said: 'Do you hear that? Do you know what it means? It means that Mr Martin will be back.'

And so I was, both in times of war and of ceasefire. Vitez was still the most convenient base from which to reach the Bosnian army's Third Corps in Zenica and its Seventh Corps in Bugojno, as well as the commander of British forces in Gornji Vakuf, not to mention the Turks, New Zealanders and Malaysians, among others. Never in my life had I gone to war in the company of quite so many armies.

Looking back on it, we probably paid too much attention to

the valley and the towns around it, as the press in Sarajevo did to the capital, and not enough to the other major centres, Mostar and Tuzla, where events of great and grim consequence were taking place, often unreported. People blithely imagine that journalists are where the news is. Alas, not so: the news is where journalists are.

And during the war which all but destroyed Vitez, while we still kept our permanent base there, they flocked to it. Both Kurt Schork and Christiane Amanpour came out to us, as if their own front lines were not dangerous enough and they had to borrow ours. Kurt did his dedicated best to get himself killed, then camped for ten days in a half-ruined hotel in Bugojno, living on a diet of fried eggs and stale bread, in search of a pass to the Seventh Corps' forward positions.

Christiane's visit was more like a one-night stand. She had just renegotiated her contract, and since she was now known as the best field reporter in any of the American networks, they were all competing for her services and offering large quantities of dollars. She eventually elected to stay with CNN – at a price which, knowing the network's star system, I guessed to be close to the seven-figure mark.

It did not change her way of working, or the drive and insecurity which kept her going when others had given up. At Santici, as ever, she got closer to the action than I had dared to, and I knew the ground and the people. It was late in the day, too late to return to Sarajevo, so she and her team asked to spend the night with us. The producer slept in the kitchen, the cameraman in the office, and I gallantly invited her to share my room: she in her sleeping bag, of course, and I in mine – we in the BBC do have our standards. I was just drifting off to sleep when I heard an unexpectedly timid voice in the darkness piping up beside me: 'Martin, you're not going to jump my bones, are you?' It was that insecurity again.

'No, Christiane, I am not insensitive to your charms and don't want to seem indifferent to them, but I have absolutely no intention of jumping your bones as you so sweetly put it.' At times like this, in front-line relationships, I tend to retreat into Britishness. It is safer that way.

She may have sensed a note of apprehension. 'Sorry,' she said. 'Just asking.'

And that was how I came to sleep with the million-dollar woman.

Both Christiane and Kurt, being restless spirits, defected for a while to other datelines – she to Port-au-Prince and he to Grozny. But Bosnia drew them back, and changed us all.

5

STAYING ALIVE

I may seem an unlikely expert on war zone survival, having nearly blown my chances more than once. But I have at least studied with the experts. One of these is Dragan Havzijevic, a Belgrade Serb whose untamed beard makes him look like the ultimate Chetnik from Central Casting. He learned his craft as a documentary cameraman in the Third World in the years when Yugoslavia aspired to leadership of the non-aligned movement. Because he worked where film and batteries were scarce, he was famously economical in his shooting habits. Our usual shooting ratio is about ten to one: twenty minutes of tape are edited down into a spare two minutes of news. His was nearer one to one. Two minutes would be edited from two minutes and a quarter – more or less as he shot it. One of our best staff cameramen used to seek out his work for its composition and framing. If Dragan couldn't do it, it couldn't be done.

I first came upon him in the Croatian war, in November 1991, during the last desperate hours of the battle for Vukovar. After three months of siege and terrible casualties on both sides, the Serbs had blitzed their way on to the ridge in the centre of town. From here they overlooked the Croats' last line of defence, from the burning Hotel Dunav to the ruined police station: bodies were left unburied on waste ground near the hospital, for the cemetery itself was being fought over – this was a war in which it wasn't even safe to be dead.

Dragan was dodging incoming sniper fire around an old field gun which the Serbs were using laterally, like a heavy machine-gun, to flatten what remained of the town. He had a 'CBS News' sign on his camera, but the CBS interest in global news had waned to a marked degree and he was working for himself. His camerawork and courage were a rare combination. I have known good technicians wilt under fire, and brave men fail to do the business technically. He had both. I hired him on the spot.

So we took him with us to the next war, in Sarajevo. From our first base there, in the Serb-held suburb of Ilidza, he was our essential link with the Serbs, whose relations with the foreign press were already becoming strained. His ferocious appearance disguised a gentle character: I suspected him of being a closet liberal. But the Serbs accepted him as one of their own, and invited him on to their forays into no man's land. He did not hunt alone, but always with George, his silent soundman. Inevitably they became known to us as George and the Dragan.

They had their own way of firing themselves up for these assignments. They would drink coffee for the first two hours of the day and whisky for the next two. Then they would disappear. Some time later they would return with three minutes' worth of the most vivid combat footage, which breathed the fear of death and the triumph of survival – a bit like a war movie without the sense of contrivance – and it made up in impact for what it lacked in length.

One day they came back not just with the tape, but with two bullet holes drilled neatly just below seat level in the driver's door of their unarmoured Volkswagen Golf. I measured it: death had been one inch away. After that, I ordered more scotch and grounded them for a while. Even Dragan was shaken: 'Mr Martin,' he said, 'compared to this, Vukovar was Disneyland.'

For the small but growing press corps in Sarajevo, the risks were far greater than any of us had imagined when we embarked on what had seemed at the time to be just another war. Nothing we had ever lived through prepared us for it. The phoney war of early April was over, and the city resounded more fiercely each day to the rattle and thunder of open warfare as the Serbs and Muslims fought for it, street by street.

The pressures were deadly and further compounded by the competitive nature of the TV news business itself. This was especially true of the two agencies, World Television News and Visnews (which later became Reuters TV). They operated under separate rules, devised by the European Broadcasting Union, whereby they would offer their images of the day's events on the Eurovision News Exchange – a market controlled by a cartel of national broadcasters. On the basis of the agencies' pictures, and of their local producers' promotion of them while they were yet an unseen commodity, one side's edit would be accepted and the other's rejected – and most of Europe would use one sequence of images. (The national networks which were already in place, such as ourselves and TF1 of France, of course had a much freer hand, and would also trade images with each other.) In the agency game there was a winner and a loser, with many a tear and tantrum at the feed point – from the men as well. The pressure on today's losers to become tomorrow's winners, by venturing that half block further where the fighting was thickest, was clear and unconscionable. Head office was urging them on to greater heroics. There are casualties inseparable from this business anyway, and probably have been since Alexander the Great set out for the wars with an official historian, Callisthenes, in tow. But if we went on like this, someone was going to be killed who need not have been killed. It was time to put an end to it.

I hate meetings. One of my reasons for staying in the field and avoiding desk jobs is never to have to attend them. I prefer war zones to offices, for I would rather watch only my front and not my back. But I organized a meeting of the TV news agencies and other broadcasters in Sarajevo to terminate this lunacy. We decided there and then to do something that had never been done before, and declare a voluntary 'pool' of all our coverage. Anyone's footage could be used by everyone. In the next battle for Grbavica, or Zuc, or wherever else was being fought for, there need be only one camera team in the line of fire. It made arithmetical sense. But it wasn't popular. It penalized the brave. It rewarded the indolent, who need not leave the hotel or their bunkers at the TV station, as many did not and yet were fêted as heroes in their home countries. It went against the traditional grain of winner-takes-all journalism. And the news agencies' managers did not approve at all, at least at the outset. One called his producer in Ilidza and demanded an explanation (the privilege of staff officers in their well-stocked châteaux the world over). 'What's got into you guys?' he asked. 'Have you lost the killer instinct?'

Journalists are not by nature team players, but competitive people with a natural resistance to pools and cartels and special arrangements. But this was a risk-reduction agreement which did not take long to prove its worth. We were staying at the Hotel Serbia in Ilidza, where our wake-up call that morning came from the barrel of a gun – or rather of many guns, since the hotel grounds and the Serbs defending them were the target of a sustained infantry attack by Muslims from the neighbouring suburb of Colonia Sokolac. We had questioned the wisdom of the United Nations Protection Force basing itself in the very front line of the Bosnian war; and now, it seemed, we were making the same mistake.

Of the cameramen available at the time to our new TV coalition, perhaps the most experienced – and certainly the most intrepid – was Rob Celliers of Visnews, who had covered many wars in his time and emerged unscathed from all of them. But Bosnia was different, and having heard of his heroics on a Sarajevo front line the day before, I had tried to impress this on him. It was a waste of breath. With no regard for his own safety he rushed forward with the first desperate wave of Serb defenders, being threatened by one of them for good measure, to the hotel building closest to their perimeter. In search of a vantage point with some kind of cover, he crouched next to a drainpipe at one corner of the building. An incoming round shattered it like shrapnel into his right arm. He dropped the camera, of course. It was intact, but he was not. (Typically, his one complaint was that it ruined his golf swing – to which those in the know replied that he never had much of a golf swing anyway.) After the accident, he was persuaded to go into management for a while. But it didn't suit him, and out of sheer restlessness he transferred to Associated Press Television, for whom he was last seen patrolling the war zones again. For some, war reporting is like a habit – and the more dangerous the war, the harder it is to break. But Rob's injury impressed on us as nothing else had that this was a war which all of us would be lucky to survive.

It was recorded from further away and on a wider angle by Victor Nikolaides of WTN, with other members of our newly arranged pool chipping in with other episodes from a fierce day's combat. The French, as so often in Bosnia, were particularly effective. The system worked, and continued to work. The Sarajevo Agency Pool was in business – the first and only one of its kind in the world. Its permanent camera team of Muharem Osmanagic and Semsudin Cengic, whom we knew as Hari and Cenga, did more for Bosnia than all the rest of the press corps put together.

It was dismaying that after the pool had been in operation for three successful and life-saving years its existence was threatened, as the agencies' 'killer instincts' reasserted themselves. Now there was a third player in the game, Associated Press Television, hungry for contracts and eager to challenge the established order of things. It did that by standing apart from the pool and competing with it. At that point Reuters Television, the most powerful of the three, capitulated to the pressure and announced its intention of breaking the pool it had founded.

The timing could not have been worse. It was May 1995, coinciding with the end of a truce which had moderated the fighting on most of the battlefields since the previous December. All restraints were now off as both sides prepared for the final battle, with Sarajevo probably at the heart of it. I found myself on a street corner close to the Serbs' Grbavica salient where I had first dodged the bullets in 1992, and crouched beneath a volume of fire like a sandstorm of instant death. It was both more intensive and more accurate than the fire last time. I wondered what the consequences would be if, instead of having one camera team shooting for everybody, we were to have three competing with each other. How many of my friends would be killed and how many wounded before the insanity ended? I attempted to intervene for a second time, and won the agreement of an old friend in Reuters to extend the pool informally at least for a few more weeks. But the agencies are commercial ventures, not charities, and in the long run the old competitiveness reasserted itself. In August 1995 the accountants prevailed, the journalists lost and the pool went out of business.

Television news is a lethal business, and we have to work out ways of making it less so. The pool reduced the risks, but other events beyond our control were increasing them exponentially, and we were still on a sharp learning curve. One of the hardest lessons we learned was about live shots.

In TV news, a live shot is when a reporter has told the story with the benefit of the best pictures available, and then is asked to do it again without them. It is a technique favoured by programme producers, since it carries an air of up-to-the-minute urgency, and by studio-bound anchormen, since it involves them at least superficially in the flow of the news. I myself have always sought to avoid it, since I lack the ingrained fluency of a Dimbleby, and live in fear of electronic stage fright. (My personal nightmares have nothing to do with war zones and everything to do with TV studios: I will wake up in the small hours of the morning in a cold sweat having dreamed of 'drying up' on the *Nine O'Clock News*.)

At the start of the Bosnian war live shots were fashionable. They originated with some kind of a TV witchdoctor in Iowa, then came to us by way of the American networks and ITN. When I met my rival from ITN I would irritate the hell out of him by asking whether he had been 'Well Trevored' yet. This was because the answer to every question by Trevor MacDonald at the controls of the *News At Ten* spaceship would begin with the words 'Well, Trevor . . .', while the hapless hack collected his scattered thoughts.

The contagion spread. And so it was that one morning, on the balcony of the Hotel Serbia, I was collecting *my* scattered thoughts preparatory to being 'Well Nicked' on the BBC's *Breakfast News*. It had been a quiet night with a definite slackening in the tempo of the fighting, apparently the result of some local agreement or the latest ceasefire *du jour*. But I should have known that at the very mention of a Bosnian ceasefire you head not for the nearest balcony but the deepest bunker. For no sooner had Nick Witchell begun his questions than the Third World War appeared to break out around us: all fields of fire seemed to lead to our over-exposed position. Nick didn't get a sensible answer out of me – not that it made any difference, for the answers were mercifully inaudible above the sounds of battle. When I heard a bullet strike the wall beside me I decided that this was definitely the kind of live shot I could cheerfully live without. Pleading the safety of all of us out there, I brought the interview to a rapid end and bolted for safer territory, tripping over the prostrate form of field producer Sean Salsarola, who was on the floor of the control room trying to coordinate the feed and avoid the incoming fire. Later I collected the spent bullet; it seemed worth saving simply because it was the one that *didn't* have my name on it. I kept it in my pocket along with a silver dollar until losing both in the mortar incident three months later – by which time it was also quite clearly a spent force as a good luck charm. But the BBC was properly and seriously concerned about the risks we were running. And that was the end of live shots on front lines.

News is an itinerant business – the moving camera rolls, and having rolled moves on – and it was in motion that we were particularly vulnerable. We took the risks for granted, like the weather. None of us up to that point had even *thought* of using armoured vehicles. We travelled in a miscellaneous fleet of hire cars, from limos to Ladas, which might have been open-topped convertibles for all the protection they offered against shrapnel and sniper fire.

An early and tragic casualty of our unpreparedness was Margaret Moth, the black-clad raven-haired Texan–New Zealander who worked as a camerawoman for CNN and whose courage under fire had impressed us all, and General MacKenzie too. She ventured down sniper's alley in a 'soft' vehicle once too often, and was hit in the jaw by a bullet near the building that housed the offices of the newspaper *Oslobodenje*. It was a truly horrific injury which she was lucky to survive, and which required more than two years of reconstructive surgery. The correspondent with her at the time, Mark Dolmedge, did all he could to help, but afterwards quite reasonably decided that this Bosnian war wasn't worth it, and quit the field – and he was a tough ex-

Marine. Margaret, by contrast, returned after surgery, and even between operations. I never really understood why. But it was her life, and she wished to go on living it her way.

My own experience was as nothing compared to hers, but scary enough all the same. In order to avoid having to match ITN in what I felt to be a mawkish and exploitative story about the rescue of Sarajevo's orphans, I followed General MacKenzie across the airport runway (which was also the front line) for a negotiating session with the Serbs on top of a small mountain in Jahorina. (The *quid pro quo* for this was that I would not show him having lunch with them – a sensitive issue in starving Sarajevo.) On the way back, without the firepower of the general's escort and in our battered unarmoured Vauxhall Carlton, we were targeted by a burst of fire from Muslim positions in Dobrinja. The easy cliché would describe it as a 'hail of bullets', but it sounded more like a gentle patter of raindrops on the windscreen – except that any one of them could have been fatal. One was stopped by the metalwork of the driver's door, showing that in this respect Vauxhall had made us an armoured vehicle without knowing it, for which I wrote and thanked them afterwards. Another came in at head height between myself and cameraman Nigel Bateson, who presents an uncommonly large target at the best of times, and lodged in a corner of the window frame.

We both swore, he more colourfully than I, for he had once served as a regular in the South African army, where they must hold a master class in bilingual expletives. In the back seat the interpreter, Vladimir Marjanovic, being international, said '*Merde*'; and the soundman, Rob Feast, being English, said 'Exactly'. One of the things that we all swore was that under no circumstances would we go through that again. I was on the phone to London immediately, demanding an armoured vehicle in short order.

I hadn't really expected much to happen. I know and love the

BBC, but at the approach of the challenge direct it tends to duck and weave like a television reporter under fire. It hides behind a blizzard of paperwork and disappears into a maze of interdepartmental committee meetings, probably culminating in a rolling seminar at a country house hotel.

But not this time. This time we had 'Miss Piggy' in two weeks. If it ever happens that I get married again, I shall have to confess to an earlier and serious liaison with 'Miss Piggy'. I owe my life to her, and a corner of my heart will be hers for ever. She was acquired on the second-hand market in Belfast, all four and a half tons of her – an armoured Land Rover encased in a corset of steel a quarter of an inch thick. She was proof against small arms and shrapnel, though not anti-tank or cannon fire. She was uncomfortable and top-heavy, and tended to veer off the road: she seldom passed a ditch she didn't like, and one of my colleagues was reputed to have had three accidents in her in an hour. (That may be a false report – it could have been an hour and a half.) But from inside her armoured recesses the war seemed different and somehow survivable. The name was well chosen. Like the original, she was built on substantial lines, and was, we hoped, not to be trifled with.

'Miss Piggy' may not have been the most beautiful debutante, but that summer of 1992 she set the fashion. Within weeks the other networks and agencies had armour of their own, although the photo-journalists – still photographers who probably ran the greatest risks of all – were left scandalously unprotected by the magazines which employed them and which profited financially from their courage. Anyone aiming for such a career should know that it is a cruel line of work, and unpensionable.

The vehicles chosen ranged from classier Land Rovers with the latest Kevlar armour, to the former staff car of the Chief Constable of the Royal Ulster Constabulary, to an impressive paramilitary model with gun-slits and an amphibious profile, selected by ITN. This so took the fancy of the HVO, the Bosnian Croat Defence Force, that when it ran off the road and was left in a ditch overnight they retrieved it for their own purposes and fitted its turret with a machine-gun. It was spotted on patrol near Busovaca. ITN eventually got it back, and then dumped it.

The armour saved life and limb. Without 'Miss Piggy', Kate might well have lost her right foot. And Harvey Watson, one of our intrepid engineers, drove unscathed over Mount Igman – a bit of a shooting gallery at the best of times – when a rifle-launched grenade exploded against the side of his Kevlar-protected Land Rover. The burst-pattern would make an impressive front cover for *Land Rover Magazine*: the shrapnel entered the Kevlar, but none of it penetrated.

When the war is over, if it is ever finally and conclusively over, we plan an armoured parade down Marshal Tito Avenue, or whatever it is called by then, by the assembled wagons of the Sarajevo Press Armoured Division. By rights 'Miss Piggy' should be leading it, but the fortunes of war turned against her. It wasn't that she never met her 'Kermit'. She did: our next armoured vehicle was inevitably named after him. But she was driven off the road once too often, bent out of shape, and cannibalized.

By dint of such methods, by armour and common sense, by the battlefield first-aid and fieldcraft courses with which the BBC prepared us, and by acting cooperatively instead of competitively, we managed over the months and years to reduce the risks to a point where they were if not acceptable – and I do not believe there is any such thing as an *acceptable* casualty – then at least calculable. The rate of attrition diminished; fewer journalists were killed or wounded – and in this the bureaucracy helped us. The armies organized themselves as armies do, with press departments whose purpose was to control and restrict the press, and the era of the free-running photographer was over. It became increasingly difficult to get access to the front lines; and even those who wished to get shot at, couldn't.

Of course, if *all-out* war returns and either army disintegrates, it will be different, and we will always share, as we should, the risks of the civilians among whom we live. In the meantime we continued to do what we could, on the private and personal level, to stay alive. For my own part, I came to put much faith in certain routines and rituals which may be considered superstitions, but which none the less worked for me.

The wearing of a white suit was one of these – and green socks with it: no other colour need apply. I started wearing white in the Slovenian war, because it was what I happened to have with me; also, in my previous battlefield outing, in the Gulf war, the British army had put me into camouflage uniform as an official war correspondent, which included paramilitary status and much digging of trenches and shell-scrapes, and I wished to reclaim my status as a civilian. The suit made a statement: this man isn't part of anyone's army, and definitely doesn't do trenches.

The Slovenian war, though it was over in ten days, was actually quite dangerous (four journalists were killed at Ljubljana Airport) as was the Croatian war that followed it. None of us was prepared for the volume of lead and other sharp objects that was flying through the air as part of this new world disorder, and we looked for some way of surviving it. I quickly concluded, since we were on the front lines almost daily – and sometimes the front lines had a habit of coming to *us* – that the white suit was proving to be better protection than the flak jacket. It was lighter too, making for a greater turn of speed over open ground, and excellent camouflage besides, in winter warfare. So I kept it and a number of others of its kind, and the green socks, and the silver dollar in the right-hand pocket, as a sort of additional insurance policy, and I would not leave home without them.

In the Bosnian war, the most dangerous of all, further confidence-building measures were called for. I would enter the Holiday Inn at the same time of day, through the same shattered window on the west side of the ruin (the main door was bad luck, and being closer to the Serbs it was probably bad fieldcraft too), and walk to my room clockwise rather than anticlockwise round the corridor. It would have tempted fate to have done otherwise – or to have failed to play 'The Love Songs of Willie Nelson', both sides, every day. Willie Nelson is the wandering minstrel of war correspondents, as he now knows. 'I kind of like that,' he says. His *On the Road Again* was the theme song and anthem of the Sarajevo Survivors Club. His music helped keep us alive.

After the mortar attack in August 1992, when some of these idiosyncrasies became known, strangers would send me all sorts of talismans and amulets which I put in my travelling shoulder bag. In reporting wars, as in fighting them, equipment is vital. There has to be a ruthless selection of what is necessary and rejection of what is not.

We are talking here not of packing for a holiday but of survival journalism, to which different rules apply. The essential bits and pieces fall into two categories. The first is the strictly functional: a Swiss army knife, a Maglite torch with spare batteries, candles and matches, extra shoe-laces, a bulldog clip for expense receipts, army field dressings, a large plug for baths, a small plug for wash basins, and a soft squash ball for anything in between. (Since the federation collapsed the republics of ex-Yugoslavia have very little in common except their almost universal pluglessness.)

The second category, even more important because quite clearly a matter of life or death, has to do with the tokens of good fortune: a silver threepenny bit, a four-leafed and even a five-leafed clover, a fragment of water-snake skin in an envelope, a brass pixie, countless silver crosses and Saint Christophers, and tapes of Willie Nelson. I carry them all, for with the exception of the brass pixie they don't weigh very much, and who can tell which will work and which will not? Better to be safe by accumulation than sorry by preferring one to another.

So far they have worked – like a charm. And on the only occasion when on a merely superficial view they seemed to fail me, the damage was not severe. In fact they made all the difference.

6

ONE DAY IN AUGUST

I left London on 18 August 1992. It was my ninth assignment to the wars of ex-Yugoslavia, and I had no particular fears about it. The summer had been dangerous and bloody, but the white suits had done the business for me and I had lived a charmed life, which I fully expected to continue. Indeed, the journey to Sarajevo was actually safer. Last time out, our press convoy from Ilidza to Belgrade had been halted and then hijacked by Serb bandit-militiamen. Their team leader, considerably the worse for drink, had ransacked the baggage as a matter of routine – their standard operating procedure. He picked out 9,000 German marks from a colleague's briefcase, and in my own suitcase he found the white flak jacket which was a source of some pride to me, as well as protection. The Serb indicated at gunpoint that it would make our life so much easier, and he would have us on our way to Belgrade in next to no time, if I could see my way to presenting him with the flak jacket. The local police chief acted as intermediary. 'He will give you the money back,' he said, 'but he would like you to give him the bullet-proof vest. Nobody knows about this. You understand?' The deal was sealed with a handshake, and the Serb was delighted. 'Serbia good, Serbia correct,' he said in broken German.

But now we were overflying the Serb checkpoints. Since the opening of the airport, accredited journalists were allowed into

Sarajevo on board UNHCR (United Nations High Commission for Refugees) relief flights. We came to know this service, because of the vagaries of its schedule, as Maybe Airlines, but most of the time it worked. The only hazard was occasional groundfire, from both Serb and Croat positions. But it was faster and safer than the land route, and the RAF pilots minimized the danger to their Hercules aircraft with a manoeuvre they called the Khe San landing. This took its name from a battlefield of the Vietnam war, and involved maintaining altitude for as long as possible on the approach to Sarajevo, then putting the aircraft into so steep a dive that it was almost a free fall, before a last-minute levelling out. It shook up the cargo and the passengers with it. I reckoned, however, that if the flour and feta cheese could stand it, so could I. Maybe Airlines got you there more often than not.

At Sarajevo airport I was met on the apron by Don Nesbitt, and that was the first intimation I had that perhaps this might not be a trip like all the others. Don was one of the BBC's old soldiers, a redoubtable sound recordist recruited as I had been in the old days at Alexandra Palace when news was very much the Cinderella service. Of his courage, dedication and good humour there was no doubt – and he needed all of them. For he was not the most popular man to work with, because of his reputation for being born unto trouble as the sparks fly upwards – or rather, in our line of business, as the shrapnel flies outwards. Don himself usually came through unscathed, but he made the rest of us nervous. The high point of an eventful career came during a French bank siege, where he was out of the line of fire smoking a cigarette, while his camera took a robber's bullet straight through the middle of the lens.

But Don is rather sensitive about his reputation as 'Danger Man', and I greeted him as warmly as I could. I hope the sincerity seemed genuine. I knew that I needed all the luck and help I could get. Sarajevo was at war. The Serbs and the Bosnian government forces, battling for control of the city they both claimed, were in places no further than fifty yards apart. Day and night, not a minute would pass without small-arms, machine-gun, mortar and artillery fire. The only thing that had improved since my last assignment was that we now had 'Miss Piggy', our armoured Land Rover, for protection.

We needed her. On the first day out I had an invitation from the Serbs to meet a member of their royal family at Lukavica barracks. The royal personage was actually as British as I am. Princess Belinda, the wife of Prince Tomislav, the Crown prince's uncle, is a fluent and articulate advocate of the Serb cause, though her Home Counties accent seemed somehow out of place. To reach her, I joined a troop of British Royal Engineers also bound for Lukavica, to sandbag the UN positions there. But to get to the barracks, we had to survive the sniper's alley of the airport runway with Muslim gunners on both sides and Serb gunners at both ends. Thanks to 'Miss Piggy', I was for the first time invulnerable to small-arms fire, but the Royal Engineers were not. They were on the road in the world's most hazardous war zone in a Land Rover and two trucks, all unarmoured. They were risking their lives to increase the UN's security, but no one was paying any attention to theirs.

I have noticed this before with the Engineers, that they tend to draw the shortest straw the army is dealing out. Though if it comes to a war they are actually out in front of the infantry and armour, clearing minefields and breaching obstacles, they are expected to do it with equipment a generation older than anyone else's. (I suspect that they are under-represented in the army's highest councils.) At least in warfare they had armoured protection, but here in peacekeeping they did not.

I even offered to lend them 'Miss Piggy': the press is not allowed to travel in UN vehicles, but I could see no reason why they should not travel in ours. And that evening I pointed out their predicament on the BBC News, in a way that I hoped might ring a few alarm bells. It did, but not the right ones. For the Ministry of Defence did not send the armour that its men on the ground needed: instead, it sent a public relations officer. I met him next day at the airport. 'What are you here for?' I asked.

'To set the record straight,' he answered.

'But the record is straight, in fact I have personally straightened it. The Engineers need protection, and they're not getting it.'

The episode ended well for the Engineers, in that their assignment was brought to a rapid end with only one light casualty. It also ended well for me, in that the army sent me Mark Cook.

Mark was a colonel in the Gurkha Rifles, and at that time commanded the fledgeling British UN force in ex-Yugoslavia, which consisted of a field hospital and the newly reprieved Engineers. It was not even called a force then but a contingent. This was the second time our paths had crossed. Thirty-six years earlier we had been pupils together at The Leys School in Cambridge. (It bothered me that my contemporaries – those not defrocked or in jail for embezzlement – were by now colonels or ambassadors or headmasters at least, whereas I was still serving in what my old Classics teacher told me was a 'piffling profession', and surely I could do better.) It was Mark's first visit to Sarajevo, and he was there on a double mission. Part of it was to see and experience for himself the dangers to which his troops were exposed. His first duty was to them. But he had also come to seek my advice about fund-raising for his orphanage.

Mark's specialty was hopeless causes and impossible missions. One day in Croatia, in the course of his routine UN duties, he had happened upon a pile of rubble which was identified to him as all that remained of the orphanage at Lipik. It was situated directly on the front line between Croats and Serbs; and, like the rest of the town, had been destroyed in the course of the war. Its sixty children, sheltering from the bombardment in the cellar, had been spared, and were refugees on the Dalmatian coast. It was another everyday wartime tale of death and destruction. Most people were indifferent to it. Mark Cook wasn't.

In addition to his military duties, he took upon himself the burden of rebuilding the orphanage. He and his soldiers, volunteers all, spent their spare time clearing the rubble. It was only later that he discovered that the cost of rebuilding the place would, conservatively, be put at a million pounds. By then it was too late to turn back, even if he had wished to, which he didn't. So he came to me, as the one media person within reach whom he knew, for advice on the publicity that would be needed to raise that kind of money. His faith was misplaced, since I knew no more how to go about it than he did. But it was while we were mulling over these impossibilities, in the BBC bunker at the back of UN headquarters, that the Reuters correspondent Kurt Schork came rushing in with news of the battle that he had just driven through. 'I don't know what it is,' he said, 'but maybe you had better take a look.'

So I donned the mandatory flak jacket and helmet, alerted cameraman Ian Fairclough and sound recordist Don Nesbitt, and asked Mark Cook if he would like to come along for the ride. It seemed in keeping with his principal mission, to get a feel for the dangers on the ground. We set off in the redoubtable 'Miss Piggy' and headed into town.

At this point there was always a choice to be made about whether to take the main road closer to the Serb lines or the back road that ran parallel to it. Neither choice was a good one, since both routes were enfiladed by snipers from high ground on cross streets held by the Serbs. On the main road the Serbs were in places little more than a hundred yards away: but you had to drive more slowly on the back road, and so spent more time in their sights.

In a decision I later came to regret I opted for the back road. Close to the old Marshal Tito barracks, I stopped 'Miss Piggy' and cautiously stepped outside. Kurt was right. There was indeed a battle raging – but as so often it was easier to hear than to see. For our vantage point I had chosen a spot in the lee of a tall block of flats which gave cover from sniper fire. I had used it before for the commanding view it offered of one of the city's most notorious sniper's corners: bullets aimed at speeding motorists ricocheted off railway wagons on the line beside the road. It was just here that Faridoun had crashed our Vauxhall on our arrival two months earlier. I should have known it was where my luck would run out.

Professionally it already had. After fifteen minutes of dedicated camera work by Ian and Don, we had acquired a clattering sound-track but very little in the way of pictures that told the story. One of the rules we set ourselves was to stay out of cover for as short a time as possible. Discouraged, we returned to 'Miss Piggy'.

It was then that a new outburst of fighting erupted all around us, and I had a debate with myself. I often do this, on the issue of whether to advance or retreat, as if I were two characters in a Tom Stoppard play. One voice said it was time to stop hiding out in bunkers and under armour and do the job I was paid to do. Another voice said not to be such a bloody fool. The voice of caution lost. I persuaded myself that perhaps this time something would happen within Ian's camera range that would at least *look* like news. Something did. For it was at that point that the mortars opened up on us. They were fired at random and speculatively, but the aim was not far off. The first one landed fifty yards away. I shouted at Ian to make sure he had seen it. The second one, moments later, hit me.

I had always wondered what it would be like to be wounded and now I knew – end of curiosity, for a lifetime. It was like an acute pain in the abdomen, though somewhat numbed by the shock of it. I had been struck by two or three fragments of shrapnel, falling (fortunately for me) near the end of their trajectory. They penetrated exactly at the spot where the flak jacket ended. (As it happened, new and improved flak jackets, with more 'southerly' protection, had been on their way to us that very day, but did not arrive in time; life is forever like that.)

I was knocked to the ground by the force of the impact. My helmet, which I had typically omitted to fasten – for in truth, I hardly ever wore it – fell off and rolled on the concrete. In the split second of the fall I knew that I had been hit, but I was lucky. I called out to the others, 'I'm all right. I'll survive.' I did not wish to alarm them. By then Ian and Mark were rushing forward with the field dressings we always carry – the first time that Mark had ever applied one on active service. Don continued the shooting of what would be my last news story for a while.

The rest, it seemed to me then and later, was rather shame-making. I was helped to 'Miss Piggy', rushed to the UN hospital in the basement of the PTT building, and given the best possible care. Doctors removed the larger pieces of shrapnel, nurses gently tended the wound. And within an hour I was evacuated to Zagreb, on the floor of a returning relief aircraft, together with four UNMOs (UN military observers) all hit by shrapnel fire on the same day. (Maybe Airlines also ran an ambulance service.) The UNMOs were more seriously hurt than I was: one had lost a finger. All I had lost was my ability to stand upright and my reputation for invulnerability.

I was grateful, of course – even more so when the BBC sent an air ambulance to Zagreb with three doctors and the foreign editor in attendance. It was, at a price which I would not wish to pay again, my fastest journey ever from Sarajevo to London. The BBC was magnificent in an emergency, as it always is. (It is the planned events that we who love her worry about.)

But I couldn't help reflecting on the striking contrast between my treatment and that of the ordinary people of Sarajevo, injured on that day or any other. For a short while after what happened to me there were little features and articles in the press based on the total fiction of the reporter as hero. It was nonsense, of course. We were not heroes but just journalists doing our job and sometimes in harm's way more than was good for us. But we had so many advantages that real people, facing equal dangers, did not. We were there of our own free will, they were not. We could escape, they could not. We had United Nations accreditation and the use of its best field hospitals, they did not. The lightness of my wound and the ease of the evacuation made me feel a bit of a fraud: all that care and attention for what really didn't amount to more than a puncture. But I found in later months that it gave me a special advantage in dealing with field commanders, of all armies, who had themselves been hit by shrapnel or sniper fire – some of them two or three times, since they led from the front. Ours was the complicity of the wounded.

Recuperation, at the Princess Grace Hospital in Marylebone, was an exercise in idleness and luxury: a round of medical and journalistic interventions, some more benign than others. I was grateful for the exceptional skill and good humour of the surgeon, Mr Oliver Gilmore. But I also discovered, for the first and I hope the last time, what it was like to be at the other end of my colleagues' curiosity. It was my fifteen minutes of fame, and in the course of it I made the firm decision that celebrity journalism was not for me. My favourite headline of the time alluded to the piece of shrapnel still left in me: 'It's lead-belly Martin', shrieked the Star.

I decided to leave this side of things to my formidable colleague Kate Adie, who deals with it so much better. She had replaced me at short notice, and flew into a situation at least as dangerous as the one I had been carried out of; probably more so, for these were among Sarajevo's darkest hours. Lying in my hospital bed, I was informed of an *Evening Standard* billboard that had just appeared in the street outside: 'TV's Kate in Shrapnel Drama'. It seemed that Kate's helmet had been hit by a fragment of shrapnel. Whether her head was in it at the time I did not know; but I did know that I could return, after treatment, to a life of quiet obscurity.

But not quite yet. First there was a mountain of mail to deal with. I discovered that if you have been a TV reporter over so long a period – already more than thirty years in my case – you almost become part of some people's families, and have more friends than you ever knew you had. I received over 1,000 letters, mostly from complete strangers.

The mail mountain provided an interesting 'profile' of my legion of unknown friends. They were predominantly female, and (so far as I could judge) in their mid-seventies. One wrote, 'You were my late husband's favourite TV reporter.' And another, 'Whenever I hear your voice it makes my toes curl. Don't worry, I am sixty-three and bed-ridden.' And yet a third, 'You cause many a flutter in this arthritic great-grandmother's bosom.' I had finally found my constituency. It was the nation's grandmothers. They were kind, anxious, complimentary, and very hard to answer. (Only one letter was hostile: it called me a 'white fascist pig' because I had been shot in Sarajevo and not Somalia.) I wrote back, so far as I could, to every one of them. My daughters Melissa and Catherine helped out by addressing and stuffing the envelopes. In three weeks the job was done and I was sufficiently recovered to start work again. It had not been a serious wound anyway but it had served as an attention-getting device, and it got more attention than it deserved.

The episode had a happy sequel for Mark Cook. As he was one of the few witnesses to what happened, he was interviewed live on the BBC's *One O'Clock News* shortly afterwards. This enabled him to give more than a passing mention of the Lipik orphanage, which was part of the reason for his being in Sarajevo in the first place. It gave the project the start-up momentum it needed. 'The message,' he wrote later, 'got across live to millions. It seemed that, thanks to Martin taking a direct hit in the groin, we had had our second lucky break. We now had a charity set up and running and a huge publicity plug. It seemed to me that providence really must be on our side – if not poor Martin's.'

I remembered that I had warned Mark, just a short while before, that with the best will in the world I wasn't much of a fund-raiser. A Serb mortar crew helped prove me wrong . . . Just sixteen months later he had raised his million and the children were back in the rebuilt Lipik orphanage. It was a striking exhibition, amid the chaos and anarchy of the new world order, of the difference one man can make. Mark Cook is such a man. When the children returned he had tears in his eyes – and they embraced him like the father they never had. It was a moment, he said, that gave him more satisfaction than anything he had done as a soldier.

7

TUNA

No war starts out of the clear blue. There are distant rumblings of thunder beforehand, and the art of the foreign editor – whenever he or she can take time off from portrayal committees and budget meetings and business plans and all the myriad mysteries of modern management – is to identify the cloud no bigger than a man's hand before it becomes the storm. This is especially true of civil wars, where the parties can play elaborate games of brinkmanship for months, moving two steps forward and one step back towards the edge of the precipice.

So it was in Croatia. And so it also was that, as with the Slovenian war which started concurrently, we came to it a day late and in a great hurry. The search was then on for the most important member of any TV team in an unfamiliar war zone, which is not the reporter or cameraman or producer or videotape editor, but the local contact with reality. To call these people interpreters is to undervalue them. Our man in Belgrade for instance, Vladimir Marjanovic, was fluent in English, French and German, besides being well-versed in Japanese, electronics and Egyptian hieroglyphics (he was by no means your average Serb in the street); having done his time in the Yugoslav army as a lieutenant in charge of an arms depot he also knew the calibres and ballistic properties of all the weapons being used around us. But his real value to us was his knowledge of the politics and the history and his ability to translate the people as well as the language. He was a living, breathing dictionary and encyclopedia.

We were equally lucky in Croatia. Our first find was Vera Kordic whom we stole from Australian television and who was working before that as a translator for HINA, the news agency of the newly declared independent state. I never really understood why she left a safe and comfortable job translating editorials from *La Stampa* and the *Süddeutsche Zeitung* into Croatian, for a far more hazardous occupation, running the front lines under fire with a TV team who knew little of the country and nothing of the language. It was a bit like preferring Grozny to Guildford. But one of us had to know what they were doing, and Vera did. She was as brave as a lioness and especially gifted at road-blocks, where she would slip into Serbian dialect and play psychological games with the Serbs' hidden weakness, which is a wish to be liked and to be hospitable. Thus did she earn the title of 'Road-block Vera'. Fortunately she still works for us, though after all the hazards we have put her through it is hard to understand why.

Our second find was Tuna, twenty-four years old and a graduate of the Academy of Dramatic Arts in Zagreb. His real name was Tihomir Tunukovic, but he preferred the short form, perhaps because he knew that the long one would tax our elocution to the limit. His English was fluent, but he was very much more than a translator. He was a cameraman with OTV, a newly established youth television station. He had ambitions single-handedly to revive the once thriving Yugoslav film industry, and to bring to it the special skills he had already learned, so that 'A Film by Tihomir Tunukovic' would one day roll on the credits. He was a champion skier and played at full back for the Croatian rugby team. In the course of these activities he had seriously challenged just about every bone in his body. I discovered this when he brought me to the hospital after I had done some minor damage to myself, and he turned out to be on first-name terms with every osteopath in Zagreb. He was a walking testimonial to their skills.

So the Croatian war, which was already beginning to scare me considerably, held no terrors at all for him. After a very short time we played to his strengths and let him loose with a camera. Though the pictures he shot were just for the news, their composition would have graced a feature film. Looking back on it now I can see that I was by no means as smart as I thought I was to use Tuna, rather than the BBC staff camera-man, for some of the more dangerous assignments. I did this not because he was in any way expendable – he was the one indispensable person that we had – but because he knew the front lines better, and by combining the roles of cameraman, soundman and translator into one we could operate as a team of two, thus halving the risks that we ran.

It made sense at the time but I regret it now, because I encouraged him to go where he wished to go and face the dangers that he wished to face, and I should have reined him in. Soon enough he was working as he preferred, entirely on his own. The front-line soldiers were his friends, and he could go with them wherever he wanted. His most famous coup was in August 1991, the second month of the war, when the Croatian town of Kostajnica on the border with Bosnia was close to being surrounded by the Serbs. The garrison changed every two weeks, and Tuna talked himself on board the shuttle which took in the new guard and brought out the old one. It was supposed to be an armoured personnel carrier, for the road was under Serb fire from across the Una river, but the armour was impro-vised from steel plates bolted on to the chassis of an old and underpowered delivery truck.

We had not even known what Tuna was up to until he returned to Zagreb late in the evening. He looked tired and crestfallen. 'I'm sorry,' he said. 'I've let you down. I should have made it back in time for the news.'

'You haven't let us down at all, but we were beginning to worry about you. Where've you been?'

'Kostajnica. But I got kind of delayed.'

'Delayed by what?'

'By an ambush, actually.'

Then we viewed the tape that he had shot. It would not have mattered if he had brought it in the next day or the next week or the next month: it was the most extraordinary combat footage from the entire Croatian war. Those were indeed the last days of Kostajnica. The men who went in with Tuna were to be killed or taken prisoner. Those who came out with him fought their way out from the dark and embattled recesses of the armoured truck. They had eight miles to go to their forward base in the river village of Dubica, and with the Serbs attacking from both sides it was like eight miles through the valley of the shadow of death. The hard-pressed Croats blazed away with everything they had, from handguns to assault rifles, fired through the gun-slits until the barrels grew hot. One man would rush to take another's place as he reloaded. The floor of the truck was an inch deep in spent cases.

Tuna, who was quite as much at risk as any of them, shot this scene almost entirely in close-up. The living fear was etched into their faces and driftingly glimpsed through the smoke of rapid fire. Even the kind of movie director he aspired to be could have spent millions and never quite done it as he did it. You could re-create the ambush and the hardware, but never the raw emotion: the terror of the journey and the triumph of surviving it. Indeed I have sometimes wondered whether anyone who has not been in a war knows what real fear is: in most of us what passes for it is perhaps just nervousness. (I have never yet watched a movie about any of the wars I was in, from Vietnam to Nicaragua to El Salvador, without walking out before the end. Not even Oliver Stone seemed to me to catch the essence of them. Rather, the reality was mocked by afterthought, and somehow skewed by Hollywood's political wisdom.)

After the Kostajnica episode I sat Tuna down and read him the riot act. I was more than twice his age, I had survived nine more wars than he had, and I hadn't done it by taking the kind of risks that he had just taken. But I had some difficulty in disguising my pride in his achievement, and that was something that would come to haunt me later. Tuna admitted that if he had known what he was in for he would not have gone through with it – but once committed, there was no retreat. He promised to be more reasonable in the future.

The strange thing was that along with the blithe courage that kept Tuna going there was a premonition that should have stopped him in his tracks. It was the conviction that he himself would not survive these wars, and it grew on him after the death of his friend and rival, Zivko Krsticevic. Tuna, who could tolerate anything but inactivity, was working at the time for Visnews, and Zivko for the rival agency, World Television News (WTN). Despite their friendship, or even perhaps because of it, they competed fiercely. On 30 December 1991, only four days before the ceasefire in Croatia, Zivko was working the front lines in the ruined village of Turanj near Karlovac when he was hit in the chest by a tiny fragment of shrapnel. He and his camera fell to the ground and it recorded his life's breath expiring.

Zivko's was the first death among the tightly knit group of ex-Yugoslav (and mostly Croat) cameramen and producers who did most of the front-line work for the networks and agencies. It had a shattering effect on all of them. After the funeral they held a wake. A friend gave this account of it: 'After a few bottles of wine we started to talk, mostly about Zivko, how he made us laugh all the time and the tricks he used to beat the competition. At some point Tuna said, 'Well, once again WTN has scored. It is 1–0 for WTN. It is our turn now. I will be the next one.'

There is no safety in war zones, but next time we worked together, in the battle for the nearby railway town of Sunja, we followed to the letter such safety drills as there can be, especially on the point of doing what has to be done as quickly as possible and getting out as fast as possible. We left at high speed under serious gunfire. I was highly gratified when the BBC later came to use Tuna's footage from Sunja as a model of how to survive wars as well as shoot them.

The Croatian ceasefire of January 1992 seemed to solve the problem for both of us anyway, at least for as far forward as we could see, which was about two months. The BBC lost interest in the Balkan wars for a while, and Tuna was able to return to his first love, the cinema. As a token of his ambition to shoot for the stars he bought the first steadicam in ex-Yugoslavia. He was seen with this sophisticated contraption, which takes the judder out of hand-held filming, patrolling and practising in the corridors of the Intercontinental Hotel in Zagreb. Actually he was showing it off. He was intensely proud of it, and even used it on a couple of local TV commercials. It was surely his passport to migrate from news to feature films, and we wished him well in his new career as movie mogul.

Then two things happened which changed both our futures – or rather, one did and one didn't. What happened was that the Bosnian war broke out, though my initial route to it was through Belgrade and the local help that I recruited was from that side. What didn't happen had to do with Croatia's fledgeling film industry. The shadow of war still hung over the new republic, a third of its territory was in Serb hands, and there wasn't the confidence to finance a promotional video on the delights of Dubrovnik, never mind a full-length feature film. Ironically *War and Peace* had been shot in Serbia and Bosnia, with the Yugoslav army as extras. Now some of those same soldiers were redefining war and peace in Balkan terms, using different uniforms and certainly firing no blanks. Tuna's movie moguldom would have to wait.

We went our separate ways for a while during the war's first summer in Sarajevo and until Serb road-blocks made the route from Belgrade impassable except to Serbs. It also began to dawn on us that the war was rather more widespread than we had shown it to be, and it was time to pay some attention to the hinterland. The front lines were still fluctuating in central Bosnia, and the Serbs in their last big push were closing in on Jajce, a town which was shared between Muslims and Croats but which stood across an important strategic road. Our BBC operation had moved by then from Sarajevo to Kiseljak and was much concerned – perhaps too much concerned – with the fortunes of the Cheshire Regiment, who had arrived under their blue helmets two weeks earlier. We needed someone experienced and self-starting to cover the fall of Jajce and the displacement of its tens of thousands of refugees. Tuna was willing and available. He left his prized four-wheel drive road runner – the one with all the gadgets and gizmos, the latest being a mobile fax and phone – in the car park at Zagreb airport. To him it was just another assignment, and a chance to test his skills and find things out.

I was not in Bosnia at the time, but supposedly still recuperating and on light duties, which consisted of reporting a state visit to Germany by the Queen. Royal tours are actually quite hard to write for television, since there is a fine line to be walked between the pitfalls of blandness on one hand and impertinence on the other. (Once, in Canada, I was so bored with it that I did the whole script in rhyming couplets and iambic pentameters, and no one even noticed.) I am no republican but did wonder, as so often with these stately progressions, whether in the sum of things they mattered very much. I had no such doubts about the war that I had left behind in Bosnia.

For whatever reasons Tuna had no one else with him in his armoured Land Rover when he drove out from Travnik on the road to Jajce to cover the refugee story. It was the 1st of November, All Saints' Day. He was not quite alone. A team from our friends and rivals in Sky News tagged along in their own vehicle behind him, but Tuna knew the area better and they properly let him lead. To have done what he had to do he need have ventured no further than the village of Turbe, which was still in the hands of government forces, and let the refugees come to him.

Instead he went the extra mile and crossed no man's land towards them. He had taken such chances before and come through unscathed. His clearly marked white Land Rover rounded a bend and drove into the sights of a Serb twenty millimetre anti-aircraft gun aimed laterally like a heavy machine-gun, one of the deadliest weapons of the war. For a reason which we never discovered, and the Serbs themselves never explained, the gun crew opened up on him and blew him away. The light armour was no protection against that calibre of round. The Land Rover veered off the road and crashed into a ravine. Tuna was killed instantly, and would have known very little about it.

They called me with the news at my home in Berlin, and at first I refused to believe it. Our team in Bosnia was like a league of friends, and Tuna was the real star of it. His death was unassimilable.

I booked myself on the first flight to Zagreb the next morning. I was met at the airport by Vera Kordic and taken to the one appointment that I dreaded most but knew I had to keep, which was to call on Tuna's parents. They were red-eyed and exhausted in a darkened flat, candle-lit and with its curtains drawn. They were also quite astonishingly gracious. I shall remember it as the most painful hour of my life, because although I live by words no words were adequate. There was nothing I could say about the man and his life and his work and his value to us, which spoke to the grief of these wonderful people about their loss of a loved and sometimes wayward son. It was the worse because I knew, and I suspect they knew, that I was in some way responsible for his death. I was responsible in a general sense because I represented the BBC, and if it had not been for his BBC work he would still have been with them that day. I was also responsible in a particular sense, because although I had not recruited him I had encouraged his camera-work and his venturesome exploits and signed him on as a permanent member of the team. I have no idea what his daily rate was in German marks, but I paid him also in praise and approval, which are just as important to fieldmen in dangerous places. Perhaps insidiously so. I was not being manipulative, but expressing what I felt, that he was really quite the best at what he did. Yet it occurred to me later that he may have become like one of those agents in a John le Carré spy novel, whose loyalty is absolute and who show a greater devotion to the cause than it actually deserves.

Tuna's body was retrieved with great difficulty and only after his personal effects had been plundered by the Serbs. They handed it over to the British UN troops who were dealing with the flow of refugees at the Turbe crossing. The Cheshires, still new to Bosnia and with so much else going on around them, were outstandingly helpful in coping with the administrative details and organizing his last journey home. So were the European Community monitors based in Zagreb, whom I had occasionally criticized in the past for not doing very much and doing it rather expensively, preferring the vineyards of Slovenia to the war zones of Croatia.

But not this time. This time Tuna's friends in the Zagreb press corps – and there was no one in the Zagreb press corps who was not his friend – had hoped that the arrival of the body in a returning relief aircraft would somehow be handled with dignity and even a little ceremony, but we had no clear idea how. Dudley Ells, a Royal Army Ordnance Corps officer who was now a white-suited EC monitor, organized it for us, blowing away the bureaucratic obstacles as if they were just so much old ordnance. He and five of his colleagues became pall-bearers for the transfer of the coffin from aircraft to hearse. The press remained in the background, not to record the event but to mourn it. Tears were shed on the tarmac and little was said.

I used the period before the funeral to compose a few hundred words for the *Guardian* on who Tuna was and what he did and why his death had such an impact on us. I wondered aloud how much longer we could expect such people to run such risks – both the locally recruited camera teams and those sent from London. There were very few with both the nerve and the talent for it. But the alternative was for these wars to be fought in a kind of dark ages obscurity. Something of the sort eventually happened and it troubled me.

The funeral was held under overcast skies at Mirogoj cemetery, whose pomp was rather out of keeping with the modesty and informality of the man whom we were burying. Zagreb is really two cities, the streets and squares familiar to us which are the city of the living, and the cemetery above them, with its marble halls and arcades and portals and pavilions, which is the city of the dead. There are Croatian families whose tombs are grander than their houses and it was among these monuments that a simple plot and a plain marble slab were found for Tihomir Tunukovic.

He had more friends than he knew. The death notices and news reports had appeared in the Zagreb papers, and an obituary in *Slobodna Dalmacija* noted that he was 'born in Croatia, he was shooting for the entire world, and he died in Bosnia'. Some 2,000 people attended the funeral, many more than could be accommodated in the chapel, so a sort of public meeting was held outside its gates, with microphones and amplifiers to reach to the back of the crowd. I was one of the two or three of those who knew him best who were asked to speak, but it was as hard as ever to find the words for it, and harder still to do so across the language barrier.

Under normal circumstances I would have asked Vera Kordic to do the consecutive translation for me, since she was fluent in many languages and we had worked together in good times and bad since the start of the war in Croatia. She could interpret what I meant as well as what I said, which were not always as much one and the same as they should have been; and she corrected mistakes which I never even knew I had made. But she was close to Tuna, and so broken-hearted by what had happened that it was as much as she could do to attend the funeral at all. In her place we were fortunate to have the volunteered services of Janko Paravic, the courtly and academic figure who was President Tudjman's official interpreter.

I am not much for public speaking, and it was the largest crowd I had ever addressed – or at least seen while I was talking to them, although of course in the nature of things I had been in the homes of millions without knowing them. The remoteness of television ill prepares one for such an ordeal, without a retake or switch-off button. I was aware that no words of mine would be sufficient, so after a very short tribute to Tuna's life and work I borrowed from John Bunyan's, that he should say them for me. I had no idea whether Croats were familiar with *The Pilgrim's Progress*, though Professor Paravic certainly knew it.

But it was appropriate to the moment. Tuna had something of Mr Standfast about him, and he was surely Mr Valiant-for-Truth: 'My sword, I give to him that shall succeed me in my pilgrimage, and my courage and skill to him that can get it . . . So he passed over, and all the trumpets sounded for him on the other side.'

There are people we know who have died and who fade in our memory. Tuna's presence is as enduring and permanent among us today as it was on All Saints' Day 1992. And his dream lives on, to be made reality should a real peace come to the Balkans. A company called Tunafilms exists for just that purpose.

8

OF SERBS AND SATELLITES

Nermin Tulic was an actor of great talent and with an abiding love for the plays of Shakespeare which he had learned from his university professor, Nikola Koljevic. Tulic was a Muslim and Koljevic a Serb, but in the old multi-ethnic and tolerant Bosnia that made no difference. Nor did it matter that Koljevic was contemplating a political career and standing for election to Bosnia's collective presidency, in which all its peoples were represented. The war had not yet started, and was spoken of fearfully as the ultimate nightmare which could surely be avoided by prudent political compromise – a further reason for well-regarded people like Nikola Koljevic to be taking a hand in politics. Tulic's wife Maja was a Serb, and he had no difficulty voting for a Serb candidate, for it fitted with his dream of the new republic. 'My wish,' he said, 'is for a European kind of Bosnia, cosmopolitan Bosnia, a universal Bosnia, and not some kind of a canton or province or sheep pen. That is what others want. I want Bosnia to be a European state.' In such a country there would certainly be a place for the professor-politician. 'He was simply someone I liked very much, a nice man, a charmer who knew a lot of things, who was helping us to learn about Shakespeare, Chekhov, Pinter. All of us, the students of the drama academy, we loved and adored our teacher. I voted for him, I circled his name.'

But the nightmare became the reality. The war began in

April 1992, and in August it blasted the actor's life with the fall of a single mortar. He was standing outside his home when it exploded near him, and he was so seriously wounded that he lost both his legs. When I visited him some months later, in the dead of winter, he was living on the charity of friends in a ground-floor flat so dark and cold it was more like a cave than a home. His wife and two children were with him, the younger one born in the hospital ward directly below him as he was being treated for his wounds. 'Some evil fate,' he said, 'has determined that one of our children spends half his life in war and the other to be born at war.' His concern was more about their future than his.

By this time the former professor had fled the city. Nikola Koljevic was teaching and charming no more. He was vice-president of the self-declared Bosnian Serb Republic, whose forces were encircling the city and bombing its people. Together with Radovan Karadzic as president, he held some political responsibility for the warfare and for the casualties, though he continued to maintain that the Serbs were the injured party. Tulic spoke of his former mentor and idol with difficulty, as someone who hardly was, or had never been. 'This is neither a human being nor a beast, nor anything else. He is a *thing* or a *creature*, simply he is a creature.'

'And if Sarajevo were an open city and you were able to meet him in the street?'

'I would kill him.'

What he feared most, he said, was not the pain or the suffering or the lifetime of immobility, but a capacity for hatred which he had found in himself and he had never known was there. And he had found it also in the city he loved. He lowered his voice as he said this. It dismayed him: 'Hatred is terrible, hatred is worse than cancer.'

Nermin Tulic's tragedy was one of many. There were a

legion of others, some known and some unknown, at least as insupportable. By the end of 1992, after nine months of bloodshed, hardly a family in Sarajevo had not been touched by the shadow of the war's destruction. Since the main municipal cemetery was in no man's land, the old Heroes' cemetery above the Turkish quarter was reactivated and filled with the graves of the city's defenders. Then the massed ranks of plain wooden markers bearing only a name and a date marched across the Lion cemetery and on to the football pitch below. Crosses too, for the incoming mortars made no distinction between Muslims and Croats and Serbs. I used to take visitors there, like Paddy Ashdown, to show them the scale of the war in the acres of graves.

The *nature* of it was harder to convey, especially in the limited compass of television, except by talking to the victims. This was not as intrusive as it sounds, for the victims were usually willing enough to talk, and they had surely earned the right to be listened to. It also somehow personalized the conflict, so that people elsewhere could relate to it more easily, as if it were their homes and families being targeted, and not some foreign conflict of no consequence.

One thing these stories all had in common was that they tended to reinforce the stereotype of good Muslims and bad Serbs. The ethnic and religious mix was actually more complicated than that – as indeed were the moral issues, for the Serbs also suffered. As many as 60,000 of them still lived in the city; they were either loyal to the Bosnian presidency or had been unable to get away in time; the rebel Serbs in Pale regarded them as hostages or collaborators. But the prevailing image, repeated daily in TV news reports including my own, was of Muslims attacked by Serbs. The fast-growing Sarajevo press corps soon came to be on the side of the Muslims, not only geographically but also morally. Indifference was not an option open to us. Some reporters' sympathies were co-opted so openly that they started to refer to the Serbs, in the language of the Bosnian presidency, as 'aggressor forces'. The Serbs' case, even if they had one, went unheard. The UN was pilloried for dealing with them at all. Their targeting of civilians was indeed outrageous and a violation of international law, and it was hard to report the consequences without letting the outrage show. As a kind of professional course correction, I found myself scrutinizing and censoring my own words, and the delivery of them, to make sure that superfluous emotion was filtered out and only the plain facts remained. Commentary was redundant anyway. The plain facts said it all.

It also occurred to me, though, that there had to be more to the story than we were telling, and to wonder why the Serbs were shelling this city which they claimed was theirs, which they said they loved, and to which they planned to return. As they had initiated this war and prepared for it, and had been polishing their bayonets while their adversaries were still singing folk songs, so also it would end only when they wished it to end. They were the movers and shakers, and the Muslims were the dreamers of dreams. Accordingly I broke ranks with some of my colleagues in Sarajevo, headed to Pale whenever possible, and did what I could to try to understand what moved the 'aggressor forces'.

It was not an easy course to take, especially at their many and hostile road-blocks. I was threatened and harassed and robbed and arrested more than at any time in my professional life. Compared to it, Belfast in 1970 was a honeymoon and El Salvador in 1982 was a beach. It was a costly investment in time and patience. The patience ran out, and the time was mostly wasted.

I travelled light. The Serbs were in the grip of extreme spy mania, and at their road-blocks journalists were doubly suspect for being foreigners (therefore historically anti-Serb) and for travelling from the other side of the lines. Where most United Nations vehicles were waved through, ours were subject to a painstaking and rigorous search at the point of a knife. A Croatian Airlines baggage tag was taken as clear evidence of Ustasha (Croatian Fascist) connections. A Dubrovnik hotel bill likewise. A love letter would be held up to the light and examined for secret codes. A map meant certain interrogation. A bottle of pills for a friend would be instantly confiscated. Even a teddy bear might not be as innocent as it seemed.

The bear existed; its name was Biggles. It was brown and cuddly and the property of my friend and producer Sean Salsarola, who braved more of these road-blocks than any of us in the first six months of the war. As the Serbs' stranglehold on Sarajevo tightened and they still kept some of their roads selectively open, he was the fetcher and carrier of indispensable supplies – German marks and Yugoslav dinars, jerrycans of petrol, bottles of social lubricant both Scottish and Irish, cigarettes for road-block taxes, and even (it was rumoured) white suits for the correspondent from the dry cleaners in Belgrade. I had always regarded Sean as a rather daredevil kind of character with a truly Italian flair for trading in favours, and knew nothing of the teddy bear until the Serb militiaman discovered it in Sean's baggage. Ian Traynor of the *Guardian* was with us at the time, and reported on the treatment that this button-eyed spy received: 'The Serbian commando, armed to the teeth, found what he seemed to be looking for – the BBC cuddly toy. As Martin Bell, his BBC crew, and a host of Western reporters looked on nervously, the commando drew his knife, upended the teddy, inserted the blade at the crotch, and gutted it. He found only foam padding. The disembowelled mascot was hurled aside. The frantic search for anti-Serbian material resumed.' (The bear was later restored to health by the expert needlework of Sean's fiancée Maria. After a period of convalescence it has been retired from front-line duty, having served with distinction.)

Those whose function it was to deal with the press were not necessarily more amiable than the militiaman. It was also Sean who volunteered to drive to Pale with Dragan Havzijevic, our Belgrade photographer and a man of impeccable Serbian credentials, to meet Todor Dutina, the head of Srna, the newly formed Bosnian Serb News Agency. The Serbs' rebellion was in its early stages, and he was not in a mood to waste time. 'I wish you to understand,' he said, 'my opinion of journalists and especially of foreign journalists. In principle, all journalists are criminals.'

Mr Dutina had just been appointed Minister of Information for the Bosnian Serb state, and it seemed a good moment to change the subject. 'Congratulations,' said Sean. 'You must be very proud.'

'I am not proud,' was the answer. 'It is my people who are proud.'

The Serbs in their pride and paranoia were difficult to deal with at the best of times, and downright impossible when the fortunes of war began to turn against them. The defining and most celebrated moment of their history was a battle which they lost (the Battle of Kosovo in 1389), and 600 years later it seemed that they still retained a talent for plucking defeat from the jaws of victory. It was almost as if they *wished* to be encircled and besieged and betrayed and attacked, and organized their affairs in such a way that this would happen, for only thus, with the world against them, would it confirm their heroic view of themselves and their soldierly qualities. They felt at their best when shining against dark backgrounds, and would if necessary create the darkness to shine against.

The Serbs' isolation was self-inflicted. They relished it. 'We have no friends but God,' said Radovan Karadzic, and sometimes I wondered how he could be quite so sure about God. Their own view of the world was Serbocentric. It turned around them. They liked to tell the story of the Croat, the Muslim and two Serbs who found themselves on the moon. The Croat claimed it for the Croats, because he said its barren landscape resembled the mountains of Dalmatia. The Muslim claimed it for the Muslims, because its shades of grey were exactly those of the hills and escarpments of central Bosnia. One of the Serbs then took out his revolver and shot the other. 'Now the moon is Serbian,' he said, 'for wherever a Serb has spilt his blood or lies buried is for ever Serbian territory.'

Even the break with Belgrade did not deter the Bosnian Serbs, although it did dismay them. They believed it was temporary, and that sooner or later their fellow-Serbs would rally to their cause. For this purpose too it was necessary to be seen to have all the world against them, a feat which they accomplished in short order. They also fantasized about the economic blockade and the damage that it would do to those who had applied it. They pointed out that it was a Bosnian Serb factory in Banja Luka which was once the major supplier of toilet paper to the whole of Yugoslavia. Thus it was suggested that their enemies would be brought if not to their knees at least to their seats in a state of some inconvenience.

At the same time and rather to my surprise, I found the Serbs quite easy to like, on a personal and social level. Once they even sought to use me to pass a message to the British government, though I protested to them that this was none of my business, but I don't think that anything came of it. They could be warm-hearted and hospitable and even almost innocent in a fourteenth-century kind of way – which is not to excuse them but rather to suggest that they belonged to a different age. Yet they were doing the damage in this one, and the problem was to get through to them. A few of the attempts succeeded, for the Serbs went through occasional short phases of accessibility, but many were a catalogue of failures and frustrations, some more memorable than others.

In March 1993, when the Serbs had encircled Srebrenica and the UN commander, General Morillon, embarked on his campaign to save the Muslims trapped there, it seemed the right time to leave the BBC's temporary base at Tuzla (as close to the enclave as we could get) and decamp to the Serbs' political headquarters at Pale. As usual they held the key to the crisis, and might be persuaded to grant some access or at least to talk about it. With my armoured car broken down in deep snow and the roads all but impassable, I commandeered an elderly Zastava – the people's car of the old Yugoslavia – which lacked such standard features as an ignition key, but skimmed across the rutted snow when its driver connected two wires. It skimmed even faster after I unwisely offered him a nip of the Bushmills that I happened to have with me, and from that point on he drove like a man inspired, with the steering wheel in one hand and the bottle in the other. It took two days to reach the Serb lines and much patience to cross them – and all for nothing. Dr Karadzic had left Pale unexpectedly, perhaps – it was suggested – to get his hair cut at the Intercontinental Hotel in Belgrade. No one was authorized to speak in his absence, all roads to the eastern front were closed, and the Bosnian Serb army was in one of its periods of extreme non-communication with the press – even its own tame journalists and photographers. In this it took its cue from its commander: 'The press is of no interest to me,' said General Ratko Mladic. 'I do not need the press, because I shall be vindicated by history.'

Outsiders imagine that when television arrives doors open to it, even in time of war, and that generals with an eye to their own reputation bestir themselves to be helpful. I wish that this were true but it is not — especially not with the Serbs. The whole enterprise cost me a week, at a time when I should have been filing daily, with not a frame to show for it. But sometimes, persistence paid.

Colonel Jovo Bartula was as tough a nut to crack, media-wise, as his commanding general. He had been branded a war criminal by the Bosnian government because when the war began he had pointed his guns outwards from his barracks towards Sarajevo, though he had not actually fired them. Now he was in command of two batteries of 100-millimetre mountain guns which, until the ceasefire of February 1994, were in place on high ground eight miles east of Sarajevo, and were aimed directly down the Miljacka valley with line of sight on the city centre. He was an officer of the old school, with little time for civilians and less for journalists. Major Mike Beary, the United Nations observer who made the introduction, assured me that his attitude was one of implacable hostility to the press in general and the BBC in particular. The BBC had just transmitted a profile of Radovan Karadzic, the Bosnian Serb leader, as a poet and man of letters (for which we were widely vilified: the critics charged that it was no better than making a programme on Hitler as an artist). But Colonel Bartula, who had of course not seen the piece, had no doubt that it was anti-Serb, and further evidence of a global media conspiracy against his people.

'The BBC,' he announced by way of welcome, 'is an Ustasha organization, and whatever you want I have no intention of helping you.' It was not an auspicious beginning, and I could sense the satisfaction of my UN friend that someone else for a change was on the receiving end of the colonel's paranoia. I nodded gravely and suggested that he should tell me more, and then when he had finished I would be pleased to answer him. (I also recruited the UN's interpreter, Svetlana, whom I knew well, to vouch for my political correctness *vis-à-vis* the Serbs:

that meant they had dealt with me before and had never actually expelled me – a mark of favour.)

Official Serbs like the colonel, stamped and moulded in the old Communist tradition, have difficulty in dealing with people as individuals; but they do understand *delegations*. They have spent their lives receiving delegations, or being delegates themselves. The most comfortable billet anywhere is the Delegates Club (which is why the UN command annexed the one in Sarajevo). So I appointed myself 'Head of the BBC Delegation', and gave a speech which would not have been out of place in the old days of Realistic Socialism. It started with impressive references to the ancient friendship between the Serb and British peoples, and had much history in it, for the Serbs live their history like no other people on earth. It went on to review the military situation, couched as far as possible in the terminology of the old Yugoslav people's army, in which not only the colonel had been trained but so had his former friend and now enemy Sefer Halilovic, commander of the opposing government forces in Sarajevo. It offered to pass a message to Halilovic. It maintained that the Serbs, though they had prevailed on the battlefield, had been seriously worsted in the propaganda war, which in the long term was just as important. The great Marshal Tito, whose precepts and example they studied, would not have made such a mistake. And if the colonel was angered most of all, as he said he was, by the suggestions that he was an aggressor in his own country, then here was the opportunity for him to say so.

The next thing I knew, he excused himself so that he could go and shave to look his best for the TV camera. (Mike Beary looked astonished. He said that he had never heard so much blarney in all his life. Since he was Irish, I took that as a compliment.) And we were led to the gun position overlooking Sarajevo.

The Muslims had come close to overrunning that high ground in an infantry attack a few days earlier. They were strong in infantry and the Serbs were not. The Serbs had beaten them back, but only just and with casualties on both sides. Skirmishing continued around the perimeter, and tracer fire vaulted across no man's land like a rain of molten hyphens. But the big guns stayed silent, as the UN confirmed that they had done for a while. Colonel Bartula explained why: 'All this is Serbian land,' he said. 'That over there is Trebevic. And over there on the horizon is Igman. It is not our aim to continue with the destruction of Sarajevo. We have already been called all sorts of names by the rest of the world – savages, aggressors, barbarians. But the world should understand that we are fighting for the right of self-determination and for the right to choose our own state and live like any other country in Europe.' As all Serbs did, he warned against outside intervention. 'They could not destroy us by rockets or airpower. Not all of us would die.' And another added: 'I wonder what the Americans would say when they started receiving a convoy of coffins. Let them play their war games somewhere in Somalia, or Iran, or Iraq, or Kuwait, but surely not here.'

In war reporting we are not in the business of liking or disliking, but only of understanding. Up there on the colonel's dome-shaped hill, with the city spread out below us and at the mercy of his artillery, I understood two things which I would not have understood if I had remained in the target zone at the Holiday Inn. One was that the Serbs were actually *disadvantaged* by their overwhelming strength in heavy weapons. They could level parts of the city at will, but there were civilians still living in those parts of the city; and in the long term the Serbs' actions would so outrage the world community that it would finally cease to deal with them, and lift the arms embargo against their enemies.

It was not necessary to believe the conspiracy theories about government forces shelling their own people for the benefit of CNN and the BBC, to see that the city's defenders could succeed by failing: they might launch an infantry attack which could make a great commotion and not gain an inch of ground, but yet provoke a fierce retaliation by the Serbs. Small arms would be answered by mortars, and machine-guns by shellfire. And where the shells landed and did their indiscriminate damage, the cameras would never be far away. Nor would the government spokesmen demanding action. This was the way that wars were waged in the age of satellite television and UN peace enforcement: a military victory could also be a political defeat. The Muslims could win the war by losing it. And vice versa the Serbs.

The other thing that I came to understand was that the Serbs' vaunted military superiority was actually quite fragile, and the juggernaut of their army was very far from invincible. They were fully mobilized and permanently overstretched across 800 miles of front line. They had no more resources of manpower to draw on. This was an army which already included all men of military age and some beyond it. On the front lines at Trebevic, overlooking Sarajevo, where the men served two weeks at a time in primitive conditions, it looked like a muster of grand-fathers under arms. The Serbs were heavily outnumbered by already rearmed Muslims, they were increasingly vulnerable to infantry attacks, and they were genuinely tired of the war.

After the appalling atrocities of the early months, the image of the bloodthirsty Chetnik took an unshakeable hold on the public consciousness, especially that of an already committed press corps. Yet for the first year of the war, at least until the Serbs' rejection of the Vance–Owen plan in May 1993, there was among them a clear and identifiable 'peace party' seeking compromise. Dr Karadzic himself had been prevailed on by the

European Community to accept the plan, and the Serbian President Slobodan Milosevic travelled to Pale to urge the Bosnian Serb parliament to ratify it. So did even some of General Mladic's soldiers, though he was inside the session and they were not.

These lobbyists included one of their most renowned field commanders, whose *nom de guerre* was Major Mauser. To the Muslims he was a war criminal – but so were almost all Bosnian Serb officers of sufficient rank to be noticed. We were introduced almost conspiratorially by another peace-seeking Serb outside the old ski hotel at Jahorina where the Vance–Owen plan was being debated. Such was the general war-weariness even then, that its rejection by the hard-line parliament was by no means certain. The major, who commanded the army's strategic reserve in the vulnerable northern corridor, spoke sombrely of the costs his men had already borne in this protracted war. He suggested that it would be a useful exercise, and greatly affect the outcome of the vote, if the politicians would switch places with the soldiers, and spend two weeks in the front-line trenches to see what life was like there. Of course nothing like that would ever happen: the war had actually increased the politicians' special privileges; and they decisively rejected the Vance–Owen plan – perhaps the last real chance for a negotiated settlement.

From that point on the peace people, such as they were, gave up. Those who could dispersed to Belgrade, and the rest returned to the trenches. The Serbs closed their ranks against the outside world, of which we in the press were the most visible and intrusive symbol; so they set about curbing the intrusions. Access became increasingly difficult and mainly confined to photo-opportunities outside the Presidency at Pale, as negotiators came and went in various states of frustration. (The most outspoken of them was the Russian envoy, Vitaly Churkin, a remarkable man whom I count as a true friend: he said he had never been lied to so much in his life – and he was once one of their allies.)

Our access to Dr Karadzic was controlled, and eventually cut off altogether, by his daughter Sonja. She was the tigress at his gates, a formidable lady of ample proportions and many shades of make-up, who headed the International Press Centre. Here she played videogames, cosseted her poodle, and raked in German marks twenty at a time for the singular privilege of a day's accreditation. Her favourites – and I was almost one for a while – were sometimes allowed four days for the price of one. For that, we would show up every day at the International Press Centre to be told whom we were not allowed to interview and where we were not allowed to go. If we sought out a source without her permission – and I had a particularly good one, a colonel with whom I had once shared some dangerous moments – we risked immediate expulsion. For the duration of the Gorazde crisis in April 1994, and again at the beginning of 1995, Pale and its Press Centre were closed to us altogether, though that wasn't actually Sonja's doing: it was ordered by the Bosnian Serb army, which saw a foreign spy in every one of us.

Often the Serbs had a plausible case to make, for on many occasions as the war ground on its battles were actually initiated by the government forces. But just as often their case was not heard. Instead Sonja and her cohorts played videogames and drank coffee, and distributed videotapes of alleged atrocities to gullible Greeks and Bulgarians.

I never had the privilege of knowing Sonja intimately, and for all I know she may have been a woman of great warmth and matching charm. But so effectively did she mask this, and such was the animus of the foreign press against her, that the story of the golden fish came into circulation. Actually there were a number of golden fish stories, but the one most often told concerned her father at the time he was negotiating with the

Contact Group. One day in Pale he became so incensed with the visiting diplomats and the map they were trying to impose on him, that he broke off negotiations and went fishing. On the river bank Dr Karadzic's luck turned, and he caught a golden fish with magical properties. 'If you throw me back into the river,' said the fish, 'I have the power to grant you any wish you may have.'

'In that case,' said Dr Karadzic, 'I wish you to take this map and make it acceptable to my people.'

'I'm sorry,' said the fish, rubbing its fins in embarrassment, 'I should have made it clear that my powers are great but not unlimited. Actually, I don't do maps. Is there anything else I can do for you?'

'Why yes,' said Karadzic, 'you can make my daughter the most beautiful woman in Bosnia.'

Then the fish said, 'I think I'll take another look at that map.'

Yet the irony was that for all their obstructiveness and our reciprocated ill-will, the Serbs had excellent spokesmen. Dr Karadzic and his Shakespearean deputy Nikola Koljevic were surpassed in fluency only by Haris Silajdzic on the other side, and in any exchange of soundbites could give as good as they got. Nor were the Serbs all wild men from the hills: they claimed a higher proportion of professors in their parliament than in any other elected assembly on earth. Even the wild men from the hills were steeped in their history, and the humblest foot-soldier in a trench could give as good an account of what he was fighting for as the army commander himself – probably better, because Ratko Mladic was like a Balkan Norman Schwarzkopf, the kind of general who lets his actions do the talking for him. The Serbs even tried to stop their soldiers speaking to the press, but the troops would have none of it. Once an ITN rival, during one of ITN's rare excursions into Serb-land, came rushing up to me in Pale with a look of triumph. They had this scoop, he said, a soldier had stopped them as they drove past the front line in Trebevic and insisted on being interviewed; he had explained the Serbs' war aims against the backdrop of the city that was under his gun.

'Congratulations,' I said. 'That's Boris.'

'Who's Boris?'

'Oh, Boris stops everyone with a camera, he's been doing it for months, and trades cigarettes for soundbites. How many Marlboro did it cost you?'

Just occasionally the Serbs would open up at the official level, for a limited period only. They did so to explain to the world their rejection of the Contact Group peace map in August 1994. (This was after the golden fish had failed them.) All journalists were welcome, even those on the 'Grey List'. They called it a grey list only because they didn't wish to be known to have a black list. It included my BBC radio colleagues Alan Little and Malcolm Brabant. The Serbs held a rolling series of press conferences to put their case: one day the Minister for Industry and the next day the Minister for Ethnic Cleansing (sorry, I should have said the Minister for Refugee Affairs). And on the morning of the referendum they led us to the Trebevic front line, the most spectacular in all that ravaged and beautiful war zone, to show their soldiers both voting and talking against the peace plan, which they believed to be a death certificate for the Bosnian Serb people. It was hardly an informed debate, since the case for acceptance had never even been put to them, but at least it enabled the voice of the Serbs to be heard. It was effective television, and I congratulated Sonja on having made it happen. 'It took two years, but you've finally done something right.'

The spasm of Serb *glasnost* didn't last. The Bosnian Serbs were now left standing alone, for even Belgrade had turned against them, and they owed the world no favours. They gave up on the press and the press on them – except that in December

1994, when they sought the mediation of former American President Jimmy Carter, they floated the idea through a Karadzic interview with Christiane Amanpour of CNN, who was definitely on their grey list. Otherwise the pilgrimage to Pale, even when their road-blocks allowed it, was a certain and depressing waste of time.

Mostly their fierce isolation was self-imposed: they were prisoners of their politics and their history. But I have sometimes wondered whether the mechanisms and dynamics of television may also have had something to do with it. Throughout the war we did not flit around evenly between one side and the other. Mostly, though I tried to break the habit, we did not flit at all. We stayed on the government side of the lines and reported from that perspective. For the kind of TV news operation that we were mounting is not a free-running enterprise. It has a certain centre of gravity, and that is hard to move. A self-starting and independent print reporter, like Maggie O'Kane of the *Guardian*, could travel extensively in Bosnian Serb territory, even alone and by bus, with only a notebook in hand or not even that. Her epic journeys brought her into contact with warlords whose natural sense of chivalry and hospitality inclined them to help her (most of the time), and fortunately they would never know what she wrote about them. But with television it is different. Stealth is not our style. Our equipment is cumbersome, an obvious target for obstruction and harassment, and not so easily moved across front lines.

The very minimum team is seven people: a newsgathering unit of cameraman, interpreter and reporter, a producer or 'fixer' at the heart of the operation, and at the transmission end a videotape editor (sometimes doubling as sound recordist) and two engineers with the satellite dish. Later we reduced it to six by doubling the roles of producer and interpreter. The dish itself, and the ton of ancillary equipment that goes with it, needs the capacity of two and a half Land Rovers to move it, and the best part of a day to set it up. Then as time passes, and human nature being what it is, the engineers accumulate extra gadgets and gizmos to make what works well work better. At one point we even acquired a 270-channel receiver dish which made it possible to watch news of traffic jams on the M25, or Country Music Television from Nashville. The system grows and takes on a life of its own. It puts out cables and wires and junction boxes which anchor it like roots. It prefers to stay where it is.

I noted self-critically that for weeks at a time, during the years of working from Sarajevo, we would venture no further than the airport in one direction and the Presidency in the other. Our measure of Bosnia was approximately the length of a single street in its capital. Forays into Serb-land would be day trips only, usually unrewarding, and therefore attempted less frequently. In this self-critical mode I would ask myself, when had we ever shown a civilian victim of sniper fire on the Serb side of the lines? When had we reported from their hospitals? When had we heard from the *Sarajevo Serbian News* in Grbavica rather than *Oslobodenje*, the celebrated newspaper on the government side which was an icon of journalism and a symbol of the city's ordeal?

Even to raise these questions is to risk being branded as an apologist for the Serbs, which I am not, and never was. They started this war; they killed and they burned and they ethnically cleansed; and the greater part of responsibility for it will always be theirs. But they didn't hold monopoly rights on evil. There were massacres also by Croats and even by Muslims, and villages burned by both. The Serbs were demonized by themselves as well as by others. But such is the nature of television that some of the coverage of the war was quite literally weighted against them.

9

PANORAMA – THE DESTINATION
OF CHOICE

Today's BBC is not at all the one I joined in 1962. It was run in those days like a rather large government department, unwieldy and decentralized but clubbable and benign. Power was devolved to the broadcasting barons who guarded their privileges, fought their corners and controlled their separate fiefdoms, but allowed their staff a remarkable degree of freedom. If ever there was a golden age of broadcasting, that was it. And I even had a part to play in it, as chauffeur. I drove David Frost in my mini-van to London from our home town of Beccles for the first edition of *That Was The Week That Was*. Now *there's* a claim to fame.

'Downsizing' and 'outsourcing' and 'producer choice' and all the other mantras of the new management were then unheard of, and this is not the place to debate their worth. (Besides, I like my job and would wish to keep it at least for a while longer.) But one thing the Birtian revolution in the BBC did achieve, which was of immediate and practical benefit, was to put an end to the forty-year feud between News and Current Affairs. The distinction was an artificial one anyway, for news is nothing if not current, and current affairs is news by another name. But in the BBC they were separate baronies, or directorates, competing for turf and resources and airtime, with different structures and mythologies, and an abiding suspicion of each other's ways of working.

At the time I came on board, Current Affairs was definitely

the senior service. It enjoyed enviable viewing figures, prime-time prominence and lavish budgets. All the excitement and creativity lay across London in the Television Centre and Lime Grove. News remained in exile atop its old headquarters at Alexandra Palace where television began. Thus marooned in the museum of the medium, it was restricted in the schedule to twelve-minute bulletins, delivered in a style not so very different from that of the old cinema newsreels. Our cameramen had actually come to us from Movietone and Pathé – and so, I sometimes felt, had our standards of scriptwriting.

It was a time when news reporters were generally anonymous, which in itself is no bad thing at all. The well-known faces and stars of BBC journalism (with salaries to match, I supposed) were the current affairs reporters, Dimblebys and others on board the flagship programme *Panorama*, which was an institution even in those days. Brian Wenham, one of the few editors who crossed the frontier and worked for both sides – indeed, both networks, for he started at ITN – identified the difference as one of rank. The current affairs reporters, he explained, were the officers. And we were the other ranks, the PBI (Poor Bloody Infantry) soldiering on in the unsung trenches of news.

So, of course, I wanted to be a *Panorama* reporter. Who wouldn't? I was at the time an acting probationary trainee news assistant with the BBC in Norwich. And from here to there seemed an awfully steep mountain to climb. John Morgan and James Mossman, my role models, might be interviewing heads of state and crafting memorable dispatches from Vietnam: in those days *all* doors opened to *Panorama*. *I* was reporting for the lunch-time news on a fall in fatstock prices at Acle Market. I would fantasize that this report, which was all of one minute ten seconds long and actually the first I ever did on network news, would somehow be spotted by the editor of *Panorama*, who would thereupon summon me to London, have me kitted out in a safari suit like a real war correspondent, and launch me into the wider world to make a name for myself.

In fact, the reverse of this happened. Our transmission area at Norwich included the country home of the BBC's Director-General, Sir Hugh Greene, at Bury St Edmunds. So it was that he accidentally came to see one of our productions, the regional news magazine *Look East*. It made such a deep impression on him that he at once commissioned the editor of *Panorama* to rush to Norwich and instruct the staff on some of the basics of television. It was a painful, day-long seminar in which everything we did was deconstructed and our fledgeling careers were crumbling before our eyes: mine especially, for the session ended for the reporting staff – what is nowadays mockingly called the 'talent' – with camera tests in the studio. I was told after this ordeal that even *live on camera* I was talking out of sync – that is, the words didn't actually match the lip movements. The rest of the human race could achieve this without difficulty, but evidently I could not. For a would-be broadcast journalist that was quite a serious affliction, and seemed to signal the end of my dreams of achieving adequacy, let alone stardom. Never mind *Panorama*. I wouldn't even be asked to do the fatstock prices again.

But the veteran news editor who hired me, Kenneth Matthews, kindly and loyally stood by me. The lip-sync problem unaccountably went away. I survived to report the fatstock prices, and more: even to take a further screen test on a chosen news story – mine was about the state of the East Anglian bean crop, for at Norwich we had our own distinctive view of what is news – which led to my transfer to London in 1964 as a network reporter for both radio and television. (It was a time of what is now hailed as 'bimediality' and to which the BBC returned with much fanfare a generation later; which only goes to show that what goes around, comes around.) I even got to

Vietnam in a safari suit – not for *Panorama* but for the news, which was by then under new management and beginning to break out of its ghetto-like imprisonment in the BBC schedules.

New technologies of electronic newsgathering and satellite transmission were becoming accessible or were at least in sight, which tipped the balance of advantage in the age-old battle between News and Current Affairs. We no longer had to apologize for being forever a day or two late with the pictures; the phrase 'Film has just reached us from . . .' dropped out of currency; magic lantern television was a thing of the past; the days were over, or were soon to be over, when our newsfilm was airfreighted in parcels from the far corners of the world to London, there to be baulked at the last resort by fog, or a baggage handlers' strike at Heathrow. And my exclusive interview with Idi Amin, conducted on my knees during a reception in Kampala to celebrate his marriage to Lady Sarah of the Mechanized Suicide Regiment of the Ugandan army, arrived so late that to my extreme chagrin it was dropped from the news, to accommodate a story about eleven swans found dead on the upper Thames.

By this time I suppose I was becoming more established in the business, and marginally less insecure (though I confess that to this day I live in a professional fear of being found out, as do many of my colleagues), and no one had accused me for quite a while of talking out of sync. Besides, I found that I was *enjoying* news and was no longer ambitious to join the officer class in *Panorama* (which stayed too long with the old technology of film, and was not perhaps quite the force that it had been).

News was fast and news was fun. News was experimenting with colour and graphics. It was also starting to break from its shackles, attempting a half-hour programme on BBC2 (so late at night and to so small an audience that it would have been cheaper to close the transmitter and bring them in by bus).

News was a madhouse from morning to midnight – but, beyond that, remarkably carefree: that is to say, there was very little spill-over of anxiety from one day to the next. In the longer form, like an extended *Panorama* report, your doubts and worries would stay with you throughout the whole project from gestation to transmission, a period of at least six weeks. But in news the cares would slip away more easily. Win, lose or draw in the eternal daily battle with ITN, at the end of the day it was over at least until the next day, when it would start all over again.

It was also the heyday of ITN (which has seemed to me in later years to have lost its edge, as its agenda slid down-market in pursuit of ratings). The competitiveness itself was fiercely attractive, like a game for adults which only two could play; for this was before the advent of morning television and the satellite news services. And the ITN people, so many of them friends as well as rivals, were tough and competitive players. It was a great relief to me when Alan Hart left to prosper elsewhere, Gerald Seymour, 'the whispering giant', to write his thrillers and Jon Snow to front the *Channel Four News*. All of them caused me sleepless nights, which I surely tried to reciprocate. It is a business where success is all gone by tomorrow, but failure stays with you for years.

News was also engagingly simple. And, as a general rule, the more dangerous it looked the easier it was, except for the technical difficulty of staying alive. That still applies. Just about anyone can find the words for a firefight. It takes no great reportorial skills to find out where the trench lines are and who is doing what to whom, and to describe the outcome in simple declarative sentences. But to make sense of it all, to see the war for the battle and the wood for the trees, to look beyond the 'bang bang' to the political context, and to do it not just quickly but almost instantly, requires skills of a different order. Even the shorter news report should ideally aspire to something of this dimension, but the longer form *demands* it. No one wants a finished slice of television, which ends up being about the reporter and very little else. (I once spent ten days in Sarajevo with a celebrated American correspondent who shared our bunker and ventured out of it for no other purpose than to address his camera – the cameraman had *no other function* than to frame the man's admittedly rugged good looks in picturesque surroundings: the actual pictures they used were hijacked from us.) That may work for the Americans, it doesn't for us. But the longer form, like a full *Panorama* programme on a single issue, requires that the reporter give more of him or herself to it than to two minutes on the *Nine O'Clock News*. It is not so much a matter of opinions as perceptions – and even of feelings, for reporters are human too. It needs to be more than an accumulation of incident, or the golden moments from sixty rolls of videotape. It has to have a message and a point and a purpose, or else it's a waste of time.

I know this because I tried it once, and failed. In 1974 I was lured by Brian Wenham, then the editor of *Panorama*, to become a sort of acting stand-in member of his officer class, and help fill the summer schedule while his permanent staff took their holidays. Normally *Panorama* took a break in the summer; that year it was to soldier on with the other ranks in charge.

The concept was a viable one: a programme about Northern Ireland five years after the restart of the Troubles. The landmarks were already set: it was called 'Five Years – A Thousand Deaths'. It had an experienced producer, Bill Cran; a gifted cameraman, Arthur Rowell; and a reporter who should have known what he was talking about.

My principal qualification for the job was that I may have been by then the most threatened mainland journalist in the Province. I had been sentenced to death by a group of ill-wishers in Dungannon, and escaped through a lavatory window and across a ploughed field from more of the same in Lima-vady. The Reverend Ian Paisley, for whom I always had a certain unreciprocated regard, would set his crowds on me: 'Mr Bell is falsely accusing the Protestant people of being rioters', then call them off: 'Leave Mr Bell alone. I feel sorry for him. He must be very disappointed that there was no rioting here today.' Alf McCreary, in the *Belfast Telegraph*, took a very much kinder line: 'Mr Bell has been here 34 times. He is not one of the long-haired weirdies, or one of the visiting "firemen" who have the difficult job of summing up Ulster in two days.'

My problem was perhaps that I was too well known, so the main players whom I wished to interview were reluctant to turn me down. The generals and brigadiers, the priests and cardinals, the politicians and paramilitaries duly stepped forward for their forty-five seconds of airtime. The Republicans remonstrated, the Loyalists threatened, the moderates pleaded for peace; just as they had for the previous five years, and they would for the next twenty. The piece was filled out with footage from the years before and images from the present: the Berlin Wall arrangement that protected the home of Austin Currie of the SDLP, a tense stand-to by a British army patrol in South Armagh, and a British shovel confiscated by the Irish police in a comic cross-border fiasco.

In the end it was, thanks to Bill and Arthur, a stylish piece of work. But the fault was mine: it really had nothing to say. It set out where we had come from and where we stood, and some-thing of the tears and the tragedy in between, but without any real sense of feeling or commitment that any of this mattered except as a means of filling fifty minutes of TV time. When the final titles had rolled, what had been the point of it? There wasn't one.

I kept Alf McCreary's criticism of the piece (he was the local paper's TV columnist), because he hit the target exactly:

It was curiously depersonalized, as if Bell had been determined to keep his innermost opinions to himself. Perhaps it is an indictment of the BBC news training system that when a reporter is given his head he tends to remain in the strictly impersonal area, where he presents facts and scenes for the viewer to make up his own mind.

I returned to Alf McCreary's comments nineteen years later when I got a second chance. After the war in Bosnia had been raging for eight months, a call came in from the editor of *Panorama*, for the programme was still in business after all those years. Would I 'do' her a Bosnia? No conditions, no instructions, no preconceived notions or prescriptive shadows falling across my path. It was a journalistic blank cheque.

I accepted all the same with a measure of hesitation, for I knew that there was some in-house resistance to the project on the grounds that I was not a 'proper' *Panorama* reporter – how true! I also knew that there was a great deal more to be said on the subject than I had dared to say, or had time for, on the news. But this was dangerous territory to be venturing into. Yet the offer was a good one. I accepted, and as a gesture of goodwill even agreed to write a script, which I hadn't done for years. (My usual rules of engagement are: no script, no computer, just a microphone to talk directly into. That way, it comes from the heart and sounds more natural.) For had I not dreamed of a berth on this flagship, thirty years before? Now . . . how exactly would James Mossman have gone about it?

10

FORCING THE PEACE

The weather in Sarajevo was bitter. The cold seeped out of the buildings and into the bones. A freezing fog settled in at the beginning of January 1993 and stayed for weeks, like an Arctic death-shroud over the corpse of the city. But people welcomed the fog, because it blinded the snipers. The victims – and *everyone* trapped here was a victim – moved wraith-like and half-seen about their business, which was mere survival: trading on the wretched black market where eggs fetched five German marks each, ferrying water from the few working standpipes, and cutting down what remained of the trees for firewood. The once tree-lined city was bare and ruined, and only the park across from the Presidency was spared the general destruction. It was there that the president had once told his people that they could have independence without war; he was wrong. It was the worst of times in the Bosnian capital. In a city of shortages hope was the scarcest commodity of all.

The despair was somehow contagious. For no clear reason that I could identify I was beginning the *Panorama* assignment at a personal low ebb, and unusually full of doubt. From where I was, it looked like a long-term prison sentence in a frozen punishment block, with no remission for good behaviour. Never again, I told myself. I already missed the energizing deadlines, the *purposefulness* of news. These *Panorama* people seemed un-focused, with the transmission date for the yet unshot epic a full eight weeks away. It was the sort of schedule that must have dated from the time when they travelled by slow boat to the war zones, and spliced their films together with Sellotape. I campaigned obnoxiously for a faster turn-around, and succeeded in getting the eight weeks trimmed to five.

But I could have few complaints about the team. We lacked an interpreter in the early stages, since our regular translator Vera Kordic had just finished a long and exhausting shift in Sarajevo. So I went to Kosovo hospital and pleaded for the services of Jasmina Alibegovic, a brilliant linguist and good friend, whose sense of humour made light of the direst circumstances. She was also a fully qualified doctor, but was released to take a short holiday on our behalf. We hope we made it worth her while. For her real work, the saving of children's lives, she was paid two German marks a month.

The cameraman was Brian Hulls, quiet and unflappable, and one of the best in the business – he had been an assistant film editor on my previous attempt at a *Panorama*. The soundman was Colin Jones, a good companion but probably overqualified to be recording the crump of incoming artillery fire, for he held not only a microphone but a doctorate in electronic engineering. The producer – and in effect team leader – was Eamonn Matthews, who came to us with a record of award-winning film-making from Texas to Afghanistan. That still didn't make him any easier to deal with. His previous camera crew, he told me pointedly, used to call him Pol Pot.

I threatened to resign on the first day and he threatened to resign on the second.

The fault, of course, was entirely mine. I was not, and still am not, what is called 'producer-friendly' – rather the reverse. In the news business, as its reach has spread and its operations have grown more complex, we use 'fixers' or facilitators. They organize our logistics, book satellites, trade images with friends (and even competitors) from other TV stations, plead for access and permissions, and generally make things happen. What we do not have, usually, is producers who *produce*: that is, help write the script and shape the story. From time to time they try, and I have been driven to resist by declaring the edit room a 'producer-free zone'. I reminded Eamonn, none too tactfully, that nothing of worth was ever created by a committee, with the single shining exception of the Authorized Version of the Bible. And we certainly weren't planning to rewrite that.

I was still unsure what the exact message of this *Panorama* was going to be, but I did know that the war itself was central to it. So an uncomfortably large proportion of it would have to be shot in the trenches. That was our first dispute. Eamonn of course wanted to be out there making movies as he had in Afghanistan and elsewhere. I said that in this case it wasn't an option. After my baptism by mortar fire the previous August I had grown preternaturally cautious. I preferred to work with cameraman and interpreter only, to reduce to the minimum the number of people at risk. Soundman and producer were obliged to stay behind. Eamonn was unhappy with this arrangement, but it was my war zone not his, and he saw the sense of it.

Our first venture, after a long delay in securing permission, was to the Bosnian army's front line in the suburb of Dobrinja, which for months had been the scene of the fiercest fighting, and a siege within a siege. The fighting had not abated. Eamonn wanted it shot like a documentary, with moody cinematic manoeuvres – pans and zooms and point of view shots. A point of view shot – at least in the movies – is when you cut from a picture of a soldier peering from his bunker to a picture of whatever it is that he's peering at. The problem that arises in the real world, is that the party of the second part shoots back – and not with a camera. I told him it wasn't on.

I returned intact, after a fairly hairy time out there, and

moderately pleased with myself. At the furthest point of the front line I had found an English-speaking Greek volunteer with the Bosnian forces; that in itself was unusual, for the Greeks tended to side with the Serbs for confessional reasons, in a sort of pan-Orthodox union. He gave a graphic account of what life was like in the trenches: death too, for the dead were buried where they fell – it was too hazardous to move them. 'My life here and also my friends' is very dangerous. We are in the first line of fire.'

'How far are the Serbs away on the other side?'

'Maybe fifteen metres.'

'Fifteen?'

'Yes, fifteen, in some places fifty, and for two months we've not enough weapons ... This war must be stopped. Many peoples in the world must help us. My wish it's always peace, peace and peace, just peace.'

I brought back the tape to my leader at rear headquarters. 'Was there a point of view shot?'

'Well, not actually, in so many words. If you take one of those out there you can get your head blown off.'

'But Martin, this isn't news. We're making *sequences*.'

It seems that hot-shot producers set much store by their 'S words' – structures and sequences. The basic formula is that eight sequences make a structure, and when you have a structure you have a programme. Brian Hulls and I agreed a fine of one German mark, to be levied on the spot, for the use of either 'S word'. So far we had only half a sequence, but several marks in hand.

Yet reluctantly and grudgingly I came to accept that Pol Pot knew his business: all those awards in his cabinet were not for nothing. My vote was for caution: to venture out of cover for the shortest time possible, do the minimum necessary, and retreat to the relative safety of the Holiday Inn. His preference –

and he had the casting vote – was to stay longer where the soldiers and civilians were, in the trenches and the streets and the water-points under fire, and in some sense to live their ordeal with them, to communicate it by sharing it. As a way of working it was a bit like making a movie in a shooting gallery, and I don't think I would do it again. But he was right.

Old BBC reporting habits of distance and detachment were early and instant casualties. Jasmina led us to a front-line block of flats near the stadium, where a basement standpipe was the only source of water for the entire neighbourhood. People could shelter all day in their cellars, but they had to come out for water. 'We're scared,' said one, 'of the lack of water, of the lack of water as much as the bullets. The worst thing is the water.' The snipers were lying in wait at an easy range. While we were there, one of the water-carriers was hit in the leg. The city's ambulance service, like its water supply, wasn't running any more. Jasmina returned to being a doctor; I stopped being a reporter and became an ambulance driver, as our armoured Land Rover raced to the hospital. There's nothing actually against it in the Geneva Conventions, but it is amazing how many young reporters believe it is somehow unprofessional to get off the sidelines for once and try to help people.

For a while we lived their lives and shared their dangers – but only up to a point, for we had the means of escape and they did not; also the means of protection. This was actually a source of some shame. The flak jacket was like a badge of indemnity, a status that I did not wish to claim. And there came a time when I discarded it to walk the streets of Sarajevo – except for appearances in front of the camera, to placate the safety-conscious BBC management. It may have been a lapse of security, but it was also plain good manners. In the news business it isn't involvement but indifference that makes for bad practice. Good journalism is the journalism of *attachment*. It is not only knowing, but also caring.

Newspeople like to think of themselves as shedding light in dark places. My ever-resourceful producer actually did that, by acquiring a dozen candles and bringing them to a cave beside the Miljacka river which had once been a fashionable restaurant. It was now a bunker for 200 people: damp, dark, squalid and overcrowded, but so far underground as to be the only really safe place against mortar and artillery fire in the whole of the city. We asked if we could talk to them. It was a request we made with some diffidence, for it seemed an intrusion into private grief. (In so many of these desperate places I ask myself, what business do I really have to be there?) But the candles made us welcome, and were arranged for the camera's benefit. The mother of a young girl described how during the first three months of the war for every artillery shell fired, her daughter would ask, 'Mummy, is this one going to kill us?'

'That is the most painful part. You can neither help yourself nor those you hold most precious, your own children. In such situations you do not have any strength or words to explain to her why and how. It would have been a hundred times easier if we had been attacked by some foreign power. It is very hard to fight against people with whom you sat to drink coffee only yesterday.'

What began as an interview session turned into a sort of underground town meeting, partly because the cave had some light in it for the first time in months, but also because these people knew me (my stuff used to run on the local television in the days when there still was electricity) and innocently they supposed that I could help them. We journalists were unlikely representatives of the world community, but we were just about all they had, and they needed someone. They were altogether in the dark, since they had so little contact with the world beyond the cave, no radios (because there were no batteries), and no news but only rumours. In such conditions, detached and dispassionate journalism was out of the question. We were drawn into this war as something other than the witnesses and chroniclers of it. We were also participants. The candles burned low in the encircling darkness and the roles were reversed, with the interviewees now asking the questions. How long would it last? How much did the world know of the city's plight? What were we telling them? How much more would they suffer and how much worse would it get before the international community acted to end it?

I could hardly answer that it was none of my business. It was everybody's business, even that of the journalists passing by: perhaps *especially* that of the journalists, because if the world didn't know, its ignorance was our failure. I told the cave-dwellers what I thought, and it seemed at the time a reasonable guess, that within three months the world would act collectively to break the siege, or at least to ease its consequences. I was of course quite wrong. No action of any significance would be taken for more than a year; no *effective* action for two and a half years. Had they known that, they should have lynched me.

Their isolation was reflected in the stories that they told. In the most poignant of these, Presidents Milosevic of Serbia, Tudjman of Croatia and Izetbegovic of Bosnia were summoned before God and allowed one question each. Milosevic asked, 'When will there be a greater Serbia?' God answered, 'It will take fifty years,' and Milosevic wept because he would not live to see it. Tudjman asked, 'When will there be a greater Croatia?' God answered, 'It will take twenty-five years,' and Tudjman wept because he would also not live to see it. Izetbegovic asked, 'When will there be a free Bosnia?' And then it was God who wept.

This may seem a partisan account, as if we were taking sides with the beleaguered Muslims. Many journalists did, which was perhaps the flaw in the generally crusading character of the Sarajevo press corps. But the Serbs, in their section of the city, led almost as miserable a life. They too were sniped at and mortared and wounded, though generally not under the eye of the TV camera. Their civilians were also in the line of fire. And, contrary to the general belief, they were not all wild men from the mountains. One of their front-line warriors, where the Grbavica salient reached deepest into the city centre, had been a judge before the war, in the old multi-ethnic order of things. 'We are living here,' he said. 'This part of Grbavica has been our home. It is a question of knowing why you are fighting. If the lives of the members of my family are endangered, and someone is going to cut my throat because I am a Serb, then I really do not care whether I have a knife, a gun or a cannon but I shall use it.'

The Serbs seemed to model themselves on the old Western gunslinger Wild Bill Hickok: he was said never to have killed a man except in self-defence, but to have spent a great deal of his time defending himself. And the Serbs weren't waiting to be attacked, they got their retaliation in first. From Zvornik to Visegrad to Foca and beyond, much of the 'defence' of the territory they previously shared was pre-emptive attack to secure it for themselves. And hardly a mosque was left standing.

Many of the early war crimes were already well documented, but evidence of others in remoter parts of eastern Bosnia was only now coming to light: stories of premeditated cruelty which it would have been difficult to believe – that people could do such things to their neighbours – but for the presence of so many living witnesses. We set about assembling this evidence with the help of the survivors of the holocaust: rape victims, eyewitnesses of torture and murder, and two men who escaped from a bus which was driven into the forest near Foca and systematically machine-gunned by 'weekend Chetniks' of Arkan and Seselj, the paramilitary warlords.

'They jumbled about fifty-five of us in the rear of the bus. All of a sudden I heard an explosion and screams. Two bombs had hit us on the front. All I could do was to close my eyes and await my fate. I could hear a machine-gun too, for more than twenty-five minutes. I heard people crying. Some of them were asking to be killed because they were so badly wounded. When the Serbs had finished, they left.'

Easily overlooked in all this, however, was the fact that the Serbs also suffered. Serb villages too were torched, whole communities massacred, and tens of thousands made homeless. With some reluctance – only on the grounds of taste, because the images were so horrific – we included, near the end of the piece, the scenes from a mass burial of Serbs near Bratunac. We did this not out of some reflexive sense of BBC balance, but because these further war crimes had also happened and were part of the whole picture. The Serbs had begun this war, they alone could end it; and while their side of the story needed telling, their sense of grievance made them particularly hard to deal with. In this as in so much else they were their own worst enemies.

But it was prudent as well as fair-minded to give them a hearing. Much later at a Serb road-block I was intercepted with a copy of the videotaped programme in my possession: I had been planning to deliver it to Jasmina, our interpreter. At Ilidza police station the tape was played to an audience of the Serbs' security police. I am convinced that it was the Bratunac sequence that saved me from imprisonment.

During all these travels, and others later, I tried to make constructive use of the slivovitz hour. That is the obligatory pause, before the camera is allowed to roll, when the local commander – of whichever army – sits you down, assesses your credentials, describes the other side's provocations, and serves up a fierce concoction of politics and plum brandy, each with a distinctive Balkan flavour. I would ask him *why*? Why the peculiar brutality of this war, its singular tortures and mutilations, in supposedly civilized Europe?

The first answer would always be the same, that it wasn't what his people did to others, it was what others did to them. Then, with the second or third slivovitz, a measure of candour would creep in. 'Let me tell you one thing,' said a Serb commander, an admired fighting man who in his previous life had been a social worker, 'that this is a war, and in wars bad things happen. We have emptied our prisons and asylums; what did you expect?' Another, a Croat, demolished the myth of Bosnia as a previous model of ethnic harmony: the war was probably made inevitable by the one before it, and the Titoist constructions did no more than postpone the reckoning: 'Yes, we lived in peace and harmony. We lived in peace and harmony because every hundred metres we had a policeman to make sure we loved each other very much.'

It was the end of January, and the time had come in our *Panorama* enterprise to make a reckoning of our own. I argued strongly against the obvious course, which was to construct a charge sheet against the Serbs in the form of a forty-minute video-prosecution. The Serbs had done what they had done, but there was more to it than that.

I had been deeply moved by what I had lived through, not only on this assignment. This seemed the occasion, through the documentary form which has the power to make points by the sheer accumulation of its images, to develop a certain argument: that Bosnia mattered beyond its borders, that it wasn't someone else's war in a republic of which we knew little and cared less, and that we ignored it at our peril. There were costs to taking action – UN intervention meant UN casualties, and the first British soldier to die, Lance-Corporal Wayne Edwards, was shot during the course of our stay. But there were also costs to inaction. I concluded, 'The case for intervention is not to help one side against another, but the weak against the strong, the unarmed against the armed; to take the side of the everyday victims of the war who, until now, have had no protection. It is really a question, finally, of whether we care.'

This peroration was delivered in the ruins of Sarajevo's once magnificent library, where the treasures of Bosnia's culture had been turned to ashes. Eamonn took this tape and some thirty others to London, and dispatched me on a mission to New York to interview Lord Owen and Radovan Karadzic. We needed these interviews, but it was still a diversionary tactic. My artful producer had taken to heart my little speech about no good thing ever coming out of a committee. He would edit the programme himself.

When I returned I realized his strength. He may have been Pol Pot in the field, but he was David Lean in the edit room. My only reservation was that he had left out an interview with Mike Beary, the Irish army major who led the UN military observers on the Serb side of the lines. Mike had helped us in the difficult task of getting access to the Serbs' heavy-gun positions, and I did not want him to believe that we had been exploiting his good offices. The UN operation in general ranged from the sporadically effective to the totally futile, but Mike and his colleagues had really saved lives by being there, and I had wished to tell their story.

The piece was broadcast on 8 February 1993 without much in the way of advance publicity because at my own insistence it had been accelerated into the schedule. It had much more impact than I had expected. People talked about it. Politicians' wives told their husbands about it. One MP accused me of upsetting his constituents. Diplomats discussed it across their polished tables. Not only TV critics but political columnists wrote about it. Some, such as Andrew Marr in the *Independent*, approved; others, such as Simon Jenkins in *The Times*, did not.

Mr Jenkins is the most fluent and influential proponent of the view – of Bosnia and other conflicts – that wars are fated to take their course and will only be prolonged by outside intervention. It is a serious and respectable argument, though I suspect it might be modified by a visit to these war zones, were he to make one. He wrote objecting strongly to the programme's lack of restraint:

We were given the pornography of violence and the pornography of grief in full flood . . . Mr Bell showed both Serb and Muslim atrocities . . . He showed what he saw and he saw a lot. But he was biased. He used the images to make the world want to come and stop the killing. He never said how. He wanted to blot out thought. His was a bias against understanding.

The best answer I can muster to this is that there are problems which cannot be solved, but can only be managed. Conflicts dragged on for years in El Salvador, Lebanon and Northern Ireland, before even the lineaments of a settlement presented themselves. It may be the same with Bosnia. And it will take time. But if, while that time passes, it is possible to create and maintain a climate of opinion in which the saving of lives is thought to matter, and governments are committed to it because their people support it, and survivors in the war zones are given some hope when they would otherwise have none, then something beyond mere hand-wringing is being achieved. And if journalists do it they are committing useful journalism. There is a point to it. It does something other than fill a slot in a schedule.

II

'SOMETHING MUST BE DONE'

For all of us who came to it from the outside, the Bosnian conflict was not just another foreign war, but a shocking and defining experience, which changed our way of doing things and seeing things. It was my eleventh, in a catalogue running from Vietnam to the Gulf, and it was quite unlike all the others. It had this impact on us because of its brutality and ferocity, because of its merciless targeting of civilian populations, because of a level of risk and danger that none of us had expected, and perhaps also because of its closeness to home. None of us had been prepared to see a war on such a scale in our continent and in our time.

Not only the journalists felt this way, the soldiers did too. During a rare week's holiday towards the end of his tour of duty in 1994, General Rose told an audience in Aberdeen: 'You cannot expose yourself to that sort of predicament where you are living daily with appalling death and destruction without it affecting you as a human being.' He was speaking during some of the UN's darkest days, but with a sense of mission unusual even in war-fighting. 'There are probably a thousand people a month,' he said, 'alive in Bosnia-Herzegovina who would not be there if the UN wasn't doing its job.' (The general was a convert; he was said to have been opposed to the original decision to commit British ground troops to Bosnia.)

UN soldiers were shocked not only by what they saw, but by

their own helplessness under the mandate to do as much as they wished. Their role as bystanders was hard to take. Another British officer, writing home to his Regiment from Bosnia in 1993, quoted Dag Hammarskjöld's remark that peacekeeping is a job not suited to soldiers, but a job only soldiers can do: 'This returns me to how we will be judged by history or, closer to home, how my children will regard our role in this genocidal conflict. How did we stand by and watch the systematic destruction of Sarajevo by Serb artillery? Why did we prevaricate while Sarajevo burned? What did we think while we watched entire communities dispossessed and flee into a cauldron of shellfire to die on the streets of some further besieged village of cold and neglect?'

For the men of action which they are, soldiers have a remarkable liking for the written word. Wherever they serve they will take along with them their Queen's Regulations, their Rules of Engagement, their Battalion Orders Parts One and Two, their Staff Duties in the Field, and other military scriptures. They also write letters, not only 'blueys' to their wives and families but 'round robins' to their separated brethren from the corps or regiment. One day there is surely a book to be compiled of these soldiers' written impressions of the war in Bosnia. It shook them up.

Yet another British officer, who had not so long before seen service in Iraq, wrote the following:

Nothing had really prepared me for the horror of seeing the destruction that is everywhere in Bosnia. I can remember saying to my wife when I got back from the Gulf war that no one could ever, would ever, start a war in Europe if they had seen what modern weaponry had done in an empty desert ... Well, I could not have been more wrong. The mile upon mile of and row upon row of burned out houses: the little Alpine villages, lying so remote, and supposedly snug and safe in a fold in the hillside, totally laid waste. I flew over one such, and simply could not believe that people who could build and cherish such a haven could find themselves burned out, and then do exactly the same thing to the next village down the valley.

Because journalists and soldiers were not in the end such very different people, but were equally affected by all this as anyone with a head and a heart could not help being, the relationship between them in the Bosnian war was unusual and complex. Usually the soldiers got there first. This time the journalists did. And the presence of one *determined* the presence of the other. No other war – not even the Gulf war, which took on the character of a made-for-television CNN special event – has been fought so much in public, under the eye of the camera. At least the Gulf campaign was waged mainly in the desert, and reported under conditions of military censorship. In Bosnia there was no desert except that created by the conflicting armies, especially the Serbs; and no censorship either, for it occurred anarchically in the decade of the dish, that ubiquitous concave disc that uplinks all our tragedies and connects us to them. It was this peculiarly twentieth-century combination, of the means of mass destruction with the means of mass communication, that brought the war's daily horrors into the living rooms of the world.

One effect of this was to force the policy-makers' hand, and to require of them some response, even if no more than a concerned soundbite in the White House press room. The British especially resented the pressures of television. 'There is nothing new in such misery,' said Douglas Hurd in a much-quoted speech at the Travellers' Club in London. 'There is nothing new in mass rape, in the shooting of civilians, in war crimes, in ethnic cleansing, in the burning of towns and villages. What is new is that a selection of these tragedies is now visible within hours to people around the world . . . People reject and resent what is going on because they know it more vividly than before.' (Or as G.K. Chesterton put it, long before the decade of the dish, 'It's not the world that has got so much worse, but the news coverage that has got so much better.')

In Mr Hurd's reading the messenger (television) is blamed as the instrument of our awareness, as if the world would somehow be a better place if the killing continued and yet we knew nothing of it. And such practitioners as myself are dismissed as 'founder members of the something-must-be-done club'. (But it wasn't I who demanded that something be done, it was Elie Wiesel, the most articulate survivor of the Holocaust – and he has surely earned the right to be heeded.) All these outside pressures have the effect of piling up a mountain of paper on the desk of the Secretary of State, and diverting his attention from other issues equally urgent but less in the camera's eye. The mandarins' objection is not just to the power but to the impertinence of the upstart medium, which challenges their monopoly of wisdom, and rushes in where the pinstripes fear to tread.

But the mandarins misunderstand. We have no political agenda to follow, and we had none from the start. We did not set out every day from our base in Vitez or Sarajevo, in the indomitable 'Miss Piggy' or her successors, on a mission to scour the byways of Bosnia for the most harrowing images of suffering, and to lay the blame for them at the government's door. It just did not work like that. And I am just about as non-political as anyone can be after more than thirty years of dodging not just the bullets but the charges of bias as well. (Not for nothing does the BBC give its reporters their on-the-job training in Northern Ireland.)

To explain the mindset I have invented an imaginary ceremony. It is as if, when we join, the BBC issues us with a stop-watch and takes away our right to hold opinions, still less to express them. Then when time comes to leave, after thirty years and more before the colours, the men in the Giorgio

Armani suits (our leaders) take time off from the sixteen concurrent seminars they are holding in a country house hotel into the future of broadcasting in the year 2004, they form themselves into a hollow square and hand us back our right to hold opinions. (They also retrieve their stop-watch.) It may be different these days, when reporters are hired not for life but a year at a time, but the ethos is the same.

Our presumed encroachment on policy-making isn't political but technical. The satellite is as much a weapon of war as the sniper's rifle, and the soundbite is an extension of warfare by other means. The modern-day Machiavelli or Clausewitz, instead of conceding these to his adversary, will co-opt them for himself. This has certainly been the case with the leaders of all three peoples and armies in the Bosnian war – especially the Muslims, whose eloquence in the early months was just about all the firepower they had. But Croats and Serbs too have tried to influence the peace process – and, in the absence of a peace process, the course of the war – with direct appeals to world opinion through the medium of greatest impact, which is television.

So when the fighting began in April and May 1992, there was no issue more important to the Bosnian Serb leadership – not even the fate of their own homes in the capital – than the control of Sarajevo television. To all the parties in the war the idea of television as an independent service was absurd: it was the way they informed, and so controlled, their people. To the Serbs especially it was the instrument they needed to rally their people and justify secession. Their first priority was to acquire their own television service.

In this they were unwittingly helped by the Muslims, who attacked the Hotel Serbia in Serb-held Ilidza, which was at that time the BBC headquarters. That attack was the BBC's Dunkirk: it led to our precipitate flight from Ilidza, and the abandonment of two of our editing machines. These were duly 'liberated' by the grateful Serbs, together with a great quantity of video-tapes, and became the foundation of their TV service in Pale. Years later those machines were still being used, and the tapes were being recycled. No amount of pressure at whatever level enabled us to retrieve them.

But this was the Balkans, where you could be not only robbed but wooed at the same time. Later, the Serbs turned against us, but in these early stages they made their spokesmen available to us, with the greater urgency as the tide of public opinion started to run against them, following the first wave of ethnic cleansing in eastern Bosnia. They wished us to know that *Serbs* had been victimized, massacred, driven from their homes. (All this was true, which didn't excuse the rest.)

The means of communication was also at hand, since my first action on reaching Pale in June 1992 was to seek out Radovan Karadzic, not only for the usual interview, but for permission to use the satellite dish that we had with us. Under the international rules which govern these things, it had to be authorized by the Minister of Communications. Dr Karadzic's fledgeling govern-ment didn't actually have a Minister of Communications, but he was willing to compromise. I returned to Tim Barrow, our 'dishmaster' and chief engineer, with a sense of mission accom-plished. 'There isn't a minister,' I told him. 'Will the president do?' From that day and for a long time afterwards, the dish in all parts of Bosnia operated, so to speak, under his signature.

It then became a television war, not just in the usual sense, that its battles and bloodshed for more than three years were beamed across the world in nightly newscasts, but in the addi-tional sense that the *other* campaign, for world opinion and the favour of governments, was waged on television too.

Dr Karadzic himself was known to call up the BBC's *Six O'Clock News*, on air, and demand the right to refute a statement just made. In the capital itself, the broadcasts of Sarajevo tele-vision regularly included a 'clip reel' of the reports of foreign journalists based in the city; they were studied closely in the Presidency, which in the darkest of times was one of the few buildings with emergency power, as the best available barometer of world opinion. And the Croat commander of the HVO forces encircled in central Bosnia, Tihomir Blaskic, regularly sought copies of our accounts of his soldiers in action. Television mattered to all these people. communications were fragmentary; diplomacy was distant and ineffective; but the satellite dish was their conduit to the world.

Our closeness to the warlords brought problems of its own. Those of us who worked in Bosnia were relatively few – for not all journalists were daft enough to seek a job in quite such a dangerous place – so we did not have to function very much, as in other conflicts, through intermediaries, spokesmen and spin-doctors. (At least we didn't. in the early days – the Bosnian government was later to discover the virtues of bureaucracy.) We *knew* the warlords and political leaders. We dealt with them daily in our business, and they with us in theirs. As a result we were hardly main players ourselves, but not mere bystanders either. Our role, in the theatre of the Bosnian war, was partly that of messengers, and partly lamplighters, for we tried to cast some light on those dark places.

But that was a long way from setting the agenda and usurping the functions of government. And if at times we seemed to be doing those things it was a measure not of how much we our-selves were doing, but of how little was being done by anyone else. We had our faults, but at least we were not inert in the face of genocide, and we did not run away. At some point in one of his many television interviews, Lord Carrington was asked whether British policy on Bosnia was being blown off course by the TV coverage. 'That always supposes,' he replied, 'that there's a course to be blown off.'

Kofi Annan, the UN Under-Secretary who holds probably the most difficult job in the world – that of its chief peacekeeper – makes much the same point: 'When governments have a clear policy, they have anticipated a situation and they know what they want to do and where they want to go, then television has little impact. In fact they ride it. When there is a problem, and the policy has not been thought, there is a knee-jerk reaction. They have to do something or face a public relations disaster.'*

Are we not all in some way 'interventionist'? I suppose it is only human, in the midst of so much misery, to want to see an end to it. And I for one would gratefully hang up my body armour and my microphone, after Bosnia, absent myself from the war zones for ever, and take up a post as peace correspondent (if such a job were to exist). But with the possible exception of the slightly polemical piece I did for *Panorama* in the first year of the war, I have kept my feelings out of it. They have no business there. It is not the function of a reporter to campaign. That is for soldiers, politicians, or columnists. What we should be doing, or trying to do, is to show the situation on the ground, who is doing what to whom, and with what effects, and why. If in the course of these modest inquiries it should become clear that some grand plan recently proposed (Bosnian examples include the 'no fly' zone, the safe havens and the heavy weapons exclusion zones, all advanced as positive and concrete measures to end the war) is not having even the symbolic effect that was proposed for it, then our viewers can draw what conclusions they please. Our job is to be their eyes and ears on the ground. It is the lesson of the Bosnian war that precisely when there is a policy vacuum, when governments are without a course to

* Quoted by Nik Gowing in 'Real time television coverage of armed conflicts', John F. Kennedy School of Government Working Paper, Boston, 1994.

follow or an expedient to clutch at, then television images have a jolting effect, and a political power to move them.

The conflict has yielded two classic cases of policy driven by television. The first was Operation Irma, when the plight of one five-year-old girl led Downing Street to order the airlift of more than forty wounded people from Sarajevo: never mind the thousands of others who suffered unheeded. It happened in July 1993. I was in central Bosnia at the time – a time of unusually heavy fighting with casualties to match, and the flight of 10,000 panic-stricken Croats, who were urged by their own leaders to flee from their homes around Bugojno. From our base in Vitez our array of dishes actually enabled us to see some BBC programmes, and that the BBC on that Tuesday should devote more than half of one of its main news programmes to the plight of a single five-year-old girl struck me as daft. I felt like a humble foot-soldier in an army whose high command had taken leave of its collective senses – and I told them so. The UN also wondered at it. And the UN Chief of Staff, Brigadier Vere Hayes, who had a true staff officer's feel for acronyms, suggested that Irma stood for Instant Response to Media Attention.

The second example was the mortar attack on the Sarajevo market in February 1994, in which sixty-eight people died. It was another clear case of policy driven by television. There had been other such massacres before: the bread queue in May 1992, the water queue in January 1993 – each with terrible effects and about twenty dead. Was it just the numbers, this time, that made the difference, on some sliding scale of atrocity? Or the so-called 'CNN effect', that the cameras were almost immediately on the spot? Whatever it was, this one moved the international community as earlier attacks had not.

In truth, the timing may also have had much to do with it. A new take-charge commander, Lieutenant-General Sir Michael Rose, was on the scene. The UN was fulfilling its mandate for the first time in months, and had embarked on a policy of threatening force against the Serbs, both for the relief of its garrison in Srebrenica and for the opening of Tuzla airport; but the TV images certainly made a difference. Among other effects, they brought about a change of policy by the British and Canadian governments about the use of airpower.

The change was as short-lived as a spokesman's soundbite, promising decisive action. Governments, who pride themselves on their control of events and their steadiness of course, will be reluctant to admit that the electronic interloper, television, plays *any* part in their decision-making. To do so would be an abdication of dignity – a bit like acknowledging that you changed your policy as a result of a thundering editorial in the *Sun*. You might have done so, but you would surely never admit it.

Whitehall's sense of decorum in this resembles that of Queen Victoria, who was extremely vexed that Gladstone spoke on affairs of state – still the Balkans, or what was then known as 'The Eastern Question' – from the back of a train in Midlothian. But that, in his time, was the latest medium of mass communication. And the argument, in those days as in these, was about the case for a principled foreign policy.

My friend Nik Gowing, then diplomatic editor of *Channel Four News*, took time off from his diplomatic editing to produce a Working Paper on these issues of war and diplomacy for the John F. Kennedy School of Government at Harvard. He interviewed politicians and their advisers past and present, who assured him that television's influence was not as great as he had supposed. His interviewees would have us believe in a government holding firm against the push and pull of television. One said, 'Television is a big influence on a daily basis, but the key is keeping a balanced, even keel over the long term.' And another, specifically on Bosnia, 'TV almost derailed policy on several occasions, but the spine held. It had to. The secret was to respond to limit the damage, and to be seen to react without undermining the specific policy focus.' Sir David Hannay, Britain's ambassador to the United Nations, took pride in their resistance to our pressures: 'We are a pretty stubborn lot. When it comes to an earth-shattering event we will not be swept off our feet.'

The Americans were more candid about it, more open with themselves. Television is an integral and dynamic part of their politics and their culture. They are elected by it and to a large extent they take their decisions by it: CNN's 'Newsak' is the mood music of their legislative and executive offices. 'The television sets a great deal of the agenda,' said former Secretary of State Lawrence Eagleburger, 'and then the President and his Secretary of State have to deal with it. There's just no argument.'

I am not suggesting that this is how things should be, only that it is how they are – certainly in America, and more in Britain than our professional pinstripes admit. I don't even welcome the trend. If there is a besetting sin of journalists, especially those of the television variety, it is an overweening sense of our own importance. It is no longer enough for us to be mere reporters, we must be styled as correspondents or even editors – though in my experience a correspondent is no more than a reporter who has lunch. What the world needs probably is not more of us but fewer, and humbler. We are certainly not infallible, and it will be easier for everyone when governments inform themselves better. But, in Bosnia, they left it to us.

12

COLONEL BOB

_____

The soldiers' motto everywhere is 'Hurry up and wait'. The Cheshires, the Twenty-Second Regiment of Foot, might as well have added it to their regimental crest. As a result of various uncertainties about their deployment, they were given nearly two months longer than they needed to prepare for their tour of duty in Bosnia. Since once they got there our paths would certainly cross, I took the opportunity to invite myself to their headquarters in Fallingbostel at precisely the same time as they rather conveniently asked me to come and talk to them. They were short of information about Bosnia: and actually, I wasn't so much invited as hijacked. They were really quite persuasive.

I had not been on a barrack square since being marched off one in rather summary fashion by RSM Gingell of the Suffolk Regiment in June 1959. (There had been a difference of opinion between us about the length of my 'demob' haircut.) This square was completely different. For a start, the camouflage years were over. The advance party were loading up their freshly painted white Land Rovers and stencilling on the UN signs. And the place was unnaturally quiet, with none of the parade ground bustle and barking of commands that years of chastening experience had led me to expect. The grass wasn't painted green either, or the paving stones white. Clearly this was a new kind of army, and not at all the one in which I had served.

Actually, it both was and wasn't. Many months later, I happened to be with my interpreter Anamarija Muvrin in the British base at Gornji Vakuf during the ritual of Commanding Officer's Orders. A soldier was being marched, ramrod-straight, into the presence of the colonel amid much stamping of boots and shouting of commands. To Anamarija's eye it looked like the prelude to a court martial at the very least. 'What is he accused of?' she asked.

'He isn't accused of anything. He's just been promoted.'

My main purpose at Fallingbostel was to meet the Cheshires' commanding officer, Lieutenant-Colonel Bob Stewart. I already knew enough about him not to expect a Camberley-trained automaton in uniform. I was also aware, since the army can be a gossip shop second to none, of a whispering campaign against him: that he might be a bit of a risk on so sensitive a mission, since he tended to speak his mind more freely than most. Good for him, I thought, that's what the army needs more of.

I took to him at once. He was articulate, relaxed, well informed and splendidly free of those reflexive habits of mind, induced perhaps by too many years at the army's academies, which I have come to identify as parade-ground thinking. The peacetime army is uncomfortable with charismatic officers. It is at a loss to know what to do with them. It tends to promote managers rather than leaders, and Bob Stewart wasn't a manager. He also cared and knew more about his soldiers than any other commanding officer I ever met, with the possible exception of Arthur Denaro of Gulf war fame.

His special relationship with his men was shaped not by Camberley but by Ballykelly. He had been a company commander with his regiment in Northern Ireland in 1982 when six of his company were killed and thirty wounded in the Ballykelly Bomb. It marked him for life, and produced a command style which caused him to lead from the front, attracting the dangers to himself. He would risk more so that those serving under him should risk less. In this he was probably a subaltern's nightmare, since he was all over everything and second-guessing it, but it suited the rank and file. His way of doing things was much misunderstood. It was not grand-standing for the sake of the camera, but the expression of a career-long concern that there be no more Ballykellys.

His battalion was also one of the best. It had that sense of family and of belonging that marks a really strong county regiment, holds the men together when the going gets rough, and makes them a pleasure to deal with. But the Cheshires were passing through some rough times which had nothing to do with Bosnia. As one of the few single-county regiments remaining in the British army they were under threat of extinction, or rather of amalgamation with the Staffordshire Regiment, which in their view would amount to the same thing. It had been announced as one of the army's 'Options for Change', and at the time of their deployment to Bosnia it seemed unstoppable. It would be a forced marriage, and both parties agreed – it was *all* they agreed on – an unhappy one. But at least the Cheshires, who had grown weary of the Staffordshires' stories of their Gulf war exploits, looked forward to paying them back in kind with some tales of real modern soldiering in Bosnia.

It was my job to help prepare them for it, in a small way, with a speech to the officers and senior NCOs. I did not volunteer for this, because it took some nerve for a former corporal in a long defunct infantry regiment to lecture a group of serving soldiers on what they would be doing. But I did know something about where they would be doing it, so I talked at some length about the causes and complexities of the Bosnian war. I suggested that they wipe the slate clean of their previous operational experience, which was in Northern Ireland.

It would be wise for them not to go looking for enemies, for if they were lucky they would find none. But if they were unlucky and enemies appeared they would be well served by their basic infantry skills: fieldcraft, marksmanship, battlefield first aid and map-reading. Especially map-reading. I could think of nowhere on earth where an officer and a map were potentially a more dangerous combination than in the hills and valleys of central Bosnia.

I also told them what I believed, that though I had doubts about the workability of their mandate, they were pioneers in a great life-saving enterprise; that the army's future lay in peace-keeping – or what it quaintly calls 'Operations Other Than War' – rather more than its senior commanders yet appreciated; and that they would find their tour of duty in Bosnia the most worthwhile six months of their careers. I'm sometimes wrong about quite a lot, but I am sure I was right about that. Some of them told me so afterwards.

I tried to warn the Cheshires that when they finally reached Bosnia they would find themselves at the centre of more press interest than they had ever imagined, or could deal with. I understated it. By the time they arrived in Vitez the British media were swarming all around. On one trip to Tuzla Colonel Stewart had to accommodate nine press vehicles travelling with his convoy. Far from courting the press, which he never did, his only concern was to control us sufficiently so he could do the rest of his business. Both he and his successor Alastair Duncan found that they could have spent their entire time, if they had agreed to all the requests they received, giving interviews and answering questions.

Colonel Stewart – hereinafter to be known as 'Colonel Bob' – was the natural focus of journalistic interest. He did not seek us, but we sought him out because of who he was and where he was. He was colourful, quotable and in command. He had attended the 'soundbite academy' at Beaconsfield where the army schools its officers in being interviewed for television, yet still came out of it talking like himself, and not as many of them did like Colonel Identikit. Because of his command style he was usually to be found in front lines or other newsworthy places, and seldom in his office. He personally fired more shots in anger, always in answer to incoming fire, than all the rest of his battalion group put together – but, typically, he didn't shoot to kill. In one incident, in the village of Jelinak, he loosed off eighty rounds from the chain gun of his Warrior when it came under fire from a Croat position on a rocky outcrop above him. His own account of it says a lot about him: 'I suddenly realized that I was about to execute two men. The men looked huge through the sights which magnified their image eight times. They were totally oblivious of the fact that they were about to die and, as they were not actually firing at us, I gave them a chance.' He deliberately aimed five yards wide. That was typical of him – always in the thick of things but saving lives rather than taking them.

He was also helpful to us when he could be, which – even in the modern and more media-conscious army – was not to be taken for granted. There was one occasion when the Ministry of Defence ordered him to put his base at Vitez off limits to the UN-accredited journalists. It had not been done before, and would not be attempted again. The reason was a visit to the camp by Paddy Ashdown, leader of the Liberal Democrats; the motive appeared to be narrowly political. Colonel Bob circumnavigated the problem by inviting Paddy to visit his Bosnian army friends in the front-line village of Turbe. 'Miss Piggy' with our camera team on board was folded into the convoy, and was right behind the colonel's Warrior when it came under fire from the Serbs. A mortar round landed twenty yards away, injuring no one and probably doing Paddy Ashdown's political fortunes no harm. As befitted a former captain in the Royal Marines, he didn't move a muscle. The pictures of his escape led the evening news, and we hoped they were duly appreciated by Whitehall's political commissars.

Looking back on it now, I think we probably spent too much time rolling along in the dust or the mud – it was always one or the other – behind British armoured vehicles in central Bosnia. They had little impact on the principal conflict between Bosnian government forces – mainly but not entirely Muslim – and the Serbs. Indeed most British soldiers, like most British journalists, never actually met a Serb from start to finish. And they were not able to prevent the fighting that broke out between Croats and Muslims around them. Colonel Bob and his men did indeed accomplish some heroic things, but these were achieved essentially in the margins of someone else's war. Yet to British journalists they were the main event, and would have been even with a rather less colourful character in command. One even went so far as to announce, 'We don't talk to locals' – an unusual formula for reporting a civil war.

So we stayed with Colonel Bob much more than we should have, and more than was probably good for his career. He was unfailingly good copy. Things happened around him. He was one of those people with the dubious knack of attracting incoming fire, and was extremely lucky to come through without a scratch. Also, our patrolling journalism almost always yielded results. It fortified our faltering courage, and got us to places where, without him, we would have been turned back or blown up. It was how we came upon the Ahmici massacre, in April 1993.

This was one of the turning points for the British in Bosnia, for Colonel Bob personally, and for the world's perceptions of the Bosnian war. Overnight it became more complex, harder to reckon on a moral compass, and somehow shaded in grey. For it was by now a three-way struggle, for which all blame could no longer be laid exclusively at the door of the Serbs. They were certainly not within fifteen miles of Ahmici.

The side-war between Muslims and Croats was as murderous as anything that had gone before – perhaps more so, because of their accumulation of grievances and the time they had to prepare for it. It erupted in mid-April 1993 almost on the doorstep of the British bases at Vitez and Gornji Vakuf. The Cheshires did what they could to intervene, but were brusquely ordered by local warlords to get out of the line of fire. Only when the first wave of killing and cleansing had spent itself, with the death toll already in the hundreds, did Colonel Bob succeed in arranging a local ceasefire and separation of forces.

The following morning he put together a stronger-than-usual patrol of four Warriors from his own regiment and two Scimi-tars (lighter reconnaissance vehicles) from the 9th/12th Lancers. The mission was to cross into no man's land through country lanes no wider than a Warrior, to see if the agreement was being observed. There were no prizes for guessing who was to lead this patrol, for Colonel Bob had not changed his leadership style. Under pressure from us, he agreed to include a press pool vehicle, the indomitable 'Miss Piggy'. I went along as driver, with my friend and rival Paul Davies from ITN and the ITN cameraman Nigel Thompson, who is a consummate professional but one of the few people in the business who really frightens me, since he is absolutely without fear and appears to believe that the bullets will bounce off him. That makes him a hard man to compete with, but this time we were pooling the coverage and he was shooting for us both.

The report that I produced from Ahmici became headline news in itself, and fairly controversial for Colonel Bob as well as for me. It was broadcast widely in the United States as well as at home, and was branded as 'insensitive' by an American media critic, because I did a 'stand up' in a charnel house. The pictures were edited as sparingly as possible, but it was the story itself that was shocking. Shorn of the pictures, this was how I told it:

NARRATION: It was a question of war or peace. Outside Vitez the British pushed a strong armoured patrol through a track across a ridge which the Muslim forces had captured in fighting just before the ceasefire. Under the terms of the deal they were supposed to have pulled back a mile and a half, but after what had happened to their people in the valley below, they absolutely refused to do so.

COLONEL BOB: You say there are many babies killed in the village of Ahmici. I'm so sorry.

MUSLIM SOLDIER: It is why we are not giving up and will fight to the end. No, we will not forgive them, we will not forgive them.

NARRATION: The British then took their patrol through Ahmici, where the worst of these atrocities were alleged to have occurred. This is or was a Muslim village of some 400 people. Every one of the Muslim houses was burned to the ground. Down the road, the fallen minaret was the very symbol of ethnic cleansing. The infantry then went on a foot patrol to look for more casualties or evidence of atrocities. They didn't have far to search. They came upon a house in the centre of the village where a family of seven had died, two in the stairway and five in the cellar. It is hard to look at some of these pictures, harder still to tell the story without them. What happened here can frankly not be shown in any detail. But the room is full of the charred remains of bodies, and they died in the greatest agony. It's hard to imagine, in our continent and in our time, what kind of people could do this.

COLONEL BOB: It looks like the father and the son tried to defend the mother and the daughters, the mother and the daughters being in the cellar. The father and the son possibly shot and then burned upstairs; and then some swine, someone, deliberately set fire to the cellar, and the mother and the daughters and young children, five or six, have all died. It is quite horrifying.

NARRATION: Down in the village the colonel then met a patrol of the HVO, the local Croat army. It was a tense encounter.

HVO: Do you have the permission of the HVO . . .

COLONEL BOB: I don't need the permission of the bloody HVO. I am from the United Nations. And as far as I am concerned what has happened here is disgraceful. Bad luck, my friend. You know, there are whole families up here that have been massacred, and I'd like to know who's done it, who is responsible. It's not you obviously, is it?

NARRATION: The Croats drove away. A more welcome guest was Jean-Pierre Thebault, head of the European Community monitoring team here.

COLONEL BOB: I've just had the HVO telling me no cameras. I told them to get stuffed.

THEBAULT: It's absolutely disgusting. People who have done this must be punished.

NARRATION: The massacre of Ahmici is of course a crime, and it's a crime that imperils such ceasefire as there is. For among the Muslims the need for revenge overwhelms the need for peace.

Colonel Bob's outburst was hardly the kind of measured response that officers are coached to deliver in their media training sessions. (In Northern Ireland they were actually issued with a thumb-sized yellow card listing useful answers in the event of a journalistic ambush: Soundbites, Officers, for the use of.) But Ahmici was not the place for a measured response. 'The scenes were appalling,' he wrote later, 'and I knew I was out of line to use the words "bloody HVO" but that was what I felt like at the time.' As it happened we were unable to file the story until the following day because our satellite dish in Vitez was in poor health and under intensive care. So I suppose that I acted unprofessionally. I invited Colonel Bob to view the footage with me, and even offered to delete the expletive if it really troubled him. There seemed no point in damaging a career for the sake of a single news story. (I know of one senior officer still serving who would have been retired long ago if a colleague of mine had not caught and buried an extreme political indiscretion. That videotape still lies in the desert sand.)

Colonel Bob, to his credit and my relief, stood by every word. He meant what he said. His strength, and the secret of his good standing with the warlords on all sides, was that he spoke from the heart and led from the front, as they did. It also definitely struck a chord with the public at home, and it surely did the army no harm that its most prominent field commander was seen to have emotions and feelings, and not be afraid to express them. Not to have done so, in the face of an atrocity on the scale of Ahmici, would have seemed heartless and inadequate, as if the UN stood neutrally between good and evil.

Soldiers are human, though, even those not so much in the line of fire or the media spotlight, and they do not necessarily rejoice in each other's success. Come to think of it, neither do journalists. Colonel Bob's high profile exploits had already attracted envy and disparagement from colleagues in safer places. None of this was communicated directly, but he was certainly aware of reports which stemmed from tabloid headlines and suggested that some kind of a 'cult of personality' had grown up around him. 'To start with it worried me a little,' he said. 'I was concerned that people might believe it and I wondered if indeed I had unconsciously promoted such rubbish.'

He hadn't. But inevitably the Ahmici incident only magnified his fame, or notoriety, and beamed it across borders. In the slipstream of Ahmici a new wave of journalists descended on the British base at Vitez: international feature writers, producers with the American TV networks, and reporters from every British tabloid except the one that claimed to champion 'Our Boys in Bosnia'. Colonel Bob dealt with them all as best he could. He could hardly ignore them, especially the Americans, for they enabled the case for the British presence in Bosnia to be heard in the White House and the State Department as it had not been heard before. Because he spoke plainly he was understood, and because he had earned it, he got more attention than any ambassador or secretary of state. A limousine-load of diplomats would not have accomplished half as much – but it may have hurt him professionally.

I knew of the whispering campaign against him perhaps better than he did, so I embarked on a damage limitation strategy which I code-named ABB. ABB stood for Anyone But Bob. Henceforth – and, I admit, belatedly – we would shine the light of publicity on the Cheshires more evenly, from the newest recruit to the most senior major. The campaign hit an early snag in the shape of Major Bryan Watters, who was the obvious candidate as alternative spokesman, having taken over as second in command half-way through the tour. He was articulate and personable, and – with Brigadier John Reith, formerly of the First Armoured Division in the Gulf – one of the two best military briefers I ever met. The difficulty was that he had promised his wife Elaine, who had obviously suffered at home from a surfeit of Bosnia coverage, that under no circumstances would he allow himself to be interviewed on television. Accordingly I called up Elaine at her home in Chester, and pleaded with her to revoke this severe directive. (I have never done such a thing before or since.) She kindly agreed, amid much ambient tumult from surrounding toddlers, and from that point on Bryan became something of a TV star in his own right.

But it was already too late. By the time of Ahmici the Cheshires were only three weeks away from the end of their assignment in Bosnia, and Colonel Bob had achieved a celebrity status which he had not sought, but which drew the disapproval of his superiors in the Ministry of Defence. Those with long memories harked back to the case of Lieutenant-Colonel Colin

Mitchell of the Argyll and Sutherland Highlanders in the Aden campaign of the late 1960s. He too was a brave and high-profile commander and a public relations legend. He too would have sent shudders down the spines of the ministry's pen-pushers, if only they had had spines. He too was not forgiven for his success. But he too saved his regiment.

That was Colonel Bob's real triumph and vindication, and it would not have been achieved without him, or without the Cheshires' high visibility at the time. The army found itself short of manpower, especially for new UN commitments which tended to be soldier-intensive. The Secretary of State announced that two previously planned amalgamations would not now take place. One of these was the forced and certainly unhappy marriage of the Cheshires and Staffordshires. 'It was the equivalent of death,' said Colonel Bob. 'Now that such a death sentence had been removed it was hardly surprising that we were over the moon.'

News of the reprieve arrived on 3rd February, with the Cheshires not so much over the moon as ankle-deep in the mud of Vitez. It was the brightest day of their Bosnian tour, and they celebrated it in more than lemonade. Their vast and imposing sergeant-major, RSM Charlie Stevens, caught the spirit of it in his home-made 'Ode to the Cheshires'. (The only real soldiers' poet is Rudyard Kipling: the rest they write for themselves.)

From Dettingen to Bosnia these men have made their mark,
They have passed with flying colours when the future has been dark.
There is something about these soldiers that nobody could have
    reckoned,
It's the inbuilt fighting spirit of the ever glorious Twenty Second.*

The saving of his regiment was the last good thing that happened

* *White Warrior: The Cheshires In Bosnia*, The Cheshire Regiment, 1994.

to Colonel Bob in a distinguished military career. From Bosnia he was eased out into a staff job which – it was made clear to him – would be his last in uniform.

As for his faults . . . Of course he had faults, which he knew better than anyone. He called them his feet of clay. He hated to delegate. He was impatient with detail and paperwork, and famous for walking out of negotiating sessions which he felt were getting nowhere. He was less admired by the squadron of cavalry attached to him than he was by his own beloved Cheshires. He was not at all times a model of tact and temperance. He paid more attention to the soldiers serving under him than those above him, and did not seek to win the favour of generals. But the faults were the downside of his virtues. Even his critics conceded his courage, which didn't prevent them from trying to block his award of the DSO. The army seems comradely mainly to outsiders. To those inside it can be a strangely calumnious institution. Even in the BBC it is difficult to accumulate quite so many ill-wishers.

Bob Stewart was the right man in the right place at the right time. It made no difference. Within two years of leaving Bosnia he received his notice of redundancy – which he both expected and welcomed, because it also gave him back his freedom to speak his mind. His departure from the army was its loss. Even today it needs leaders as well as managers. And in peacekeeping it needs them more than ever.

There remains the question of his private life and his friendship with Claire Podbielski. Since this is what did for him in the end, I shall here set down what I know of it. Claire was a stylish and attractive Frenchwoman, and the extremely competent delegate of the International Red Cross in Colonel Bob's area of responsibility. Whereas most ICRC delegates seem to feel that a certain aloofness and self-importance is a mark of their status in life, she was warm, friendly and approachable with not a sign of the standard ICRC Swiss satisfaction. She was also immensely hard-working and conscientious in her overseeing of prison conditions and prisoner exchanges. Both she and Colonel Bob saved lives. They were co-negotiators on a range of sensitive issues. They dealt with warlords who trafficked shamelessly in the misery of their captives, and in bodies both live and dead. ('A dead body,' wrote ICRC historian Jean-François Berger, 'has a market value of, say, two cans of petrol.')* As the war erupted around Claire and the colonel in the Lasva valley, they inevitably spent much time in each other's company. And to be closer to her work, Claire moved into the colonel's house in Vitez – which of course set all sorts of tongues wagging.

Actually it wasn't so much a house as a hotel, for Colonel Bob played host to a wide variety of guests, from generals to journalists, with business to do in the camp. I was a regular guest in the evening for what was always a mixture of business and pleasure, as the colonel reviewed the day's events over a glass of whatever was available. It was quite obvious that a strong bond of friendship had developed between him and Claire, perhaps all the stronger because of the difficulties and dangers that they shared. I think that he loved her even then. But these were two people with the strongest sense of duty and responsibility; and I am equally convinced that nothing happened between them which should not have happened, unless it was an offence for him to offer her a thimbleful of Bailey's Irish Cream as he helped her draft her overnight report to Geneva.

The friendship was widely known in the camp, just as it was an open secret that Colonel Bob's marriage to his wife Lizzie was in trouble even before the Cheshires' deployment to Bosnia. To me it hardly rated as news whichever way you looked at it – a point I discussed with an old friend from Belfast days, Ted

* Jean-François Berger, 'The Humanitarian Diplomacy of the ICRC', ICRC, Geneva, 1995.

Oliver of the *Daily Mirror*, who was well connected in the Sergeants' Mess, the best source of gossip in any battalion. What would be the headline, we wondered:

'British Colonel in Love Drama'? 'Bosnian Bob Finds Romance in the Trenches'? And what would be the point of writing this stuff, or of causing much pain to three decent people for the sake of a front-page splash? The front page wraps the fish and chips, but the hurt can last for years. I have a theory which I know may be heretical, but which holds that what you don't file as a journalist says quite as much about you as what you do. Ted Oliver is one of the best around.

The story came out anyway after the Cheshires' return to Fallingbostel in Germany. News of the colonel's impending divorce was not well received by his critics – or rather, they pounced on it. The armed services went into one of their periodic fits of hand-me-down righteousness, and produced a new set of moral guidelines more appropriate perhaps to a priesthood than an officer corps. These rules, incidentally, were the petard on which no less a figure than the Chief of the Defence Staff was hoist for a *real* breach of ethical principles the following year. They have also been so rigidly applied that they are known to have wrecked some service marriages which would otherwise have stayed more or less intact.

On all of this I have just two reflections as a semi-detached observer. One is that Colonel Bob was treated ungratefully, though very much in line with traditional practice: the army rewards its heroes by retiring them. The other is that the army which holds its officers to such a high standard of behaviour is also the army which places an intolerable strain on their families, and those of the men serving under them, when it sends its soldiers on a sequence of back-to-back unaccompanied tours away from home. It thus becomes commonplace for the casualties of a battalion's six months in Bosnia to include not only its dead and wounded, but ten per cent of its marriages and usually more. *That* was the real scandal, and it arose from the ethos of the downsizing exercise known as 'Options for Change', which required the army to do more with less, and at whatever cost.

Soldiers and their wives have sought me out and spoken about this – they believe, quite falsely alas, that I have some influence. Their words are shot through with sadness and despair, as if they belonged to some lost and forgotten regiment, as perhaps in a sense they do. As a result of a series of concurrent emergencies, from Bosnia to Belfast, more than half the British army is on active service or imminently preparing for it, with all the strains and separations that this involves, but none of the recognition that should go with it; and decisions are taken by a generation of politicians who have never served in uniform, and whose principal experience of separation from their families is a two-day jaunt to Brussels. The army deserves better. It is a still admired institution. It does not exactly reflect the society that it comes from, but it does reflect the *best* of that society. Yet many is the soldier whose only reward, having gained a medal and lost a marriage, is to return to a broken home.

Here is an idea for the next Defence Review: that it include *as a starting point* not just the nation's defence needs, but the welfare of the servicemen and women who meet those needs. And that this part of it be conducted by a caring and respected officer with recent front-line experience: someone like Colonel Bob Stewart of the Cheshire Regiment.

13

SOLDIERVISION

In war reporting access is everything, or nearly everything.

There have been exceptions – notably a *Daily Mirror* reporter in Africa, in the days when the *Daily Mirror* took note of Africa, who covered the Nigerian civil war from the bar of the Federal Palace Hotel in Lagos, which was much frequented by journalists returning from the front. He was generous and they were thirsty, and he had a knack of filing their stories even before they did. Such was his way with words and his economy with the truth, that by the time he had finished it was as if *he* had dodged the Biafran bullets and *he* had swum the crocodile-infested rivers. (In the coinage of Fleet Street in those days all rivers were crocodile-infested.) But he was one of a kind.

The general rule holds good: especially in television, although we intercept what we can when we can, there is no substitute for being there. And *being there* is an art of its own not taught in the journalism schools, but only in the real world beyond them. It is hard, and getting harder all the time. The days are long gone when you hailed a taxi and asked its driver to take you to the war, although I have done something of the kind in El Salvador and towards the end of the old regime in Saigon; and the late great James Cameron claimed to have done it in the Arab–Israeli war of 1967 – and if he claimed to have done it, then he had.

In Bosnia the war began with a free-for-all on all sides, in which journalists could roam where they dared, which was why the initial casualties were so high. But soon enough the road-blocks went up and multiplied; access was increasingly restricted; permissions were required, and hard to get. The commonest Catch 22 was that you weren't allowed through without a pass, but you couldn't get a pass without going through. Each of the armies had different reasons for keeping the press at bay: the Bosnian Serbs from their deeply ingrained distrust of foreigners, the Croats because of their need to mask the involvement of main-force Croat units from Zagreb, and the Muslims out of a sense of anger and betrayal, as they had expected the world to come to their rescue and the world had turned its back. (Lord Owen had told them, but they didn't heed his warning, because they didn't believe it: 'Don't live under the dream that the West is going to come in and sort this out. Don't dream dreams.')

But still there were ways of getting through. It took patience and persistence, plus an ability to absorb large quantities of coffee and slivovitz. It was also important to be known to the warring parties: newcomers had a hard time of it. So it was that an American network producer, assigned to Sarajevo to work with a correspondent who knew little about television and less about Bosnia, was heard on the phone to his mission control in New York complaining that he had not been hired to run a journalism school in a war zone. 'How,' he asked, 'is she supposed to compete with war zone thugs like Martin Bell and Tony Birtley?'

Never in my life had I been described as a war zone thug before, and I took this as quite a compliment – especially the bracketing with Tony Birtley. Tony is everything I am not: blond, young, good-looking and suicidally brave. After an uncertain start at TVAM, he had been given a contract by ABC News of America to cover the war, partly because few of their highly paid staff correspondents, with the exception of anchorman Peter Jennings (and he is actually Canadian), were willing to set foot in Bosnia. Not only were there no American ground troops in Bosnia, there were few American journalists either. The flame of Ernest Hemingway burned low.

Tony solved the access problem dramatically and it nearly cost him his life in March 1993. He hitched a ride on a Bosnian army helicopter flying into the besieged enclave of Srebrenica. There were only two such helicopters operational, soon to be reduced by the fortunes of war to one. They flew in with arms and ammunition and flew out with the most severely wounded. I told Tony he was as daft as a brush to try it. Even if he survived the flight in, which was like travelling in a slow-moving time bomb through Serbian anti-aircraft fire, he would be stranded in Srebrenica indefinitely, unless he also became a stretcher case.

Which of course is exactly what happened. He got in un-scathed, and was the only journalist on the ground when the intrepid General Morillon reached the enclave and offered it his personal protection under the UN flag. 'I am Srebrenica,' he announced in Gaullist fashion. Tony's reports, smuggled out of the enclave through UN channels, were not just the only ones available, but brilliant and vivid journalism by any standards – and as one of the new breed of cameraman-correspondent he had done it all by himself. But the Serbs knew that he was there – he had, perhaps imprudently, also been broadcasting on the 'ham' radio – and their mortar crews were looking for him. They found him, twice. On the second attack he was badly wounded in the leg. His only good fortune was that two United Nations soldiers were hit at the same time, and the UN was able somehow to spirit him out with them. But it was only in hospital in London that he knew for sure that the surgeons could save his leg.

A little over a year later, against all odds, he was back in the war zone again. I met him on the ramp to the UN's Sarajevo sector headquarters at the PTT building. We both limped up it like the walking wounded which in a sense we were, and each of us reproached the other for being there at all. I think we both felt, if *he's* not giving up, I'm damned if *I* will either. We war zone thugs stick together.

Tony then proceeded to solve his access problem for a second time. He had never worked much on the Serb side of the lines (in 'occupied territory' as the Muslims put it), and after his exploits in Srebrenica the Bosnian army accorded him special status: after all, he even had a street in the town named after him. Accordingly he was sometimes allowed to the front lines, especially with the Bosnian army's Seventh Corps, when they were closed off to all others. His reputation continued to grow, and rightly so. But he had paid a high price for the privilege.

Something of the same kind happened to me, on a rather more modest scale. I had haunted the Bosnian army's Third Corps headquarters at Zenica for three days, drinking their coffee, completing their paperwork, and schmoozing with the necessary people – all to no avail. Then by chance we ran into one of their commanders heading out to newly liberated territory. My interpreter, the persuasive Anamarija, pleaded for access. He shook his head. She tried again with an exaggerated account of my standing and influence in Britain. Still he wouldn't budge. Then she mentioned that I had once been wounded in Sarajevo. Immediately he softened and smiled and gave his agreement, as if that somehow made all the difference, and why hadn't we told him before?

To receive the authorization is one thing, but to make it work is another. Bosnia is a country of home-grown Napoleons, one at every road-block. It takes a fair slice of luck to get past them.

Our next stop was in a plastic cave on the road to Zepce. It was a restaurant built like a Gothic grotto to attract visitors to the 1984 Winter Olympics. Though it looked from the outside like a normal road stop, its vaulted interior was hung profusely with pink and green stalactites. If it had been a horse not a house, its pedigree would have been by Disneyworld out of Winter Wonderland, but it was the headquarters of the Third Corps' Northern Operating Group, which had just driven the Serbs out of fifty square miles of territory they had held since the war began.

The colonel commandant sat us down, offered us coffee, and with it a gravely delivered lecture about the responsibilities of the international press. We had, he said, a duty to be correct. All officers who once served with the old Yugoslav army do this, whatever their present allegiance. With General Gvero, General Mladic's deputy on the Serb side, the correctness lecture lasts at least an hour, and ends with a message of friendship to the British people. I rather like it: it is a fragment of the old Communism frozen in time.

Then came the interrogation: 'Why does the British and French government policy favour the Serbs? And why is the BBC pro-Serb?'

'It isn't. So far as I know my own government doesn't have much of a policy except to save lives where possible. As a reporter I really am independent. But I know that the Serbs don't like me very much; and for that matter, neither does the British Foreign Office.'

'Then what would you wish us to show you?'

'The territory you've captured.'

'We haven't captured it. We've liberated it.'

'Then the territory you've liberated.'

'And I suppose, you are only interested now, because the Serbs are losing?'

'No, Colonel. I'm interested because it's my job to be interested, and it seems to me that the front lines are moving for the first time in two and a half years – though whether you let me get at them is up to you.'

I don't know how it is with other war correspondents – it may be they question themselves less – but there are times when I find it hard to explain even to myself why I do this for a living. These moments of self-doubt tend to occur in the quieter interludes, not rushing the trench lines under fire, but sitting beneath a pink and green stalactite and trying to convince a sceptical commander that the BBC is not the public voice of the British government. If I fail to persuade him I shall at least spend the rest of the day in relative safety. If I succeed, my reward will be to advance past his last road-block towards the sound of gunfire, into some of the most dangerous territory in all Bosnia.

In this case we succeeded, with misgivings. But there was another headquarters still to be negotiated – there almost always is – that of the Seventh Glorious Muslim Brigade in the area just liberated, or captured. It lay up a newly carved mountain track so steep as to be almost perpendicular. Our three-ton armoured Land Rover failed the challenge – indeed, all our armour was useless in that terrain. The brigade commander, Colonel Halil Brzina, rescued us by sending down his mountain-climbing command vehicle, overpowered and underweight as ours should have been if we had known what we were getting into. Memo to the BBC's Transport Department: next time send us a Lada Niva or a Land Cruiser, unarmoured.

'What kept you so long?' the colonel asked. He was a courtly, stooping man with a humorous eye and a well-trimmed beard, and an interest in the world beyond those valleys. (Soldiers are progressively easier to deal with the closer to the front line you go.) He seemed genuinely if surprisingly honoured by our visit, and greeted us without the standard correctness lecture, for he was not at all in the mould of an officer trained in the old Yugoslav army. He was an engineer from that part of Bosnia

Herzegovina where, in the merciless side-war between Croats and Muslims, the Muslims' houses had been blown to pieces and .the Croats' left intact; and when they later turned from being enemies to allies, the Croats explained that the explosions had been the result of a very unfortunate problem with the gas pressure. It was a problem that left the colonel, and countless others, with no home to return to were this war ever to end.

'So what is your opinion,' the colonel asked, 'of the Seventh Muslim Brigade?'

'Very professional,' I replied with care, for this was a booby-trapped question if ever there was one. 'I can tell you that in two and a half years of reporting this war, it is the first time I have seen the Serbs being pushed back.'

'Chetniks,' he corrected me. Only the civilians may be Serbs, the soldiers are always Chetniks.

'Sorry, Chetniks. And if I were allowed to express an opinion (which of course I am not) I might even congratulate you for it. It's been a long time coming. And as for the Seventh Muslim Brigade, I am sorry to disappoint you, Colonel, but I had never really believed that you were a bunch of ferocious *Mujaheddin*.'

That was the point of it, of course. He had an agenda: they always do. Military commanders don't necessarily invite you forward out of a touching faith in the freedom of the press. In Colonel Brzina's case, it was to counter the Serb account of the offensive, that his men had burned and looted their way through defenceless villages, and were now poised to wreak their funda-mentalist vengeance on the Serb-held town of Teslic. He wished the world to know the truth, and gave us the run of his 'liberated' valley.

Though the Muslims now held it, it had historically never been their territory; there was not a mosque on those hillsides. But of course he drew no distinction between 'theirs' and 'ours': he was fighting for One Bosnia. 'Look,' he said, 'we are not like

An earlier war. At the trial of British mercenaries in Angola, 1976.

In Belize, 1981. No computer then, no computer now.

The media war with ITN on Arthur Denaro's tank – Saudi Arabia, November 1990.

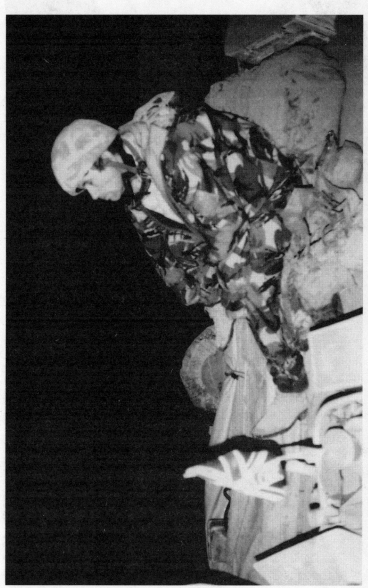

With the Irish Hussars on the assault into Iraq, 28 February 1991.

Lukavica Barracks, 1992. With Colm Doyle, Lord Carrington's representative, during a break in negotiations with the Serbs, who were then holding President Izerbejovic hostage.

With General Lewis Mackenzie on the BBC balcony. Illidza, June 1992.

At Sarajevo Airport, June 1992. President Mitterand's damaged
helicopter in the background.

With Croatian warlord
Sinisa Dvorski, in
Kostajnica Croatia,
July 1992.

With BBC Foreign
Editor Vin Ray,
putting on the flak
jacket, two days before
it failed to protect me.
August 1992.

Being interviewed by
the Bosnian newspaper
'*Oslobodenje*,' at the
BBC bunker in
Sarajevo, two days
before the mortar
incident.

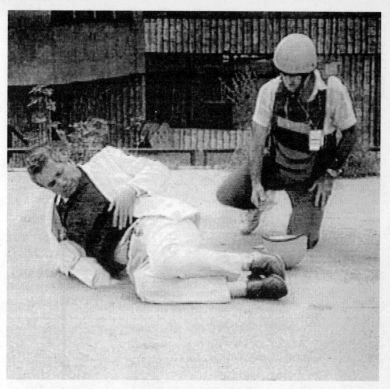

My least favourite photograph. Sarajevo, August 1992.

In the HVO (Croat) trenches near Vitez, August 1993
(photo: Anamarija Muvrin).

On Maslenica Bridge, Croatia, 1993. Rebuilt by the Croats and destroyed a week later by the Serbs.

Negotiating with London for one minute and forty-two seconds of the
BBC *Nine O'Clock News*. Vitez, 1993.

Outside UN headquarters in Kiseljak, January 1994.

First meeting with General Rose, UN headquarters, Kiseljak, January 1994. In the centre, Major Mike James, Army Public Relations.

With Christiane Amanpour of CNN. At airport negotiations, Sarajevo, April 1994

In a front-line Bosnian army stronghold, formerly a Roman fort and a
crusader castle. Prusac, Central Bosnia, November 1994
(photo: Anamarija Muvrin).

In a ruined mosque in the front-line village of Prusac, November 1994
(photo: Anamarija Muvrin).

Armoured vehicles of the Sarajevo press corps
outside the TV station, 1994.

A road still open to the intrepid 'Miss Piggy,' on a blown-up
bridge near Zenica, 1994.

Chetniks, slaughtering and burning. We are very sorry that the Serbs left their villages, and we invite them to return; we shall protect them. We have a thousand years of living together. The world should know that this is a fight of all Bosnians for the defence of their bare lives.'

The words had a familiar ring, for the Serbs of course had no intention of returning. They too had been persuaded that this was the final battle for their homes and lives. 'Their propaganda makes them crazy,' remarked the commander, sadly. But it was a battle that they chose to fight elsewhere, for the villages were indeed untouched. Especially in this low-tech and brutal war without distinction between military and civilian targets, it is easy enough to see when a place has been fought through and when it hasn't. These places hadn't. Here the Serbs had clearly known what was coming. The civilians had left with their furniture and animals, and the soldiers apparently had not been far behind. If they were going to make a last-ditch stand they would find another ditch at another time. It was as if, in unspoken complicity with their enemy, they had agreed to surrender land that would be taken from them anyway under the Contact Group plan. The Muslims had captured Serb field orders more or less conceding this. The same had happened, on a larger scale, at Kupres – the first break in the Serb ascendancy and the military stalemate.

We filmed and interviewed and did what television people reflexively do; and before we left the valley, towards nightfall, the colonel insisted on presenting me with a captured Chetnik bayonet, its handle carved with the Cyrillic acronym, 'Only Unity Saves The Serbs'. I accepted reluctantly, since BBC guidelines allow us to receive nothing of greater value than a ball-point pen, and a cheap one at that – but I persuaded myself that the bayonet would be safer in retirement as a paper-knife, slitting envelopes rather than throats.

Apart from that trophy, what had we come out with? In TV terms, as cameraman Tony Fallshaw pointed out rather mournfully, very little: images of the unburned villages and abandoned farms, of Muslim soldiers cleansing the surrounding hillsides, some minor damage when the Serbs had struck back with a wire-guided anti-tank missile, and a burst of fire above our heads when we ventured too far forward. But not much else: no tanks, no trenches (for there were none yet in this fast-moving mountain warfare), no dead, no wounded, no combat – nothing that would jostle for its place in a crowded half-hour of news. So I did what I often do when hard-pressed. I filled it out with soldiervision.

Soldiervision, if not one of the dirty secrets of war reporting, is at least among its rather less heralded practices. It is the footage which we don't shoot for ourselves, but a man in a uniform shoots for us. He will be serving other masters and other causes: the military archive, the greater glory of the general officer commanding, or the local TV station by way of corps headquarters. The management of news is part of the new world order – and the people must be told of their army's victories whether or not these victories have actually occurred. One army I know calls the unit that does this work its Moral Regeneration Department.

In the Bosnian war soldiervision eventually passed into the public domain, usually through one of the TV news agencies and after a number of German marks had changed hands. Because our own access was more than ever restricted, we tended to make increasing use of it, especially on the Serb side. Their cameras were where ours were not. And every Sunday night in Sarajevo we put our editing machines into the record mode, as their twin TV services of Pale and Banja Luka broadcast an hour of edited highlights from the previous seven days' combat. It was not so much *Match of the Day* as *Battle of the*

Week, an extraordinary sequence of vivid images for which great risks were obviously taken, backed by an uplifting commentary and a sound-track straight from the strings of Mantovani. (It also assured the Bosnian Serbs that their army was invincible, which proved to be an error and an illusion.)

We recorded this and re-used it (minus the Mantovani) selectively and without moral qualms – for it was the TV service of an unrecognized state, and it broadcast besides with some of our pilfered equipment. We labelled it clearly, because we could not always be sure that it was what it said it was. But if, for instance, it showed its own people, the Serbs, in clear breach of the Geneva Conventions, it was unlikely to be lying.

At the height of their assault on Bihac in November 1994, the Sunday night *Battle of the Week* showed some remarkable scenes of Muslim prisoners being threatened by the Serbs, and then paraded in companies in front of their new masters and forced to chant the catechism of captivity. 'We are the prisoners of the Serbian republic,' they repeated in fervent unison. 'We are the prisoners of the Serbian Republic.'

'To whom does Bosnia belong?' demanded their Serb tormentor and chorus-master.

'Bosnia belongs to the Serbs as much as Moscow belongs to the Russians.' And on and on: 'Bosnia belongs to the Serbs as much as Moscow belongs to the Russians.'

What made this particular sample of soldiervision so compelling and spine-chilling – our reason for both using it and labelling it – was that these were the images that the Serbs chose to show to their own people about the treatment of prisoners of war. If this was what they felt to be credit-worthy and good for morale, then what else might they be doing in darker places which they would rather hide? We were given the feeling, not for the first time, that we were reversing rapidly into the world of the Great War. Some of the weapons were actually the same, and so were the barbarities and ways of thinking. The only new ingredient was television.

In the best of all possible worlds the soldiers fight the war and the journalists report it — except that war, by its very definition, is the *worst* of all possible worlds. So the interaction between us occurs in an ambiguous grey area. Soldiervision is part of this. Some of it is genuine and some of it is staged — except that a soldier who is under fire, or expects to be, will not usually look and act like one who is blazing away for the camera's sole benefit.

Even when we have solved our access problems and are shooting our own video rather than intercepting someone else's, we can find ourselves on equally uncertain ground. At one point in Croatia, with my friend and cameraman Tihomir Tunukovic — who survived that war but not the next — I was visiting the town of Sunja, where the Croats' front line of defence was the old railway station, already half ruined. When we arrived it was quiet, but as soon as we started shooting so did the Serbs and Croats, with fierce intensity. The battle for the station lasted a full two hours, with the BBC pinned to the ground in the middle of it. The Croats claimed that they were under a full-scale infantry attack. They may have been right, but I was too close to the floorboards at the time to assess the battle impartially. Slobodan Praljak, the Croats' commander in Sunja, had been a noted theatrical director in Zagreb in his former life (he was to go on from there to higher command in the Bosnian theatre of war), and it did occur to me long afterwards — though not at the time, for I was far too busy surviving — to wonder whether the old showman might have staged the whole battle for our benefit. The Croats were campaigning for international recognition, and it suited their purpose to be seen fighting off the marauding Serbs. Coincidence or conspiracy? Did the battle occur just *while* we were there, or *because* we were there?

This business I am in is not just physically dangerous, but morally dangerous too, and anyone contemplating a career in it could do worse than to ponder the following anecdote, which I hope is apocryphal, but believe is not. It is about a journalist who wished to write a profile of a sniper on a front line in Sarajevo. It doesn't matter on which side the sniper operated, for both sides have them and each side fears the other's as much as it values its own. The sniper was peering out from between two bricks in his forward defences. 'What do you see?' asked the journalist.

'I see two people walking in the street. Which of them do you want me to shoot?'

It was at this point that the journalist realized too late that he was in absolutely the wrong place at the wrong time, and engaged on a story that was fatally flawed and that he should not even have considered. He urged the sniper to shoot neither of them, fabricated some excuse and turned to leave.

As he did so, he heard two shots of rapid fire from a position very close to him. 'That was a pity,' said the sniper. 'You could have saved one of their lives.'

14

COURT MARTIAL BY BLUE-EYED STARE

When I first met Michael Rose he was commandant of the army's Staff College at Camberley, traditionally an appointment for upwardly mobile generals, and one that gives them a chance to rethink and reshape the training of future commanders. On the issue of peacekeeping, there was plenty of rethinking and reshaping to be done, yet peacekeeping played a very small part in the syllabus. Even by the beginning of 1994, when General Rose moved over from theory to practice, and the Bosnian operation was coming to preoccupy Whitehall's planners and policy-makers, the army's academy paid it very little attention. The time set aside for it had risen from two hours to two days and finally to two weeks out of a thirty-six-week course. The rest of the time was devoted to the study of command in conventional warfare. With an ex-corporal's deliberate intention to provoke, I told my army friends that since their professional future clearly lay in operations other than war, they could surely divide their time more profitably than to spend two weeks studying their future and thirty-four weeks studying their past. But old habits are hard to break. Their library was overflowing with volumes advising them on the great land war in Europe which they would never have to fight, but on peacekeeping its shelves were all but bare: there were few textbooks of value except the memoirs of former UN commanders, not all of whom found favour in Camberley, and the maxims of Clausewitz were of little use in settling an argument between Serbs and Muslims at a mixed military working group.

By this time General Rose was already in Bosnia, and learning about the job the hard way, by doing it, in the manner of all UN commanders. His formidable reputation was also earned the hard way, as the man who broke the Iranian Embassy siege in 1980, and as a secret soldier in conventional warfare. He led the SAS component in the Falkland Islands Task Force, assigning both it and himself to the mission with a fine disregard for bureaucracy. His record was that of a tough no-nonsense soldier who champed at bits and suffered no fools near him. His extra qualification for the UN's Bosnia command was not his know-ledge of peacekeeping but his knowledge of French. Having studied for a year at the Sorbonne, he was the only senior British officer with fluent enough French to brief and be briefed in it.

In Sarajevo that mattered, as the encircled city was, in UN terms, a French fiefdom. It had not been intended that way, but the French had replaced the Canadians in July 1992 as part of a trinational brigade so daft in its conception that only the United Nations' ivory tower, its thirty-eighth floor, could have dreamed it up. When the then UN commander, General Lew MacKenzie, first told me about it, even he had difficulty believing it. It was known as the 'confessional deployment'. The French were in-cluded because they were Roman Catholics, the Egyptians because they were Muslims, and the Ukrainians because they were Orthodox. All it lacked was Copts. The plan was that all the city's constituent peoples would feel in some way spiritually befriended. Of course, it didn't work. And the principal contribu-tion of the Egyptian and Ukrainian battalions was to ease the hardships of those citizens with German marks by selling their food and fuel on the black market. Senior officers tried in vain to suppress this traffic. When the small Ukrainian contingent in the enclave of Zepa radioed that they had supplies enough only for one more day, their battalion commander was unsympathetic: 'Then tell them that they'll have to buy it back.'

When General Rose arrived in January 1994 the black marketeering was only part of the problem. United Nations troops were blocked everywhere, their peacekeeping was ineffective, their morale was low, and the outgoing commander, General Briquemont – sacked by the Secretary-General over a dispute about command and control – revealed that some of the national contingents were refusing to take his orders.

Even those who did took a minimalist view of their mandate. The Coldstream Guards confined themselves to escorting the aid convoys, ignoring the war that was raging all around them in central Bosnia. 'Our task,' said one of their majors, 'is the road and not the war.' The Canadians alongside them were apparently under orders from Ottawa to do nothing to offend anyone, and their weakness was seized on instantly by the Serbs. One of their patrols was submitted to a mock execution, and an entire platoon was kidnapped in broad daylight.

General Rose then came on the scene and surveyed the shambles. He started in Kiseljak, at the cliff-like hotel which was the home for an entire transplanted NATO corps headquarters. He inspected this vast UN paper factory, overstaffed and underperforming, with the blue-eyed stare he normally reserved for journalists and insubordinate officers. And I knew its days were numbered – as they were. The few individuals and sections which found favour were moved to his forward headquarters in Sarajevo. The rest were dismissed as surplus to requirements.

He announced a new robustness of attitude. An aide whispered to me that certain battalions who had thought they were doing well in Bosnia would be informed that General Rose didn't share that view. He had himself been a Coldstream Guardsman, but the Guards were not exempt. He dispatched a platoon of them immediately, outside their operational area, to unblock the crossing known as Sierra One, where for three days the Serbs had stopped all UN traffic between Kiseljak and Sarajevo. The Guards took well to their new combative role and roared up to the road-block armed to the teeth and with four Warriors ready to do battle, if necessary, to force a way through. The Warrior is a high-impact vehicle, and the nearest to a tank that the UN could muster at that time. The Serbs gave way, and the general's 'get tough' policy seemed instantly vindicated.

I asked him if, when it was all over, he expected to leave Bosnia as yet another frustrated UN commander. I was rewarded yet again with the blue-eyed stare. 'Definitely not,' he said.

He had momentum, now he needed luck. He got it in a way he could never have wished. On the 5th of February 1994 a mortar bomb exploded in Sarajevo's main market. It was mid-morning and the market place was crowded. Sixty-eight people died, making this the most terrible single atrocity in all the city's chronicles of mass killing. The TV cameras were on hand almost immediately which the Serbs quite falsely took to be some kind of a media conspiracy against them. And though most of the pictures were to my mind simply unviewable, those that were shown had a transforming political impact.

The result was the first effective ceasefire in twenty-two months of war. The agreement, stitched together in a little over two weeks, provided for an almost total end to hostilities, the opening of crossing points between Muslim and Serb sections of the city, an end to its blockade, and the withdrawal of all heavy weapons from a twelve-mile zone around it, with the exception of those held at collection points under UN supervision.

General Rose was everywhere, the UN incarnate: cajoling, persuading, striding the streets with his arms folded and assuring the people that their long ordeal was over. Came the hour, came the man. The swarming media were as ready to salute a new hero as they were later – as he would discover to his cost – to discredit an old one. It was his heyday and honeymoon, his fifteen minutes of fame.

He was not by all accounts an easy man to work for, and commanded a division as if it were a platoon. To his staff, or at least those in the inner circle, every day was a roller-coaster ride, sometimes terrifying and sometimes exhilarating, but never dull. His language was colourful and he was not a glad sufferer of fools. A computer-written slogan on his office wall said: 'Bollocks to the lot of them'. He played the political game when he had to. But as events unravelled and air strikes became an option, you knew that if he praised the unity of purpose between the United Nations and NATO, it was a signal that there had just been the mother of all rows between them, and a NATO commander might even have been told undiplomatically where to park his aircraft. The inner circle loved it, were fiercely loyal to him, and did whatever damage control was necessary. Those not in the inner circle might as well have gone home for all the use he had for them.

For a secret soldier without previous experience of public diplomacy – a man who knew more about dealing with terrorists than journalists – he had a remarkable and intuitive grasp of the importance of information policy, of leading from the front, and of the politics of peace by announcement. All this is vital to the art and practice of peacekeeping. If you wait for bad things to happen, bad things *will* happen. Better to seize events by the throat, and have them respond to you. (This actually comes straight out of Staff College doctrine, and is one of the few theoretical continuities between peacekeeping and war-fighting.)

For the first time since the war began, Bell's Law of Bosnia was confounded. This proposition, based on close and sometimes painful observation, states that in general the worst that can happen will happen. But now, for a season at least, it no longer applied. The principal ceasefire agreement was supplemented by a separate and unlikely deal, brokered by the Americans and Germans, between the Muslims and Croats who had been engaged for ten months in the brutal and costly side-war in central Bosnia. And this agreement was not just for an end to hostilities, but actually for a political federation between these two bitter enemies.

If that was possible, anything was possible. It was a moment of rare opportunity, but the UN commanders knew that it would pass and be wasted without the reinforcements that they needed – as many as 35,000 to police the agreements in central Bosnia and Sarajevo, and to protect the endangered Muslims in the eastern enclaves. The most critical of these, because the largest, was Gorazde, where some 65,000 people short of food and ammunition had held out for a year and a half against the encircling Serbs.

The UN Security Council is better at passing resolutions than at providing the means to implement them. If words alone could keep the peace, then peace would have prevailed. Over the months it had delivered about a hundred resolutions and statements, often vague and conflicting, and never matched with the necessary strength on the ground. The Gorazde crisis was described by a senior UN officer, Brigadier Charles Ritchie, as 'a classic case of what happens when what is expected of you exceeds your ability to do it. We do not have instantly the troops available that we would like to send to Gorazde.'

Even so in early April 1994, by the sheer force of personality and power of optimism, General Rose was within an ace of securing a wider agreement for the withdrawal of forces from all lines of conflict, while another search would be made for an overall peace settlement. The only dispute was about the length of the interim regime between the withdrawal and the settlement.

The two sides agreed to adjourn their airport talks for the night, with the apparent intention of signing on in the morning. General Rose believed that the peace he had worked for was but seven hours away.

The Serbs, however, thought otherwise. That night they stormed the Gorazde enclave in force. They came at it from both sides of the Drina river, with armoured and infantry attacks supported by heavy artillery. The defences crumbled. My Bosnian Serb friends explained it to me later, with bitterness and regret, as not just their army's long-planned spring offensive, but a deliberate peace-wrecking manoeuvre by the war party in their leadership. It was more than war; it was sabotage – and principally the work of General Ratko Mladic, their army commander, who accepted the political instructions that suited him and disregarded the rest. His forces had undoubtedly been attacked from inside the enclave (the word the Serbs always used was 'provocations'), but their response was – as usual – disproportionate. He wasn't interested in peace on the terms available.

His assault had important consequences. It left General Rose isolated and embattled on three fronts, none of them directly involving the Serbs. First, he was conducting a running skirmish with the Sarajevo press corps, who refused to believe the UN line that the Serbs' attacks were local and limited, and their objective was not to overrun the enclave. In this we were supported by the reports of a team of four UNMOs who were on the ground in Gorazde and outraged by what they saw as their commander's attempt to downplay the crisis. Their point was that *they* knew what was happening and he didn't. Their message, leaked to the press, of course, further eroded General Rose's credibility: 'It is a grave situation. The continued assessment for loss of civilian life is very high. The city centre of Gorazde is now only three kilometres from the Bosnian Serbs' front line. To say it is only a minor attack shows absolutely no understanding of what is going on.' To this the general replied that he did take the situation in Gorazde seriously, but he would not react to the first reports he saw and add to the panic.

His second area of conflict was with NATO, which was by then deployed in its new role as the UN's Bosnian enforcement agency. The Serbs at this time had their tanks already in the outskirts of Gorazde, and the city centre under small-arms fire. They were checked and halted by NATO air strikes on 10th and 11th April – the first time that the alliance had used such force in its history. The results were mixed. The NATO ground attack aircraft, flying at low level in foul weather, destroyed an elderly tank, some trucks and a communications centre, at a cost of one British Sea Harrier shot down. In the days that followed they were looking for more targets, while General Rose was urging restraint. He spent an entire day on the telephone to Brussels trying to persuade NATO commanders that the Serbs had halted their advance, it was time to give negotiation a chance, and UNPROFOR was in any case a peacekeeping not a war-fighting force. Also, he was responsible for the safety of his troops, who were endangered by over-reaction. In the words of Colonel Simon Shadbolt, General Rose's military assistant, whom some saw as the brains of the partnership: 'A preemptive punitive strike against the Serbs might make people happy over their cornflakes in the morning, but it is not going to help peacekeeping.' Or, as the general himself put it, 'Patience, persistence and pressure is how you conduct a peacekeeping mission. Bombing is a last resort because you then cross the Mogadishu Line.' (M words were much invoked by both sides in the debate on General Rose's steward-ship. His defenders praised him for avoiding the errors of Mogadishu. His critics attacked him for repeating the errors of Munich.) NATO commanders, steeped in the doctrines of overwhelming force, were unimpressed by General Rose's case for restraint – and especially the idea of limited response, or 'proportionality' in the selection of targets for air strikes. 'Proportionality,' exclaimed one of them, 'I'll give you proportionality. Han Pijesak (headquarters of the Bosnian Serb army) *and* the Pale ammunition dump *and* Lukavica barracks. That's proportionality!'

Finally, General Rose found himself enmeshed in difficulties with the governments of the troop-contributing nations – including, to his great dismay, his own. By this time the Serbs had reluctantly agreed to allow a token UN force into Gorazde. It was to be only a company strong and lightly armoured, and composed in equal parts of Ukrainian, French and British infantry, with a Norwegian field hospital attached. By late afternoon they had reached their assembly point on the airport taxiway – and that was as far as they got. The Norwegians and Ukrainians were willing to go, but the British and French governments denied permission for their troops to join in. General Rose had not expected this. (It was St George's Day, and he would rather have spent it socializing with his Coldstream Guards on their Regimental Day.) That evening, subdued and seething, he described the refusals as disgraceful and made his protests directly where he could, through the French ambassador, and by back channels to Whitehall where he could not. It was a classic case of the frustrations of UN command. Though both governments later withdrew their opposition, the entire life-saving operation in Gorazde was compromised by political foot-dragging and loss of nerve at a high level. Nor could the blame be offloaded, this time, on to the smaller contributing nations. A British general had been unable to deploy even the British troops supposedly under his command. (Much later, in July 1995, the defence of the UN's safe area of Srebrenica, garrisoned by Dutch troops, was ended by order of their Chief of Staff in Holland, who was far outside the UN's chain of command. It was not so much a chain of command as a web of incoherence.)

To be fair, the role of the press throughout this episode was hardly an instance of consummate professionalism either. We may have been lied to and were certainly misled. We had no independent and accurate sources of information. None of us was present on the ground – the Serbs saw to that. The reported casualty figures on the Muslim side – 750 dead in the Serb assault and 1,900 wounded – were unverifiable. All that we had to go on, beside the clearly incomplete UN accounts, were the excitable and highly political 'ham' radio broadcasts beamed daily out of the city, which was said by then to be a total ruin:

The situation in Gorazde is dramatic and deteriorating fast. The hospital has been hit again by tank fire. Nineteen villages within the safe area have been burned to the ground since the offensive was launched. The result of the arms embargo is that it has deprived us of the right to defend ourselves. The embargo must be lifted immediately. Tomorrow may be too late.

It sounded authentic and some of it was true, for the plight of Gorazde *was* worsening. But our own taste for the dramatic may have seduced us into giving it more credence than we should have. I am not blaming others here, but only myself.

The cries for help from Gorazde were supplemented in Sarajevo by daily statements from the Bosnian Prime Minister, Haris Silajdzic, who was an easy man to like and a hard one to keep off the screen. By his mastery of the soundbite he probably did more single-handedly to affect the course of the war than anyone else except General Ratko Mladic on the Serb side: Mladic did it with guns and Silajdzic with words. The combination of his eloquence and our own exclusion from Serb-held territory meant that the Bosnian government's view of events prevailed.

The Serbs agreed to a voluntary withdrawal, their only one of the war. By 27 April the UN force was well enough established in Gorazde (though the French had still not arrived) for the UN commander to visit. As usual the press was shut out on Serb insistence – and the Serbs controlled the access. But at least one camera, resting on a military shoulder, accompanied General Rose. A copy of the tape reached me later that evening without the caveat which was supposed to accompany it that some of it was politically sensitive and 'off limits' – not to be used (since the tape was the UN's own, it could set such conditions).

It was certainly strong stuff. General Rose was with British and Ukrainian troops on a three-hour tour of the scene of battle. Casting his soldier's eye over it, he concluded that the Muslims had deliberately collapsed their defences. 'They think we should be fighting the war for them,' he said. 'I mean, how the hell they let a tank down that goddamn route. One man with a crowbar could have stopped it. It's a five-mile road down a wooded ravine; they could have just dropped a boulder on it. I think they basically turned and ran and left us to pick up the bits.' On his tour of the hospital he was equally unimpressed by the unsubstantiated casualty figures. 'We were getting these reports, and yet the people who came off the helicopters, some of them were young men who hopped off the stretchers.'

Because they caused quite a stir, the general later described these remarks as 'tittle-tattle', and just about court-martialled me for broadcasting them; the blue-eyed stare pronounced me guilty as charged. In my defence, they were not conveyed to me as off the record, they were clearly his considered view, and they put him back on speaking terms with the Serbs. Gorazde and its people *had* suffered severely, if not as severely as first reports had indicated, and they had successfully campaigned to draw the United Nations to their defence.

General Rose set great store by his press relations, which he saw to be central to the success of his mission. He rightly perceived that we were not adversaries but partners, but the Gorazde episode was an object lesson in the tensions that could still arise between the UN and the press. Their primary objective was peace and ours was truth. We were journalists not propagandists. And from time to time, we collided.

15

OF MEN AND MANDATES

Long after the Bosnian conflagration began, many of the UN soldiers trying to extinguish it were heard wondering why a *preventive* UN deployment had not been considered – a force that would have been in place *before* the resort to arms. Actually it was considered, by President Izetbegovic himself, towards the end of 1991 during Bosnia's last winter of peace. The European Community was under pressure to recognize the independence of Slovenia and Croatia, and he knew what the likely consequences were for his own powder-keg republic. But if he were offered independence, he had to take it. So he suggested a modest UN force to police his borders, and the UN responded by proposing that the headquarters for its planned Protection Force for Croatia be sited at Banja Luka, a stronghold of the Serbs in northern Bosnia. Those were days of relative innocence, and it was really felt that this modest deployment would be enough to hold the Serbs in check.

In a country where the rewriting of history is a growth industry, the story was later circulated that President Izetbegovic had asked for an entire UN division of some 14,000 men to be sent to Bosnia before the fighting began; and that Cyrus Vance, the chief UN negotiator, had warned him that it could only happen after the event, and would take 10,000 casualties. This story seems to be largely fictitious, except that Bosnia did in the end qualify for its UN division. But by the time they arrived the situation was already beyond their control.

Bosnia was a classic case of what is known in UN operations as 'mission creep': a force goes in to do one thing and inexorably ends up doing another. Whatever the instructions from New York, it more or less has to reinvent its mandate in the light of events that New York could not foresee, or should have foreseen and didn't. In Bosnia the mission crept both ways, from doing rather more than the mandate authorized to doing a great deal less.

The UN's operation there was from the start probably the most *ad-hoc*, makeshift and ill-considered in its history. It was not just badly planned, but *unplanned*. As the slide into war continued and the capital itself came under threat, the UN moved its proposed headquarters from Banja Luka to Sarajevo, hoping to provide a sort of white security blanket for Bosnia's ethnic and tribal groups to clutch at. But it made no difference. 'Militarily it was a dumb order,' said General MacKenzie, the UN Chief of Staff, who was perhaps in the best position to know, as the walls of his new headquarters crumbled around him. For when the fighting began he had just a platoon of combat troops available to him, the Swedish security detail commanded by the valiant Captain Thomas Jarnehed, where he needed at least a battalion.

After six weeks even General Nambiar's optimism evaporated. The force was literally blitzed out of the city, leaving only a few UNMOs, who were unarmed, to pick up what pieces they could. The first ever UN field headquarters in Europe fled in disarray to Belgrade. The withdrawal was so precipitate that even the UN's civilian spokesman, the dapper Fred Eckhard, was seen risking the integrity of his Brooks Brothers suit by helping to move boulders from the path of the retreating column.

As far as the Secretary-General was concerned, that was that.

Dr Boutros-Ghali had no great enthusiasm anyway for intervention in the 'rich man's war' of ex-Yugoslavia. The Sarajevo experiment had failed; his mandate and mission were in Croatia; and he recommended to the Security Council that no peacekeepers be sent back into Bosnia.

He had not reckoned with the power of television or the wiles of the Bosnian Serb leadership. The blue helmets might have pulled out, as indeed did the BBC for a while, and in equal disarray. But other agencies and networks remained, including – to their great credit – our rivals at Sky News. The fighting intensified around the Marshal Tito barracks, the landmark twin towers beside the Holiday Inn were on fire, and the plight of the city's trapped civilians was so acute and conspicuous as to create an irresistible pressure for intervention. If the UN wasn't for this, what was it for? And it didn't even have to be mustered from distant capitals. Its armour and infantry were six hours' drive away.

The other new element was the unexpected willingness of the Serbs, perhaps with an eye to the public relations dividend, to allow Sarajevo airport to be put under UN control and used for humanitarian flights. It was an offer that the UN could hardly refuse, and did not. It hurriedly put together its first specifically Bosnian force, of Canadian troops under the command of General MacKenzie. It opened negotiations for a land corridor through Serb-held territory. In a series of incremental and 'mission-creeping' resolutions it enlarged the mandate and strength of UNPROFOR, and authorized the use of necessary measures (which is UN-speak for the use of force) to deliver humanitarian aid.

The UN Secretary-General, Dr Boutros-Ghali, who had opposed the whole enterprise, now described it as 'pioneering a new dimension of UN peacekeeping'. The British government, which had set itself resolutely against the deployment of its ground troops in Bosnia, reversed course. Was this done in principled defence of the war's victims, or also (as some of the soldiers themselves suspected) in defence of an endangered Security Council seat? In the arcane world of UN politics, if a country seeks to punch beyond its weight (a much favoured phrase in the Foreign Office), it tends to need a battalion or two to punch with. The new UNPROFOR, 6,000 strong, consisted principally of British, French, Canadian and Spanish battalions, with contingents also from Holland, Belgium, Denmark, Ukraine and Egypt. It was a force of very mixed quality.

And as the months of peacekeeping passed into years, the discrepancies between the contingents multiplied and increased. Nation by nation, the good units learned and improvised, and devolved responsibility downward, to the corporals and lance-corporals, where it belonged. The bad units went to pieces. No one dared to point this out, because it was politically incorrect to do so and against the mind-set of the UN's cave of winds – in which respect political correctness was as much the enemy of good peacekeeping as of good journalism. But it reached the point of scandal and débâcle. The hardest case was that of the Ukrainians, once an important part of the vaunted Red Army. They entered the enclave of Gorazde in April 1994, alongside the British and the French, with twelve heavy-duty armoured personnel carriers, an infantry company of ninety men and all the equipment and armament that went with them. Fifteen months later they came out with one rifle and a broken-down truck. That was all they had. Everything else had been traded with or sur-rendered to the Serbs and the Muslims, in equal proportions. At least the UN was principled: even its fiascos were even-handed.

All of this was predictable. None of it was predicted, except privately by UN commanders on the ground. Yet they had no choice but to go along with Dr Boutros-Ghali's 'new dimension of peacekeeping'. It looked like firm action by the world commu-nity, but was very much less than that. It was the politics of the lowest common denominator. The real new dimension was that it was the only military intervention in UN history where the sole declared objective was to help the victims of war, and that in a very limited way, so that at least they should not be starving when they were shot. A Bosnian army officer dismissed it scornfully as 'a spoonful of aid so that we can be healthier when we are hit by mortars and grenades'. They wanted guns but were getting feta cheese. And Médecins Sans Frontières asked, 'How can we think of passing food through the window while doing nothing to drive the murderer from the house?' General Philippe Morillon, who was the UN's commander in Bosnia at this time, coined his own word for it. He called it 'a mandate of *angelism* – an illusion that the mere pretence of UN soldiers with blue helmets and the blue flag would help to prevent the explosion'.

The mandate, literally interpreted, did not provide for peace-keeping or peacemaking, for mediation or the separation of forces, but only for the provision of humanitarian aid. Later, when peacemaking and peace enforcement became necessary, they would seriously conflict with the humanitarian mission. UN soldiers in Serb-held territory would be held hostage as a guarantee of UNPROFOR's 'good behaviour', its reluctance to take on the Serbs. As the force was originally constituted it was like an armed Red Cross, with its weapons only to be used to protect itself. To true interventionists like Dr Alain Destexhe, Secretary-General of Médecins Sans Frontières, the course that was taken was not intervention but non-intervention, not action but inaction:

Humanitarianism has served as an alibi for political impotence. It has never been further removed from what it asserts itself to be: a signific-ant gesture of fraternity and hope. When the accounts are drawn up, when we finally know Bosnia's fate, humanitarianism will find itself sitting in the dock with the accused . . . a companion to the territorial conquest and ethnic cleansing, even, to a certain extent, making them possible . . . The Serbs soon realized the advantages to be gained from this approach: no matter what they did, the humanitarian bridges would never be destroyed. The only thing that Europe seemed to be asking of them was the passage of a humanitarian convoy from time to time.*

The commanders of the newly arriving UN battalions thus found themselves in an impossible position: not only were they mandated to deal with the effects of aggression rather than with the aggression itself, but they were involuntarily acting as agents of ethnic cleansing. As usually practised this was not so much a killing as a squeezing process. The Serbs would overrun a town, then leave open one road out through which non-Serbs would be expelled.

So it was that the Cheshire Regiment arrived in central Bosnia just as the town of Jajce had fallen, and the thousands of Muslims and Croats who had shared it were being pushed across the confrontation line at Turbe, having been pillaged and robbed by the conquering Serbs in the process. In all the British army there was not a more humane and caring commanding officer than the Cheshires' Bob Stewart – perhaps even more so sometimes than his superiors would have liked. He was outraged. But he had no alternative but to help the refugees with transport and medical aid at the crossing point, and no mandate even to do that.

And that was just the beginning of his problems. For the Serbs, in pushing the minority populations – and in the case of Jajce, the majority – out of their territory, upset the delicate ethnic balance of central Bosnia. Tens of thousands of Muslims and Croats came flooding into valleys which the two communities had shared in relative harmony for centuries. Now each felt

* *Yugoslavie: la politique de la bande velpeau*, by A. Destexhe, Paris, Armand Colin, 1993.

threatened by the other, and the newly arrived UN force had the task of patrolling the flashpoints, countering the rumours and trying to hold back the tide of war. None of this was in the mandate, but it had to be attempted.

When it failed, and the Croats fell on the Muslims in mid-April, Colonel Stewart and his men found themselves in the middle of a crisis which the UN's copious paperwork had not anticipated. Under the terms of their mandate they would have been justified in retreating to their bunkers and staying there. Instead, and at great risk to themselves, they intensified their patrolling to try at least to contain the fighting; they rescued the living and retrieved the dead from burning villages under fire. The soldiers themselves were deeply shocked. One said, 'This is Europe in 1993, not 1943. I just can't believe what I'm seeing.'

I came upon Colonel Bob at Kakanj, while all of this was going on, and asked him what he thought he could do to stop it. Usually he was a man of immediate fluency, but he paused a long time before answering. 'I have decided,' he said finally, 'not to play this "UN safe". We are patrolling constantly. We are doing everything in our power to save all the lives we can. There is nothing more we can do.'

'If we find an incident,' added his second-in-command, Major Bryan Watters, 'all we can do is report it, if we cannot get access. If we can, we will position ourselves between the fighting forces and extract the women and children.'

They were acting out of common sense and common humanity. After one of the worst of the barbarities, a truck bomb which demolished the centre of Stari Vitez, a crowd of desperate Muslim refugees laid siege to one of the British camps demanding to be let in. The UN mandate had no guidance on that one either. Bob Stewart had tents put up to shelter them, and circled the Warrior fighting vehicles as a ring of steel around them, while he negotiated to transfer them to the relative safety of Zenica.

Because he needed some guiding principle to work from even
if he had to make it up for himself, Colonel Bob invented the
concept of the 'implied mandate'. Since the mission was humanitarian, he would help the victims and broker local ceasefires
wherever possible, and so create the conditions under which aid
could be delivered. It made more sense and was more likely to
succeed than simply opening a road into a war zone, which was
all that the original instructions would have allowed. These UN
officers were soldiers of conscience, deeply troubled by the
inadequacy of their mandate. They pushed it to the limit, but
even at the limit it allowed them to do very little. Bryan
Watters distinguished between recent 'clean' wars between combatants, such as the Falklands and Gulf wars, and the savagery of
the civil war raging around him:

There are few noble acts in a civil war. I suspect some people will be
troubled by what we have been powerless to prevent and I think there
lies the rub. I suspect history will not judge the world community on
what it has done but on what it has failed or will fail to do. We are
powerless under the present mandate to prevent this genocide taking
place on a holocaust-like proportion.*

The commander of the next British battalion in central Bosnia,
Lieutenant-Colonel Alastair Duncan of the Prince of Wales's
Own Regiment, managed to push the mandate a little further
when he took over in May 1993. He was a quieter character
than Colonel Bob, but combined an equal courage with a flair
for staff work. By making contact with the UN's legal experts
in New York, he found that he was able to invoke the Geneva
Conventions to identify and then defend a safe area for the
protection of the civilians living in it. This also saved lives which
would otherwise have been lost, and was applied by the UN
Security Council on a much wider scale nearly a year later.

* *White Warrior: The Cheshires in Bosnia*, The Cheshire Regiment, 1994.

What the UN never did, however, was put its mandate to the test that the wording implied. It had clearly threatened the use of force. That was what 'all measures necessary' meant in the authorizing resolution of 1992, just as it had in the build-up to the Gulf war in 1990. The wording was almost identical. Though the UN's convoys were blocked and turned back by the Serbs almost daily, in violation of constant assurances of freedom of movement, it never once used force in Bosnia to deliver so much as a packet of sugar or a box of pills.

There would almost certainly have been casualties if force had been used: but there were also casualties because it was not. Yet these were casualties which it was perhaps easier for the world to live with, because they were people suffering and dying out of sight of the cameras in the obscurity of the blockaded enclaves. The most eloquent witness to this was Larry Hollingworth, the former Ordnance Corps colonel and Father Christmas look-alike who ran the UNHCR's operations in Sarajevo for the first year of the war and in central Bosnia for the second. In a conflict with few real heroes, he was one. Like Colonel Bob, he was in the business of saving lives. And to save them he was as willing to take on the Serbs as his own organization's bureau-cracy in Geneva. He was not much loved by either. He would spend days in argument and frustration at the Serbs' road-blocks – so much time at Rogatica that he practically lived there – cajoling their bandit-commanders. His only weapons were his bottles of whisky, which he used to lubricate the negotiations, to keep out the cold, and to save himself from the slivovitz. His impressive armoured escorts, usually French or Ukrainian, were a bluff, for they would not be used to force a way through as under the mandate they could have been. He knew that – and the Serbs knew that, and exploited it.

Zepa was typical – a Muslim town to which the Serbs made no territorial claim, which didn't prevent them from seizing it in the end. They laid siege to it and strangled it for more than eight months, and when Larry Hollingworth finally negotiated his way into it, in January 1993, after a nightmare journey through Serbian lines, he found that the staple diet for the survivors was cattle fodder and bread made with straw. He gave me this account of conditions at the hospital: 'They've done thirty-six amputations without anaesthetic, and all using what I can only describe as a carpenter's saw. Of these thirty-six, seven were on children of whom three died. The problem is that they try to give the adults as much of the local alcohol as they can and then make them sing or shout prayers, but they can't give the alcohol to the children.' Larry felt that the time had come, if not for a change of mandate, at least for the existing mandate to be made to mean something. 'I want to stop being messed about,' he said. 'I have negotiated my way through many, many road-blocks, and I've played the willow tree most of the time. But looking back on it now, the more I played the oak, the better it was.'

It wasn't war in the enclaves: it was murder. People there were being killed by the Serb blockades through malnutrition, starvation and medical neglect, as surely and deliberately as if they had been singled out and shot by firing squad. It just took longer.

It was at this point, and with the collapse of the Vance–Owen plan, that the United Nations, having failed to deliver on its previous mandate, decided to come up with a new one. This time its mission didn't just creep; it jumped. It authorized NATO to shoot down aircraft violating the ban on flights in Bosnian airspace. And it declared the towns of Sarajevo, Tuzla, Zepa, Gorazde, Bihac and Srebrenica to be safe areas defended if necessary by force against further attacks. This was the Washington 'Action Plan'. Under it, the UN was like some sheriff of a Wild West community, announcing that henceforth there would be protection for all its people; and NATO was its enforcement agency, its hired gun.

To be fair to both organizations, this time at least they followed their words with actions, though a long time later. Air strikes were used against the Bosnian Serbs near Gorazde in April 1994 and near Sarajevo in August, and against the Croatian Serbs on the Udbina airfield in November. The latter was a major air raid involving thirty-eight aircraft of four nations. It created a considerable political impact, and a quickly repaired crater in the runway. It was also the last air strike of the year, though not of the war.

It was done in defence of the safe area of Bihac; and Bihac was the classic case of UN weakness and self-delusion. The crisis, which resembled the earlier one in Gorazde, began with a break-out by the Bosnian army's Fifth Corps against the encircling Serbs. They achieved an immediate and unexpected success, which they lacked the strength to consolidate. The Serbs then regrouped, helped by Croatian Serbs from across the border and by the rebel Muslims of Fikret Abdic, a businessman-turned-warlord, in loose alliance with them. It was a complex and very Balkan imbroglio, and increasingly dangerous as the counter-attack drove into the safe area.

The UN threatened to use airpower to stop the Serbs, as it had done in the similar case of Gorazde; it also misread their intentions. The Serbs have a reputation for being devious, but are usually quite straightforward. First they announce what they intend to do. Then they go ahead and try to do it. In this respect – and this respect only, of course – they reminded me somewhat of Margaret Thatcher in government.

The announcement of their intentions on Bihac came from Jovan Zametica, the Cambridge don and Serb nationalist, who was Radovan Karadzic's principal adviser on foreign policy and sometimes on relations with the United Nations. His phone call from Pale to General Rose was somehow intercepted by Kurt Schork of Reuters. Its publication may even have suited the general, though he said that if it happened again he would sue for breach of copyright, for it showed what he was up against. It followed the air strike on Udbina, to which the Bosnian Serbs reacted as angrily as if the airfield had been theirs.

'I shall use some very undiplomatic language,' said Zametica. 'Don't fuck with us. Don't mess about. If you hit us this means all-out war. This has come from the Head of State, President Karadzic. He is in a furious mood.'

A placatory General Rose was more concerned about the Serbs' advance into the safe area, and went so far as to suggest that it could have been a map-reading error. 'If you could please ensure,' he pleaded, 'that if they overrun the line, they could remove themselves from the zone.'

But it was of course no map-reading error, and Zametica told him so: 'Our intention is to demilitarize the area because you're obviously unable to do it. We wish to disarm every armed Muslim there. Should you attack us it means very bad news. I think you should use all your formidable intellect and authority back in London to state exactly what is at stake here . . . My President is passing the message to you – don't mess around with us.'

The signals from Pale could hardly have been clearer, yet General Rose dismissed them as rhetoric. He held one of·his occasional press conferences in front of the sand-bagged Residency where he worked, and assured us that the front lines in Bihac had stabilized. It was as if Mr Zametica's threats were inconsequential. General Rose maintained, as he had in the Gorazde crisis, that Bihac was a tactical battle for local advantage. But whereas in Gorazde the limits of the safe area had never been exactly defined, in Bihac they had, and he suggested that they might be redrawn on the map a few hundred yards one way or the other.

A few hundred yards was not what the Serbs had in mind, though. Even as the general was speaking they opened an assault which put them by nightfall two miles within the safe area. That was beyond the scope of even his cartographic diplomacy. His quite unjustified optimism turned to anger. 'They have clearly crossed the line,' he said, 'beyond which the safety of the population of Bihac is now threatened. This is a very grave development which we have to act upon ... A flagrant and blatant violation of the UN designated area.' It was also a defeat and humiliation for the United Nations, compounded by renewed heavy shelling of the capital the same evening – all of which I set out in what I thought were rather measured terms on the BBC news.

The following morning the general's spokesman, Jan-Dirk von Merveldt, made a beeline for me. 'I have been instructed,' he said, 'to give you a rocket.'

'Thanks, Jan-Dirk, it happens quite often. What is it about this time?'

'I don't know. All I know is to give you a rocket.'

Actually I knew very well. It was always the same, when the general thought my reporting had been negative about the UN's achievements. (He had actually withdrawn an earlier rocket after seeing the report himself. He didn't apologize – generals don't – but he had his military assistant do it for him.) He received his journalistic feedback at home from his wife, whose displeasure was not lightly to be incurred. On her one visit to Sarajevo I had been obliged to promise, under pressure, to try to look more cheerful in delivering the news from Bosnia. (She brought the same message from their two sons: it seemed I had the whole Rose family on my case.)

This time it was going to be difficult. For the Serbs, unlike the UN, were not bluffing. They responded to the threats of more NATO air strikes by activating their ground to air missile systems – SAM2s, SAM6s and SAM7s. The systems' radar 'illuminated' patrolling aircraft, and a missile was fired at a British Sea Harrier over the Bihac pocket, but missed. That raised the stakes considerably. The NATO command concluded that the next strike would have to be a massive and simultaneous one against the missile sites on Serb-held territory.

At that point the UN backed down again. It was a peacekeeping not a war-fighting force. It had 500 of its men held hostage by the Serbs. Its Bosnia command not only vetoed the proposed air strikes, but asked NATO for a 'cooling-off period' in which its aircraft would cease to patrol the skies above Bosnia, and would enforce the 'no fly' zone from somewhere round the edges.

All this was done discreetly, even secretly. It became known only when the UN's Director of Air Operations was persuaded to give a briefing to the press about the Serb missile systems, and perhaps unwisely strayed into other areas. He was after all a wing-commander not a politician. I sincerely hope he is still in a job, for candour is always to be encouraged. He told us what he knew: 'NATO has stood down at our request just to help get the peace process going on. Clearly we want to restart good communications with Pale so that our normal operations can go on.'

In short, overflights, air strikes and air drops to the besieged enclaves were all suspended. The UN's safe areas weren't safe, and its Protection Force wasn't protecting. Its policy imperative was, even after all that had happened, *not to upset the Serbs*. To revert to the Wild West analogy, it was as if the sheriff had asked his hired gun to please go away because the bad guys were cutting up rough. The transformation of the sheriff (General Rose) was fascinating to behold. He had arrived in January 1994 calling for a more 'muscular' and 'robust' attitude to the Serbs. Yet by the time he left a year later there was little muscular or robust about the force he led or his leadership of it; for the Serbs held the initiative. Even his body language was defensive. He walked with his arms folded.

What went wrong? How did January's promise become December's deadlock? General Rose's supporters believe that he was the victim – his critics would say the *author* – of a fundamental misappraisal of the situation that he inherited. All incoming commanders examine their options – and, in peacekeeping operations, tend not to think much of them. General Rose's, as set out in the Campaign Plan that he commissioned, ranged from the total withdrawal of the UN force (for which there was no political consensus) to total peace enforcement (for which there was also no consensus, and there were no sufficient resources either). The status quo option was equally unappealing, because the status quo not only was not working, but had proved to be the downfall of his predecessor. But the campaign planners identified an option which they called 'Towards Peace', and guided his hand towards it as a conjuror might towards a pre-selected card. 'Towards Peace' was no more than status quo plus: it would make the existing operation more efficient, and 'even compel to some extent the cooperation of the belligerent parties'. It supposed that peace was possible incrementally, from the exhaustion of the combatants and through a step-by-step process on the ground. It wasn't – at least without the use of more force than General Rose would allow. On Bihac especially he shrank from enforcement with an Akashi-like disdain. The Americans believed that he ordered his SAS men on the ground, the forward air controllers, not to identify targets for NATO air strikes. There was much activity in the air. But the F16s circled aimlessly and returned to base.

The Bihac fiasco was certainly the low point of his term of office, which included some real achievements. It was also the occasion of his famous ambush by Haris Silajdzic, the Bosnian Prime Minister, in the halls of the Presidency. Silajdzic was genuinely outraged by the UN's appeasement of the Serbs, to the extent that he cast diplomacy to the winds. From a ritual hand-shake with General Rose, Silajdzic turned through forty-five degrees and harangued the cameras directly, not in spite of the general's presence, but because of it: 'I am sorry to say this, General Rose is right here, standing right here, and I am telling him it is your responsibility to call for the air strikes and you are not doing it. Thank you.'

In the end the Bihac pocket, or what was left of it, did not fall, just as Gorazde had not. But the cases were different. The Bosnian army's Fifth Corps did not collapse its defences, but fought on tenaciously. Bihac was saved both by the Serbs' reluctance to engage in costly street fighting, and by the Christmas truce brokered by former American President Jimmy Carter. It was certainly not saved by the United Nations.

In peacekeeping, no operation will be quite like any other; each will have its own complexities; missions and mandates creep and change. But some lessons have been learned the hard way from the Bosnian experience, and are still being learned, which could usefully be applied elsewhere.

First, a merely victim-based strategy doesn't work, and probably prolongs the war. It is misdirected in practice, because it tends to feed the front-line troops. And it is morally objectionable, because it stands impartially between good and evil (those old-fashioned concepts are realities in Bosnia) and unwittingly helps the aggressor by acting as his welfare agency.

Second, humanitarianism conflicts with peacekeeping, and still more with peace-enforcement. The *threat* of force, if it is to be effective, will sooner or later involve the *use* of force. At that point the UN, as an aid-delivering entity, has to go out of business. Its troops have the choice of being taken hostage, or moving into more of a war-fighting mode, at least defensively. And the contributing governments must be ready for this: it is not a risk-free enterprise.

Third, the credible threat of force can yield results. The authorization of NATO air strikes in June 1993 pressured the Serbs into relatively cooperative behaviour for ten months, until the crisis in Gorazde which they did not actually initiate. The air strikes on Gorazde in April 1994 resulted in a local agreement and a Serb withdrawal. And, most spectacularly, the arrival of IFOR in December 1995 – the same UN soldiers under a different command and mandate – turned belligerence into compliance overnight. The fainthearts said it couldn't be done. It could be – and it was. This was the lesson of Bosnia, that force prevails.

Fourth, all threats will be tested; and if they are bluff they will be seen to be bluff. That was the lesson of Bihac. If you *declare* an area safe you have to *make* it safe. As it was, by firing at one aircraft and 'locking on' to others, the Serbs saw off the mighty power of the Atlantic Alliance. The UN wasn't prepared or equipped to move to the next level of escalation.

Fifth, peacekeeping is a soldier-intensive business in which the quality of the troops matters as much as the quantity. In Bosnia the quality varied and the quantity fell short of what was needed. One UN commander said that one third of his staff officers might as well not have been there for all the use they were to him. Bosnia also showed, again, that a Security Council resolution without the means to enforce it is just another worthless piece of paper blowing around in the UN's cave of winds on the East River. I was accredited there for more than ten years, and have seen it from both sides.

Finally, peacekeeping is not just soldiering under a different-coloured helmet. It differs in kind from anything else soldiers ever do. It has its medals and rewards – chiefly the satisfaction of saving lives – but it also has its casualties. And no victories.

16

SHADING THE TRUTH

Professionally I see myself as a footnote. I belong somewhere towards the end of the second generation of BBC war reporters, heirs and successors to a great tradition which began with Richard Dimbleby, Frank Gillard, Godfrey Talbot and many others, on and above the battlefields of the Second World War. They worked exclusively in radio – a medium then of unparalleled reach and influence (as its present practitioners maintain that it still is). We who came later will for ever stand in their debt and under their shadow. Ours was a smaller canvas. We dealt for the most part with local tumults, regional conflicts and various kinds of insurgency. We never faced the dangers they faced, or tangled with the censorship they tangled with.

For those who labour in the field today – a different-looking field strewn with satellite dishes – one of the incidental benefits of the fiftieth anniversaries of the Second World War was that they unloosed a tide of reminiscence of what war reporting was like for our founding fathers. Most interesting of all was their own judgement of their work, of what they did and were allowed to do. We honoured it and praised it; they did not. That was par for the course: the constant mark of good journalism is its discontent with itself, which is also why journalists and diplomats are such very different people. Richard Dimbleby, who reported the North African campaign until just after the fall of Tobruk, recorded in his diary his frustration with the censorship imposed by Middle East Command: 'It really is disgraceful to deceive the public, to cover up failures, and I really believe that's what Cairo is doing.' He fell foul of the rift between Churchill and Auchinleck and was withdrawn from the campaign.

Another of the great legends of BBC radio, Frank Gillard, was widely praised for his reporting of the Dieppe Raid, which he observed off-shore from a Royal Navy ship under fire and described as an all-time model of combined operations. (It is fascinating to me how all that generation when actually broadcasting, and only then, felt obliged to slip into the accents of the ruling classes.) What he was not allowed to do was to describe the sea running red with blood, or the raid as the fiasco and disaster which it was. In the television programme broadcast by the BBC in May 1995 to review its own war record, *What Did You Do in the War, Auntie?*, this wonderful man demolished his own legend with moving and absolute honesty. 'I feel ashamed now,' he said, 'that I was not able to tell the true story of Dieppe to people. And I read in BBC literature about my memorable report from Dieppe. To me it's memorable in all the wrong ways. It's memorable with shame and disgrace that I was there as the BBC's one and only eyewitness and I couldn't tell the story as I ought to have told it.'

But that was then and this is now; that was a war for national survival, and nothing like such a conspiracy of untruthfulness could happen today. Or could it? I am actually not sure. The test of any censorship regime is the way it handles setbacks and reverses, and the last time the British army went to war, in the Gulf in 1991, the victory was so swift and complete there was hardly time for either. But rules were at least worked out in advance, during a long negotiation in a tent in the desert, which would in theory have allowed for more openness in the reporting of failure.

For those of us who succeeded the Richard Dimblebys and Frank Gillards, and who worked in later years and greyer areas, the dangers probably lay less in censorship than in self-censorship. Beware the siren calls for responsible journalism for beyond responsibility lurks mendacity. In my own case I plead guilty not just to self-censorship but even (as a lawyer might say) to aggravated self-censorship. And since this is the only book I intend to write, it seems the best place to set out the details of how I lied in public, or at least allowed such shading of the truth that it had the effect of a lie. I do this both as a reproach to myself and a warning to others. And unlike Frank Gillard I had no excuse: there was no government censorship forcing me into it.

There were, however, the BBC's powers that be – or rather the powers that were – in Northern Ireland. It happened in August 1969, when sectarian tensions which had been simmering for months spilled over into open conflict in Belfast, and Roman Catholics were burned out of their homes in border-line streets between the Shankill and Falls Roads. I was out and about in the ruins with my friend and cameraman Peter Beggin, whose images caught the plight of these desperate people. They returned to their homes only once, to leave again with what they could carry or push in a pram. Later in the day we were minding our own business and editing these pictures together for the evening news, when I felt the presence of Authority in the cutting room behind me. 'Martin,' said the voice of Authority in its distinctive Malone Road accent (which is quite the other side of town from the Shankill and the Falls), 'I'm sorry, but you can't say that.'

'Can't say what?' I inquired innocently.

'You can't say that they're Catholics. You will have to call them refugees.'

'But you know they're Catholics and I know they're Catholics and just about the whole of Belfast knows they're Catholics.

Look at that picture there – are you trying to tell me it is a *Protestant* woman pushing a pram-load of her belongings with a crucifix on top of it?'

'Look, I live here and you don't, and I'm responsible for what is broadcast here. Our duty is to calm things down, not to provoke another riot. Those people are refugees.'

As it happened I rather liked this Authority and had worked for him in London. He was right on one point, that Ulster was the closest we had had to a civil war, and there was a dynamic relationship between what people did on the streets and saw on the television. The rioting tended to abate around tea-time, as the rioters went indoors to watch the instant replay on the evening news. And if they didn't like what they saw they would come at me with fists and voices raised at the very least, to make sure that I had seen the error of my ways by the time of the main news three hours later.

In this case we made fools of ourselves to no purpose. We outraged the Catholics, failed to appease the Protestants, and generally short-changed all our viewers by denying them the truth. It was not a deception on the scale of Dieppe, but it was still quite a serious falsification. To this day I don't know why I went along with it, except that I was young and inexperienced and impressed by Authority, who must surely know his Belfast better than I did.

That was not the end of it, though. The shocking part of it was not Authority's behaviour but mine, and I then compounded the felony by lying about it. The chattering classes were in business even then, and because the troubles in Ulster were all over their television screens they began a debate about whether the medium was acting responsibly and whether or not the coverage was being censored. I was invited to contribute a piece to *The Listener*, which was then the weekly bulletin board of the chattering classes, and this was the conclusion:

The problem of communication is one of the chief frustrations of the job, though perhaps the least tangible. The others are more direct and pressing. There are many difficulties both logistic and journalistic. But, in my experience, censorship is not one of them.

I still don't know why I wrote that, since censorship had been a difficulty at least once. But the incident had a sequel to it, and what I took to be a kind of nemesis. In those days, rather than wait for the army and RUC reports to come in, we used to take the camera car on evening patrols through the streets. These ranged from the routine and uneventful to the downright terrifying, according to the climate of the times prevailing in Belfast, and they got a number of my army contacts into trouble, who were falsely accused of tipping me off when mayhem was afoot. It was on one of these patrols that we came upon a pub on the edge of Ballymurphy which had been bombed just minutes before. There was an epidemic of such bombings at the time, for Belfast was sliding into sectarian warfare, and this was how it was waged. The attack that night was one of the few without casualties, because for once some warning was given. It was just after nine o'clock. The alarm bells were ringing and what remained of the pub was completely deserted. As I entered what used to be the lounge bar I noticed that the lights were still on and so was the television. I thought that I heard a voice I knew. I did know it. I looked up and realized that it was my own, and the face that went with it, on the BBC's *Nine O'Clock News* – broadcasting in the ruins and to an audience of no one. It was an other-worldly scene that left a deep impression on me. And I drew a lesson from it: if you shade the truth as I had done, there will be nobody out there watching. (Perhaps this is how the world will end: the interactive screens will be talking to each other, but the people will have fled.)

A quarter of a century on, the lesson still applies as much to Bosnia as it did to Belfast. The ruins are on a larger scale, and the truth is harder to establish. Or rather, all parties hold to their separate truths, which they will cheerfully lie to promote. Habits of mendacity and deception are deeply ingrained, and especially difficult for outsiders to deal with. There was an UNPROFOR staff officer who used to add a motto of his own to the daily situation reports which he circulated. 'Everybody's lying,' he wrote, 'but it doesn't matter, because nobody's listening either.'

In our Bosnian war coverage we no doubt made mistakes, but they were not the mistakes of political direction or surrender to government pressure. For my own part, I hardly belong on Whitehall's list of the dozen most troublesome journalists, but I can think of nothing in my reporting of this war which found favour around its polished tables, or was intended to. I was not seeking approval, but attention.

The mistakes that we made were different mistakes, and if we shaded the truth we did it in different ways. These had to do with the nature of the medium itself, its thirst for immediacy and its idolatry of the live shot. We are driven too much back on to our communications and not enough out into the world around us. The *reductio ad absurdum* of this comes with those network promotions – which began with CNN but have now affected others – in which we congratulate ourselves on our talent and technology, on how fast and wonderful we are, on how we can pitch our dishes wherever the news breaks, and how we can bring you the world in twenty-two minutes. It is true that Sarajevo can now talk to Atlanta, but what has Sarajevo got to say to Atlanta that it has been given the time to find out?

Since we at the BBC are now threatened with having to take the road of rolling news ourselves, I studied the CNN operation alongside us with particular interest. I learned about it from my

good friend Christiane Amanpour, and looked forward to learning even more when Peter Arnett visited Sarajevo in June 1995.
I had known Peter during his first career, as a brave and brilliant
Associated Press reporter in Vietnam in 1967. Now he was at
least as successful in his second career as a TV reporter, up there
with Christiane in CNN's stellar firmament. The Sarajevo
assignment was his own choice, and his way of reimmersing
himself in the real world after perhaps too long on the celebrity
circuit promoting his autobiography.

I am not myself a new-fangled sort of reporter, and would
probably have been more at ease in the days when the transmission systems were cleft sticks and packet steamers. But as it was
clearly time to have the waves of the new journalism washing
over me, I looked forward to watching Peter Arnett at work.

His day began – and for that matter continued and ended –
on the roof of the TV station, whence CNN beams its reports
to Atlanta and the world. The first thing he did was to produce
a small bag from which he extracted a hand-mirror and powder
puff. With these he prepared himself for his stint at the CNN
coalface – fourteen live shots, one after the other, in which his
task was to use news agency reports to brief his viewers on what
was happening on the battlefronts. If he could see or hear
anything from his rooftop perch, that was as close to eyewitness
reporting as the rules of the game allowed. He pleaded with
Atlanta to be let out to the front lines, in the traditional mode of
war reporters, to find things out for himself. It was what he was
good at and how he had made his name.

'Of course, Peter,' they said. 'That's fine. Just be back in forty
minutes.'

I felt for Peter. He is really terrific at what he does, but was
not allowed to do it. And though I am fortunately much less of
a celebrity than he is, I have felt some of the same pressures. The
low point was during one of the NATO air strikes against

Serb positions in 1994. The air strike was known to be imminent, and I went through the motions of sounding authoritative about it. But since it was NATO and not the United Nations which dropped the bombs, the news came out of Naples rather than Sarajevo. So it was that a producer from London fed the Naples communiqué into my earpiece which I then repeated verbatim and live on camera. It was like a sort of news bypass operation, in which only the ear and the mouth were actively engaged – not journalism, or even show business, but puppetry.

So our first admitted failing was that because of the ever-pressing rush of deadlines we didn't get out and about as much as we should have. Our second failing was that because of certain internal constraints we were not always able to present events in Bosnia quite as we found them. This was not political censorship. It was 'good taste' censorship. And since it is an issue on which I am totally at odds with my leaders, I shall deal with it chapter and verse.

17

WAR IS A BAD TASTE BUSINESS

In the second winter of the war Paul Goodall was killed.

The Bosnian war, even at this stage, was one with few heroes. Those it did have included the sixty British drivers from the ODA (Overseas Development Administration) who drove their unarmoured trucks through active war zones to bring aid to people who without it would have starved; heading east through Gornji Vakuf they actually made a right turn in no man's land, directly in the line of fire where fighting was fiercest between Muslims and Croats. They did it in all weathers and all phases of the war. Their leading light and inspiration was a junior government minister, Lady Chalker, to whom they were devoted. Once, stranded with them in a snow-drift on a mountain road, I noticed that one of them had christened his cab 'The Baroness Chalker of Wallasey'. Not many politicians in office draw that kind of compliment.

Up to that time the ODA drivers had survived the hazards of Bosnia with remarkably light casualties. But their luck was about to change. Paul Goodall had delivered his load to the UNHCR warehouse at Zenica and secured his vehicle for the night. He and two other drivers were on their way by Land Rover to their hotel when they were hijacked by four *Mujaheddin*, later joined by a fifth. (These Islamic fighters-to-the-death, from a number of Middle Eastern countries, were supposedly allied to Bosnian government forces, but accepted no orders from them.) The *Muj* ordered their captives to drive out of town, forced them at gunpoint to the bank of the river Bosna, where they were told to kneel in the snow, and then were robbed. Paul was executed at point-blank range by a single shot in the back of the head. The other two ran for it and both were wounded as they plunged into the icy river. They swam underwater and surfaced downstream with the cold helping to numb the pain; in the manner of ex-soldiers (which they were) they encouraged and helped each other, and struggled to safety. Their wounds were dressed by the family who found and sheltered them. They were taken first to the civilian hospital in Zenica, then to the British field hospital in Vitez. Both were extremely lucky to be alive.

From our vantage point in 'TV Alley', outside the gates of the camp at Vitez, we didn't get to hear about it until next morning. Details were scarce and pictures scarcer. It was going to be a difficult story to tell on the evening news.

In normal times, we enjoy a blessed measure of freedom; our editors in the BBC newsroom leave us alone to get on with the business. We are spared the American system of 'script approval' where – whatever the status and salary of the correspondent – every dot and comma and nuance of the script is debated with headquarters in New York. Our only negotiation, usually, is about length – an issue which I generally resolve by settling for one minute and forty-two seconds whatever the story. (I was much impressed by an old BBC news editor whose professional life was a long campaign against the prolixity of his writers. In his view, more meant worse. 'Son,' he would say, 'the greatest story in the world was told in two words: Jesus wept.)'

But these were clearly not normal times. There was an anxious voice from the duty editor in London asking what I had got to offer. I told her, not very much. (At that time even the survivors were too ill to talk.)

'You are not including any' – there was a hush in the tone and a long and awkward pause – '*bodies*, are you?'

'No,' I said. 'There's only one. It's in the camp, and the subject of an autopsy. Absolutely no bodies, I assure you.'

'Nothing that will upset people?'

'Well, the story itself is pretty upsetting, especially to the families, and they've been told. It *is* a murder you know, and a particularly brutal one.'

And then the voice said, 'Is there *blood*? We don't want to see any blood, at least not before the nine p.m. watershed. It's in the guidelines, you know.'

Actually, I didn't know. And of course there was blood. While I was broadcasting live for the *One O'Clock News*, our friends and allies from Reuters TV had been to the scene of the crime, which they found with some difficulty. Inevitably, the shooting had left blood on the snow; fatal shootings tend to. There followed a day-long argument in which my point, that when people are shot they bleed, was answered by hers, that she did not want to upset the viewers, especially in the early evening, when more children would be watching. New guidelines had been issued to this effect and were being strictly followed. Indeed, they have since been tightened.

To be fair to my masters, their nervousness was based on audience reseach. The new BBC, whatever its faults, is a great deal more accountable than the old one. It listens to what its viewers and listeners are telling it. And one of the things they are telling it most insistently, in letters and phone calls and audience research interviews, is that they are deeply concerned about the level of on-screen violence – not so much the stylized violence of fiction as the real violence of the world around us. In this new climate of sensitivity the BBC could hardly stage the last Act of *Hamlet* – still less report the death of Paul Goodall in any recognizable way.

I believe we should listen to the audience and respond to its concerns, but in the internal BBC debate about the depiction of real world violence only one side has been heard, and it hasn't been the side of the BBC's troops in the trenches. The point we would make, and which has gone by default, is that the new world order is much more dangerous than the old one, that it has to be seen as it is rather than as we would wish it to be, and that in our anxiety not to upset people we are running the risk of misleading them quite dangerously.

The issue came to a head for me in Bosnia, because the murder of Paul Goodall was not an isolated case. It was January 1994, at the height of the fighting between Muslims and Croats in the Lasva valley, and we had access to the most extraordinary images of front-line combat that I have ever seen. To be honest, we did very little of this for ourselves (I had perhaps become over-cautious since my collision with the mortar fragments). It was done for us by Kresimir, a gentle soul and professional musician who carried a camera on our behalf, though he would accept no payment. His motive was that he wanted the world to know what was happening to his people. He was a Croat trusted by the HVO's front-line commander Tihomir Blaskic, the soldiers in the trenches were his friends, and he went where they went.

The result was a series of images of raw power and great impact: winter warfare in a First World War landscape of barbed wire and trenches and bunkers, an advancing infantryman hit and killed in the snow under the eye of the camera, and street fighting in the ruins of Santici with the Croats winching out their casualties under fire. Kresimir was also lucky to be alive. In Santici he was hit by an AK47 bullet at a hundred yards, but it struck him on the front plate of the flak jacket we had given him only the week before. (Much later, I took the damaged ceramic plate to the RBR Armour Company in the Old Kent

Road, where these things are made by an entirely Ghanaian labour force. I was led down to the factory floor, work stopped for a moment, and in a heartfelt but inadequate speech I thanked them for saving his life.)

His pictures were the very model of what is known in the trade as 'bang bang': so close to the action, indeed *part of* the action, that no news editor would think of dropping them from his programme. But in their raw form, the 'rushes', they showed the costs as well as the courage that this kind of combat exacts. As the Croats advanced, they recaptured a house where a dozen of their comrades in arms had been surprised and their position overrun in the first assault, then apparently tortured and executed: their bodies were found stacked in a room and bound together with wire. Kresimir's coverage showed that too, and the grief of the mothers and wives in Vitez when they found their worst fears confirmed.

These images also fell foul of the 'good taste guidelines': even mourning was put out of bounds. The reports still ran, of course – thanks to Kresimir, they were too vivid not to. But all that was left in them was the 'bang bang', apparently heroic pictures of camouflage-clad figures blazing away amid the ruins; and even the ruins seemed picturesque, being sunlit at this season against the snow. It was about as close to reality as a Hollywood action movie. Indeed at times fact imitated fiction: one of the Croats' warlords, Darko Kraljevic, would dash out of cover and fire both his weapons on the move, revolver in one hand and sub-machine gun in the other, in the manner of Arnold Schwarzenegger terminating something.

What was missing in all this, and in our reports of it, was a sense of the human price being paid, the irredeemable waste of young lives. I am a fierce BBC loyalist; it is an institution that it is easy to be proud of even today, and a force for truth and freedom in the world; also, at the personal level, I am fortunate to have worked throughout my career for caring and decent people, and I bite the hand that feeds me very seldom. But it did seem to me and still does that in this case, in our anxiety not to offend and upset people, we were not only sanitizing war but even *prettifying* it, as if it were an acceptable way of settling disputes, and its victims never bled to death but rather expired gracefully out of sight. How tactful of them, I thought. But war is real and war is terrible. War is a bad taste business.

Television by its very nature has an aptitude for illusion anyway. Reality is somehow diminished by being framed in the modest rectangle in the corner of the living room. Images from the front line especially lose something in the transfer, and take on the quality almost of travelogue, as if in a scene from one of P. J. O'Rourke's *Holidays in Hell*. So often in the course of this war, harried by the ever-imminent deadline, I would rush from battlefield to cutting room — often a journey of only a few hundred yards — clutching my field cassettes with a survivor's pride and eager to get at them. Then, having viewed them, I would ask myself, is that really all there was? Was that it? Something was missing, something that will always be missing in the compressed world of the tube: the sense of the surrounding reality, the sharper perceptions of the eye as against the camera, the sights and sounds and smells of actually being there. For this there is no video substitute, not even the 'virtual reality' of TV news.

And yes, we do self-censor. Even those of us who resist the external censorship of real-life violence find images that we have to leave, as we used to say, on the cutting-room floor. Nearly all the TV pictures of the mortar bombing of the market place in Sarajevo — indeed of all that city's mass killings — seemed to me to fall within this category. So did the scenes in the cellar in Ahmici where a Muslim family of seven, including mother, grandparents and small children, were burned to death by the

Croats. In the end I used a single picture, a close-up of a burned hand, as emblematic of the rest, and even that was hard to include though necessary. I have become, I suppose, more hardened than most to man's inhumanity to man – or, at least, less surprised by it. But when in that setting I tried to utter a few words to the camera (as in most reports from far-flung places we are expected to) I found that for the first time in my life the words would not come out. Horror paralysed thought. I was reminded of Elie Wiesel who said of some events that he had witnessed, 'There are things I cannot say . . . I cannot say them.'

In the same way there are things we cannot show . . . we cannot show them. And others that lie beyond the range of our cameras. Television often stands accused, at least in the military circles in which I move, of exaggerating the events it relates and wrenching them out of context, but in Bosnia it has consistently understated the facts where it did know them and under-reported them where it didn't. The massacre at Ahmici became as notorious as it did, not because it was the worst of its kind (though it was certainly among the worst), but because it occurred just off a main road within three miles of a principal UN base. The village's toppled minaret was a grim advertisement of what had happened. It positively invited further investigation. And the victims were found by men of the Cheshire Regiment in their subsequent search of the ruins.

It took no great courage for the press to drive in with Warrior armoured personnel carriers fore and aft, and two platoons of infantry all around, but it was a completely different matter to go in where the UN feared to tread – or having trodden, withdrew. There came a point in the fighting between Muslims and Croats where even the dauntless Colonel Bob, pinned down in no man's land after repeated ceasefire attempts, concluded that he was keeping his men in the line of fire to no purpose. That left the press – especially the picture-driven elements of it, the TV crews and photo-journalists – in an exposed and dangerous position. The army had absolutely no obligation to protect us, especially along a confrontation line from which they themselves had pulled back. Yet we could hardly report the war from their bunkers and billets. Almost every day we were faced with difficult decisions about how far to go, and whether we should try it at all.

We were probably over-cautious. I certainly was. I could feel the war of attrition grinding me down, and I found myself grasping at any available pretext to dodge the column – which in this case meant staying away from the front lines at all costs. Feature stories about the state of aid supplies, or children learning their lessons in cellars, or the visit of some minor politician, were recommended to our editors in London as a refreshing change from the daily drumbeat of bombs and bullets. What I didn't tell them was that I was becoming almost too scared to go out.

This feeling was strongest among those of us whom the war had already marked in one way or another. It made no difference that the three armies in the field were using old-fashioned weapons systems: an old trench mortar can ruin your day just as surely as a new cruise missile. We knew from personal and painful experience that it wasn't a fireworks party: also, that the categories of journalist most at risk were those taking their chance in a war zone for the first time, and those others – such as Sebastian Rich and myself – who had been playing the odds for too long.

Sebastian came to us on contract from ITN, and worked with the zeal of a convert. He had a reputation as something of a 'headbanger', a war-loving, camera-toting character who would venture into the cannon's mouth without a thought of the risks. But he wasn't like that at all. I found him as cautious as I was, and with reason. He had been quite seriously wounded by a rifle grenade in Beirut some years before, he had survived a brush with death in Afghanistan, and he had had some close calls in Sarajevo too. During an exchange of fire at the Holiday Inn his face was pierced by a shard of glass at least an inch and a half long; as a result he partially lost his hearing – a particular handicap in a war zone.

He was an uncannily accurate predictor of incoming fire. After an unnerving journey at night through Gornji Vakuf, with explosions all around the convoy and tracer fire above it, we paused at the entrance to the British UN base at the moment it became the target. Sebastian as usual sensed the dangers before he saw them, as a mortar exploded fifty yards away. We were saved by the guardhouse sandbags, but his camera took a fragment of shrapnel directly through the lens hood; another inch and he would have collected another injury. His voice, all over the sound-track, said the rest: 'We're out of here. This is crazy . . . Into the camp everyone, NOW.' At such a time, you don't go into committee. You run for it. Our interpreter, Anamarija Muvrin, who was as fearless as she was beautiful (she left a trail of broken hearts behind her), would look at us reproachfully as if to wonder what kind of stuff these British war correspondents were made of. We told her that we intended to survive this war, and whether she liked it or not she would survive it with us.

The BBC, like all considerable news organizations, was caught in the contradiction of sending its journalists to war zones while at the same time imploring them to stay safe. A cameraman was not allowed to stand on a ladder in London, but was expected to run the trench lines of Lukavica. In one of his attempts to square this circle, our Head of Newsgathering, Chris Cramer, who really did care about safety having once come through an extremely unsafe place himself, sent a memo which I treasure to this day for its ringing declaration that 'Macho journalism will not be countenanced.'

He should have countenanced my kind, and I suppose he did. It was the very reverse of macho journalism. It was let's-get-the-hell-out-of-here journalism. And therefore, since finding fault with television has become something of a growth industry, I am taking the opportunity to set the record straight. On the issue of our coverage of the Bosnian war the true charge against us is not that we misrepresented it by seeking out the horrors and ignoring the context; or that we somehow short-changed our public by telling them less than we knew. It is that for reasons of prudence we didn't know, and therefore didn't tell, the half of it.

18

ARM YOUR CHILDREN

There was just one moment when I thought I had realized my long-standing ambition to become a peace correspondent. It was in November 1989. I was serenely completing a twelve-year shift as the BBC's chief North America correspondent – twelve not entirely peaceful years, since they included rather too much dodging of bullets in the wars of Central America. It occurred to me even then that more of my fifty-one years than was good for my health had been spent in the world's war zones, from the ditches of Vietnam to the sands of the Sinai to the *barrios* of Nicaragua, and that too many of the friends I had shared them with had paid the price. I remembered Neil Davis of NBC News, killed in a tinpot coup attempt in Thailand. I remembered David Blundy of the *Sunday Times*, killed in El Salvador. And I remembered Mohammed Amin of Visnews, maimed in Addis Ababa and now back in action working his camera with an artificial arm. Journalism attracts some strange characters, but it has its heroes too. Since I did not aspire to be one of them, I felt it was definitely time for a change of life.

Quite by chance, I was offered one. The Berlin Wall had come down, the cold war was ending, and there was a definite slump in the British market for North American news. Tony Hall, who was head of everything at BBC News, summoned me to London *en route* to a super-power summit in Malta and suggested that I move at once to Berlin, for a six-month secondment to report the democratic revolutions in Eastern Europe. I could hardly answer that it didn't seem much of a story.

The job did not have a title, though in function I suppose it was something like new world order correspondent – even peace correspondent at last, if all went well. The bureau was in BBC terms an illicit one, without brass plate or headed notepaper, and for some obscure bureaucratic reason we were obliged to work from a false address. But it was a great opportunity to kick-start a career which was by then almost on cruise control. I paused for a full thirty seconds, in order to be seen to be making great sacrifices and giving them serious thought, but for no more than thirty seconds, in case he changed his mind.

I then returned to Washington in short order, and set about discarding my worldly possessions until all that remained could fit into four dark blue Globetrotter suitcases. (I am superstitious about suitcases: it is a truth universally acknowledged, at least by me, that dark blue Globetrotters bring good luck in dangerous places.) Actually there should have been only three of them: the fourth was entirely filled by a vast black leather greatcoat given to me as a going-away present by my friends at PVS, the BBC's facilities house in Washington. It was supposed to protect me from the blizzards blowing into central Europe from the Caucasus. I wore it only once in front of the camera, in the ruins of Dresden, and it drew the instant disfavour of the BBC's Head of Newsgathering. He said he didn't expect his reporters to look like U-boat captains, especially in Germany, not now and not ever. (The Head of Newsgathering has a certain way with words.) The coat was not worn again.

My career as new world order correspondent turned out to be a brief one. I dutifully did the circuit of Eastern European capitals, froze in Warsaw, explored secret and sinister tunnels in Bucharest, and fell in love with Prague. I was just in time to be accredited to the Volkskammer, the fading East German parliament which was furiously trying to vote itself into oblivion, and to have my passport stamped by the border police at Checkpoint Charlie, before it too went out of business. It was the best six months of my working life, for I was witnessing history at every turn and doing it for once in conditions of relative safety.

What the BBC didn't tell me, quite reasonably because it didn't know, was that it would quickly lose interest in the more successful revolutions, and the least successful were about to slide into war. Already in those early months there were intimations of what was to come; and though I hardly caught the significance of those omens at the time, it did begin to dawn on me that the new world order might turn out to be more dangerous than the old one. In the cobbled town squares of the former German Democratic Republic, at the election rallies of the new political parties or the old ones now opening to the East, I would look out over a sea of white faces and realize what an homogenous society this was, or had been – without freedom and real democracy, for sure, but without ethnic tensions either and with the ghosts of the old Germany laid to rest.

Now they were stirring again. The borders were open and foreigners, especially Romanian Gypsies, were pouring across them. The hatred of the *Ausländer* revived as if nothing had been learned and nothing forgotten, and with it a small but significant Neo-Fascist movement, which drew support especially from the young and the unemployed. With our small BBC team, chiefly camerawoman Katharina Geissler and producer Sean Salsarola, we paid them some attention. It was hard not to as they marched behind their banners of hatred, their boots and drums beat out a primitive rhythm, and shouts of '*Sieg Heil*!' were heard again in streets which had once been citadels of Fascism.

In my conversations with London I sensed an understandable concern that this was a low-life phenomenon that thrived on publicity and might be better ignored. Perhaps, if we didn't look at it, it might even go away. On one occasion I did a report from the open-air black market in Berlin's Alexanderplatz, which was dominated by swarthy Romanian traders. East Germans around them were puzzled and angry, and already nostalgic for the old order, where these things were not allowed. One of them spoke bitterly about 'Jews and Gypsies who have no intention of working here'. The report duly ran on the *Six O'Clock News*; it was one in a series on the new Germany, and they were more or less committed to it. But the remark about Jews and Gypsies was taken out. The feeling seemed to be that the Germans of today should not be thinking like that – and if they were, we had no business showing it. It was a slight but, I thought, dangerous act of timidity, and it was picked on by Peter McKay in his newspaper column. 'There are bound to be difficult moments in Germany's unification,' he wrote. 'Some very ugly people will emerge from the old communist cocoon in the East. However much we approve of unification, we should take care to report accurately – regardless of taste – what is being said and done there. We don't want any more surprises from Germany.'

It was a small enough incident, but I think it illustrates a general truth, that political correctness conflicts with good reporting. Personally, I have nothing against political correctness, and will stand shoulder to shoulder with the chattering classes on a reasonable part of its agenda. But the trouble with it is that it masks the truth – truth that may later do us damage because we chose to ignore it. In television news we are already denied the use of the full range of images available to us to depict the world as we find it. We *deny ourselves* these images for the most compelling reasons of taste, that we ourselves can hardly bear to look at them, and it serves no purpose to try and inflict them on others. But when we start excluding *words*, on the grounds of supposed political correctness, we are in deeper trouble than we need to be.

On this I offer a Bosnian example from the war between Muslims and Croats. At a time when it was raging most fiercely in September 1993, the front line shifted to the grounds of a mental hospital in the old spa town of Fojnica in central Bosnia. The Bosnian army held one side and the HVO, the Bosnian Croat Defence Force, the other. The hospital itself was in no man's land, its staff had fled, and its demented patients were wandering about in both sides' line of fire as helpless as children, and yet it was notable that there was no operation Irma, no international campaign on their behalf. I had wished to end my report with the thought that this was what the conflict had come to, and there could hardly be a crueller image of it than a madhouse in a war zone. I was told that the use of the word 'madhouse' was no longer admissible: there were people who might be offended by it. I tried to make the case but in vain. The issue was a small one, but it seemed to me to be symbolically quite important. If the strengths and cadences of plain English were denied us – the English of Cobbett and Dickens and Orwell – then our focus on the world around us would blur still further. It was Orwell himself in his classic essay 'Politics and the English Language' who spotted the link between the corruption of language and the corruption of thought. There wasn't political correctness in his day, but there was what he called 'orthodoxy'. 'Orthodoxy, of whatever colour, seems to demand a lifeless, imitative style ... If you simplify your English, you are freed from the worst follies of orthodoxy.' And there wasn't ethnic cleansing, but there was something presciently like it: 'Defenceless villages are bombarded from the air, the inhabitants driven out into the countryside, the huts set on fire with incendiary bullets: this is called *pacification*.'

By the time of the Fojnica incident my working life was

spent almost entirely in the war zones. I did little else for nearly four years, and might as well have restyled the job description as new world *disorder* correspondent. I had never expected to be living quite so much on my nerves, and really didn't know whether the nerves were up to it, or had too much mileage on them already. The dangers were routine and usually manageable. The disturbing part of it was the constant exposure to the suffering of others, with a measure of guilt thrown in. On a front line in central Bosnia, cameraman Sebastian Rich and I were reporting on a sudden flight of Croatian refugees. An overburdened old lady and her granddaughter were setting out with faltering steps along a cart track through a no man's land that was known to be mined. Seb said, 'You know, there are times when I *hate* this fucking job.' I agreed. We shouldn't have been filming those two, we should have been helping them. Yet had we done so we would have missed our feed, and if we had survived we would certainly have been arrested by the Serbs on the other side. It seemed a lame excuse then. It still does now.

Because of these pressures and a certain coded way in which my employers started talking to me about this time, in the autumn of 1993 I became aware that they might be beginning to wonder whether I was not myself a candidate for admission to some kind of a British Fojnica. And I was not the only one. There is an established medical condition of battlefield stress, which might as easily affect a journalist as a soldier. On returning from Bosnia, I found myself summoned for consultations with the BBC's chief medical officer, a kindly and expert Irishman, for what I supposed was a post-operative session on the war wound. But that was just for the record and the opening civilities. The questioning then turned to the main event, which was my state of mind – in fact, my sanity. I was further quizzed on this in public by Dr Anthony Clare, another penetrating Irishman, in one of his mind-related radio programmes; and he had a specialist in battlefield stress beside him. I could have talked myself out of a job right there and then. They were indeed hard questions to answer, for to be unaffected by what one had lived through might itself be taken as evidence of some kind of lapse from a medical state of grace. And although I claimed to be more or less sound in mind as well as limb, might not battlefield stress be rather like alcoholism, and denial one of its symptoms?

I did admit to certain changes that I had noticed in myself. One was that when I returned from Bosnia to my cottage in a leafy corner of north London, I couldn't sleep, at least for the first several nights. The quietness was unnatural, with nothing to be heard but the wind in the oak tree and occasionally a night owl lodging there. I actually missed the crackle of small arms and thump of mortar fire which were my lullaby in Sarajevo. I could sense the wise Irishmen noting this, as evidence against.

The other change was that nothing else, outside certain personal relationships, seemed to matter very much. This was not a work obsession, for I had worked just as hard in other countries, and then stowed away those memories with the Globetrotters. It was a Bosnia obsession. I would return from a six-week stint in the burning Balkans, and from a war which threatened the security of Europe even in periods of relative lull and ceasefire, and be asked to take part in one of those talk shows with which Radio Five likes to fill its evening hours. Bosnia was an afterthought, if that. My fellow panellists, the great and the good of British journalism, were principally concerned with some business about the position of Eurosceptics in the Cabinet, and the overwhelming moral issue of the day, which was whether the winner of the National Lottery was entitled to anonymity. I remember not contributing much, but asking myself, is this my country? Is it even my planet?

The fault was clearly mine: some lack of proportion which is best identified as 'Bosnia withdrawal syndrome'. I have seen it in others, especially journalists, but soldiers and aid workers too. The Prince of Wales's Own, one of the finest battalions we ever dealt with in Vitez, found on their return from Bosnia that even their best men were scoring unexpectedly low marks on routine proficiency tests. Somehow ordinary soldiering didn't seem to matter so much. The same thing happened rather more publicly to General Lewis MacKenzie. After his recall from Sarajevo he assumed the command of a Canadian Army Division. There are not many of these, and at any other time it would have been the fulfilment of a lifetime's ambition, but after his experiences in Bosnia he found it curiously unsatisfying – frustrating too, because he could speak his mind freely in Sarajevo, but not in Toronto or Ottawa. He left the service a year early, and incorporated himself as General MacKenzie Communications Inc., beginning a new career as adviser to other nations' armies and commentator on UN peacekeeping. (He also held on to his sanity: the evidence of that is that he turned down repeated invitations to enter politics.)

I have written of the need for some kind of professional commitment and a journalism that cares as well as knows. But clearly there has to be some balance as well, or one is at risk of becoming a crusader in lost causes and a foaming-at-the-mouth zealot, and the less effective for that. I had sensed it in myself on the occasion of the Radio Five talk show. Their politics and perceptions meant nothing to me. I was in danger of ranting on like the Ancient Mariner who 'stoppeth one in three'. It would be useful to call a halt, to stay away for a while and somehow see the thing from a longer perspective.

Again I was lucky: it must have been those suitcases. Providence – also known as my benign and efficient foreign editor Vin Ray – intervened. He needed someone with old-soldierly credentials, and who knew the difference between a remembrance a celebration (it was surprising how many did not), to cover various fiftieth anniversary commemorations of events towards the end of the Second World War. I assured him that, contrary perhaps to appearance, I was not old enough to have been among those present at the Normandy landings. But I was certainly there for the anniversary, as the veterans paraded at low tide on the sands of Arromanches in front of the Queen, and marched off proudly with a spring in their step, singing the songs of two world wars and as far away from Tipperary as ever. (Unfortunately the live coverage of it all was diminished by a commentator who insisted on talking over every frame of it, though it needed no words at all. The hardest skill in television is the art of writing silence.)

Naturally I sought out my old friends from Suffolk, who had landed in Normandy with the British Third Division. There are few greater privileges than to listen to old soldiers who have come through such times: it is like the study of history without historians. They were also parading through Colville-Montgomery, which they had liberated. Their senior survivor, Lieutenant-Colonel Eric Lummis, wounded in Normandy as a young subaltern, formed up the sixty old soldiers behind him in column of march. I made sure that his word of command, 'One Suffolk quick march ...' found its place on that night's *Nine O'Clock News*. The youngest of them was sixty-eight, and this would not happen again.

The following day they invited me to join them in a memorial service at the Château de la Lande, once a German *panzer* stronghold, where many of their comrades had fallen. The band of the Suffolks' successor regiment, the Royal Anglians, marched down the château's broad driveway playing the regimental march, *Speed the Plough*; Eric Lummis thanked his hosts feelingly in home-made French, and undraped a simple plaque at the side of the road; the Last Post was sounded, and old soldiers' eyes misted up. It was certainly no celebration. Of the 925 men in the battalion, 103 were killed in Normandy and 389 were wounded – and the Suffolks were luckier than some.

I remembered these figures because not many days later, in my other life, I was present at another such ceremony – the same words, the same salutes from the living to the dead, almost the same regiment, and a strikingly similar plaque. But this was from the new world order, not the old. The plaque was in memory of Steven Wormald, a twenty-two-year-old captain with the Royal Anglian Regiment who had been killed by a mine within a week of arriving in Bosnia. It had happened during a time of supposed ceasefire, in one of the broken villages near Gornji Vakuf, on the old front line between Muslims and Croats. The inscription recorded that he had died in the service of peace. There seemed a grim symmetry about it.

After a fifty-year break, the British army was back again and involved in a land war in Europe. It was not a combatant, but its soldiers were sometimes as much at risk as if it had been. And not all the deaths, like Steven Wormald's, were accidental. Lance-Corporal Wayne Edwards, the first to die, was deliberately shot in the driver's hatch of his Warrior APC. A soldier could become a target in peacekeeping just as much as in war-fighting.

Of course the cases were different. The UN force was a small one from a volunteer army. It could be pulled out quite rapidly, though with some difficulty, or be transformed into something else. National security was not obviously involved. National survival was not involved at all. The conflict in Bosnia, however terrible, caused great upheaval but did not spread significantly beyond its borders. But there were still some disturbing continuities. The war was territorial, and began essentially with the aggression of the strong against the weak. Force prevailed. National security *could have been* involved: after 1914, we should need no history lessons on the repercussive effect of a first shot fired in anger in Sarajevo. The best analogy perhaps was that of a fire, which had broken out in the southern wing of our common European home. We had the choice of forming ourselves into a fire brigade and fighting it, or of retreating into our separate apartments and hoping that it would burn itself out. UNPROFOR was our fire brigade, however ill-equipped and ill-prepared, and would-be arsonists elsewhere in the world were watching to see how it did. It did not do well, until handing over the fire-fighting function to a much more businesslike outfit.

There was also surely the moral dimension of whether the victims' plight moved us to help them beyond any calculation of national interest. Ethnic cleansing, which in its most lethal form is updated genocide, resembles genocide exactly in that it is not an unaccompanied crime. It needs accomplices – not only the hatred that makes it happen, but the indifference that lets it happen.

Again, the fifty-year perspective is a useful one. My next anniversary assignment was a grim one indeed: the liberation of Auschwitz. I had not been in a place, not even Berlin, so haunted by the ghosts of the past. The new inscription on the memorial at Birkenau, the purpose-built death camp in which more than a million Jews perished, describes it as a warning to humanity. Survivors of the Holocaust, impelled to return for the anniversary, were not the only ones to see the continuity between 'final solutions' then and now, and to conclude that the warning to humanity had not been heeded. René Guttman, Chief Rabbi of Strasbourg in France, was leading 200 of his people in prayer at one of only two synagogues still functioning in Cracow, the city nearest to Auschwitz (and incidentally the city of *Schindler's List*). In his opening remarks he welcomed them by mistake to Sarajevo. It was more like a slip of the heart than a slip of the tongue. 'We understand,' he said, 'that what happens in Sarajevo nowadays happened because we are in front of the same intolerance and hatred of people that was here fifty years ago. The instinct of holocaust is unfortunately in the hearts of some people.'

The same connection was made by Elie Wiesel, who has surely earned the right to be heeded as much as any man alive. He did it implicitly in his speech at Auschwitz, of which he was one of the few survivors, and addressed it to the next generation: 'I do not want my past to become their future.' And he did it explicitly and outspokenly to an audience which included President Clinton, at the opening of the Holocaust Museum in Washington: 'What have we learned? We have learned some lessons, minor lessons perhaps, that we are all responsible, and indifference is a sin and a punishment. And we have learned that when people suffer we cannot remain indifferent. And Mr President, I cannot not tell you something. I have been in the former Yugoslavia last fall. I cannot sleep for what I have seen. As a Jew I am saying that we must do something to stop the bloodshed in that country. People fight each other and children die. Why? Something, anything, must be done. This is a lesson. There are many other lessons. You will come, you will learn. We shall learn together.'

We are still learning. The case against indifference, as Elie Wiesel made it, is quite unanswerable. And because it was he with his credentials who made it, we mere war zone reporters don't have to, but just go about our everyday business of assembling the evidence that makes his warning relevant and urgent and necessary. It is and should be a long way from polemical journalism, for we should find what we find and not what we are looking for, but if we are lucky we can open people's eyes to these old and dangerous currents swirling around us. If we are not, they will continue to worry more about the National Lottery.

In the case of our present experience, unlike the earlier and arithmetically yet more terrible genocide, the facts were well enough known and documented from the start. There were eyewitness reports and photographs. There was television. We do not have the alibi of ignorance. But the difficulty is the same. It is a difficulty of communication – Cassandra's predicament – speaking the unspeakable to an audience that doesn't want to hear. It was Elie Wiesel as usual who found the right words for it: 'My good friends, it is not because I cannot explain that you won't understand, it is because you won't understand that I cannot explain.'

In my temporary function as new world order correspondent, I have witnessed the first two tests and challenges of that order. One was in Kuwait, where a larger country invaded and annexed a smaller one. The Western alliance promised that the aggression would not stand, and it did not. (But Kuwait had oil.) The other was in Bosnia, where a stronger people attacked a weaker people and expelled those whom they didn't kill from land they had shared for centuries. (But Bosnia had no oil: and the American army does deserts, it doesn't do mountains – at least it didn't until its orders changed dramatically late in 1995. Even then it played for safety, performing limited functions with minimum risks behind a ring of steel, with every intention of leaving the field and declaring a victory exactly one year later. The Americans' aim in Bosnia was a take-away triumph.)

At the time of writing, diplomacy is once more engaged on the issue; there is a peace treaty in place and a force to implement it, at least in the short term. I have believed from the start that this is a crisis which will end in one of two ways: either the stability of the rest of Europe will spread to the Balkans, or the instability of the Balkans will spread to the rest of Europe. It can still go either way. If the nightmare scenario returns, and the implementing powers are unwilling to stay the course, *then* the security of Europe will be threatened, and we shall remember the principal lesson of the war that the Bosnians have learned for themselves.

It is a brutal one: arm your children.

233

19

DAYS OF FOREBODING

Four days before Christmas 1994 former American President Jimmy Carter brokered a ceasefire which the United Nations, for ever a well-spring of unfounded optimism, believed might be the prelude to a wider settlement. To the rival armies it was no more than a mid-winter break – a sort of half-time in the terrible game of war. A friend on the government side described it as exactly that, with arms rather than orange juice coming on to the field to refresh the combatants for the next round of fighting; and he correctly predicted that the ceasefire would fail long before its expiration date at the end of April. 'There now begins,' he said, 'the liberation phase of our struggle.'

The Serbs were equally combative verbally, and matched the government spokesmen threat for threat. The Serbs had as little faith, or less, in the ceasefire agreement that both sides had signed on to supposedly in good faith. But reserves of good faith had long been exhausted; each side expected the worst of the other and was seldom disappointed. So it was that on the 24th of March, when the agreement had still more than a month to run, Dr Karadzic was trying to rally his people for the final battle and victory. His forces were already under heavy attack in central Bosnia and being forced out of positions which they regarded as part of the Serb heartland, and had held since the start of the war. 'I must say to all of you,' he said, 'that we must finish this war with a victory. We are not now going to stop until we totally defeat them. There is no more ceasefire. The enemy has to be destroyed.'

For both sides, having fought so long and sacrificed so much, the peace option never really existed except as a matter of tactical convenience. For the first time in nearly three years of fighting there were no international mediators shuttling and negotiating, no functioning peace process at all. Yasushi Akashi, the senior UN figure on the ground, made a last trip to Pale to plead for an extension of the ceasefire, and was told none too politely to go away. As the clock ticked round to the end of April, he called these 'the days of foreboding'. Jimmy Carter would not be invited back – and no one else of any consequence either. A Masada complex prevailed in Pale, as much among the political as the military leadership. The Serbs were preparing for war.

So were their adversaries. The Bosnian government used the winter break purposefully, to rearm and reorganize its forces in the field. The arms embargo still applied, but was honoured mainly in the breach and had leaked like a sieve for months. The Bosnian army changed materially, with the acquisition through American back-channels – and probably airdrops – of new weapons systems including heat-seeking anti-tank rockets. The Serbs' vaunted superiority in armour would no longer count for so much, and government soldiers were relishing the coming clash of arms. One of them said, 'We shall feast upon their tanks.' The army also changed tactically, with the formation of rapid manoeuvre brigades as a mobile reserve to be switched from one front to another. This marked a real break with the past – for they were real soldiers now and no longer armed civilians defending their streets.

This new mobility and the Serbs' defences were tested for the first time towards the end of March, when an estimated 12,000 men from the Bosnian army's Seventh Corps and Third Corps, operating together for the first time, attacked in deep snow and dislodged the Serbs from supposedly impregnable positions on Mount Vlasic, overlooking Travnik. A late winter snowstorm did not impede the attackers but helped them, by concealing their advance and enabling them to walk over the Serb mine-fields without detonating the mines. Nothing like this had been attempted before, or even planned. 'Previously,' said General Mehmet Alagic, the Seventh Corps commander, 'this would not have been imaginable.'

All of this, or at least some symbolic part of it, I would expect to have seen for myself under the old order of things, where reporters thought to be sympathetic were allowed at least some access to Bosnian army positions. But that changed too. Part of the army's reorganization was the imposition of an information blockade which applied for two weeks after the attack even to its own press and television. The foreign press was kept at arm's length not only from Seventh Corps headquarters at Travnik but even from Travnik itself. The closest we got was a road-block a mile outside. Now I knew that after three years in Bosnia modern warfare had finally arrived. We would get the same hassle here as everywhere else.

Did you ever hear of an army which paraded its defeats and masked its victories? I hadn't either, until now. And yet it made a kind of political sense. For the years of reverses and setbacks, especially in Sarajevo, when Muslims were shooting at tanks with bolt-action rifles, it suited the purposes of the Bosnian government to have the press alongside. That was for the battle of David against Goliath, at the time when David was still losing it, or barely holding his ground. The campaign was on, abetted by sympathetic press coverage, to lift the arms embargo against him and equip him at least with armour-piercing sling-shot. Many journalists were enthusiastic in the cause. One even filed his reports from the Bosnian Presidency.

The campaign partly succeeded. But now that David was acquiring some of the properties of Goliath, and the armour-piercing sling-shot was in his arsenal, there were new questions arising of field security and control of the press which had never existed in the old days, and which were resolved by a policy of almost total exclusion. The men with the heat-seeking rockets, unlike those with the bolt-action rifles, were remarkably camera-shy. The Bosnian authorities came up with a number of reasons for keeping us out, mostly familiar to us from other wars: it was now too dangerous on the front lines, they couldn't guarantee our safety, we were spies and agents of foreign governments, we were security risks, we were giving away their positions to the enemy. But they also offered a completely new reason, or at least one I had not heard before: that we were bearers and tokens of ill fortune. 'Look,' said one of their soldiers at First Corps headquarters, 'we appreciate what you have done in the past, but while you were doing it we have noticed something. We noticed that when you were with us we were losing, and that now you are no longer with us we are doing just great. Come back and see us when the war is over.'

The information blockade also saved the government side from repeating some of its more spectacular past blunders. In the early days its successes had been so few and so slender that it had tended to trumpet them before they had been consolidated or even while the Serbs were busy reversing them. A mighty triumph would be proclaimed, and then turn out after a day or two to be rather less of a triumph than at first supposed, or indeed a total defeat. This kind of public information débâcle, as damaging to morale as the defeat itself, would not occur again. A friend with a sense of humour still unimpaired by the war described it as 'premature exhilaration'.

The information blockade was something of a professional crisis for the few war reporters still in business in Bosnia at the end of the war's third year. It was less of a problem for the print people whose simpler logistics and ways of working I had never envied more. Not only did they carry no tripods, but because they lived by words alone they could still glean those words, even in times of restricted access, from the United Nations, from the few liaison officers still working in Pale, from diplomats and relief agencies, and from Bosnian government sources of varying credibility. And if all else failed, they could apply the knuckle to the forehead in the time-honoured manner of foreign correspondents the world over, and think their thoughts out loud. The resulting 'think-piece' or 'analysis' would be at least a passable substitute for the missing front-line dispatch.

But television was different. With us there was neither fudging nor forgiving. Either we were there or we weren't. Either we had the pictures or we didn't. In this case we weren't and we didn't. All we had, recorded after some delay from the television services of both sides, was what I have described as soldiervision, images shot in the snow of Vlasic or the mud of the Majevica hills south-east of Tuzla showing heroic and casualty-free advances against an enemy which had fled in panic and left its weapons behind. Someone had to be lying.

I remembered the wisdom of Tip O'Neill, former Speaker of the American House of Representatives, who observed that all politics is local. The same is surely true of war. All war is local. For the individual soldier it is the wood where he bivouacs and the ditch or trench where he fights and maybe dies. Nothing else matters. The war may begin as a fight for his country, but it ends as a fight for his life.

I thought a lot about this during the spare time imposed on me by the information blockade, of the frailties of my craft which it had rather cruelly exposed, and of how perhaps I had been hoist with my own petard. For television is also local. It deals in particular incidents and moments. That is its strength and its weakness. There had been a time, during an earlier phase in the war, when we had privileged access to a battle between Croats and Muslims for the control of sixteen houses. That's all it was. Yet so extraordinary and heart-stopping was the footage that we filled our news programmes with it for more than a week. That simple skirmish represented the war – indeed, for us it *was* the war – and it substituted for other actions of much greater consequence where the cameras were not. Now, fifteen months later, the cameras were also not at main force engagements taking place between formations of many thousands on both sides. These could well be the turning point of the war, but as far as the outside world was concerned they were ignorant armies clashing by night, and the world knew nothing of them. All we could be sure of was that when they were over the winner would write the history.

There are few more disgruntled characters in journalism than a war reporter on the wrong side of a road-block, and I was on the wrong side of too many. I had perhaps been spoiled for access in the early months of the war, and I took it badly. I felt I had the choice of giving up and going home and hanging up boots and helmet once and for all, or else of staying on for just a while longer and trying to understand things from afar. It was at that point that my luck turned. Not that the road-blocks lifted – they didn't – but I did meet Enver Kazas.

Enver was thirty-eight, sparely built and fair-haired, with an air of unvaunted authority and a swift and sudden smile. He was a captain at the Bosnian army's First Corps headquarters with a political influence far beyond his rank. Generals listened to him as they do not listen to captains in, for instance, the British army. As a front-line soldier he had commanded a company and led it through two hard years. Since he led from in front, his own survival was much against the odds. In combat successively against the Croats and then the Serbs he had lost sixty of his ninety men. He still believed in a European and multi-ethnic Bosnia, and was not enthusiastic about the army's tendency to form all-Muslim units. He was especially proud of his loyal Serbs – as distinct from the 'Chetniks' or 'Karadzic Serbs' on the other side – and of the two loyal Serbs in his company who had been awarded the Golden Lily, the Bosnian army's highest award for valour. He spoke at length about this, about the problems of success that arise when a unit claims the credit that properly belongs to another, and about the sense of outrage felt by the front-line troops when they learned that their parliamentarians were trying to claim military status. Then his attitude softened and his eyes brightened, and he said, 'Now let's talk about poetry.'

For Enver Kazas, in his other life, was a poet and literary critic. He had written the introduction to the Bosnian, or ex-Yugoslav, translation of Laurence Durrell's *Alexandria Quartet*, but it was unlikely to be published for it had still been at the printers when the war broke out, and the printers were in Serb-held territory – or, as he put it, PZT, which was the acronym for *Privremeno Zauzeta Teritorija*, Temporarily Occupied Territory. Now, with his larger literary project on hold, he was composing a philosophical essay on the war and its effects. He was concerned in an almost Orwellian way with its perversions of meaning and language. He wrote:

In besieged Sarajevo, life is being mocked. Death in the war loses its meaning, it becomes a habit, a number in a news report, a countdown of people who are missing. I have even read in the newspaper not just death notices but *congratulations* on someone's death in this war. War, like death, changes the meaning of everything.

He also – and most unusually for a soldier – questioned the

long-term significance of the present cataclysmic events. It was the kind of perspective on war that will not be found in the text-books or memoirs of professional soldiers, since it can come only from a citizen army such as the Bosnian army – or for that matter the Bosnian Serb army – where a whole people is mobilized and writers become soldiers (whereas in a volunteer army soldiers sometimes also write, which is a very different matter). Enver was no warlord but a one-man paradox: a decent and reflective trained killer. He continued:

History writes events as they happened and art writes them as they could have been. We have learned history as a sequence of battles. But war is not history, nor is history the history of wars. Historically speaking, one of the principal events that has happened on our continent has been the transplantation of the potato into Europe. That made a change. But what change did the wars make? No change. War is just war: a break between two periods of peace.

As a writer he could distance himself from the conflict around him and perceive that potatoes mattered more than battles, but as a soldier he had to see it differently. It was a war for the survival of the Bosnian people and one they must win. Since defeat meant extinction and extinction was unthinkable, the only available options were a negotiated peace or war until victory, and Enver was among a growing number of Bosnians who genuinely and alarmingly believed that victory was possible – by 1997 at the latest. They were willing to fight on that long, and longer if need be. He based his confidence partly on the new-found strength and armament of the Bosnian army, and partly on other sources that he had in his keeping. For among his many functions and duties he was the custodian of captured documents.

He produced these selectively and to promote his thesis of Bosnian Serb decline. Out of the pile he drew the personal diary of a young conscript from Serbia who found himself drafted into the Guards Brigade of the Bosnian Serb army. (Enver claimed that despite the break with Belgrade there were still entire units of the Yugoslav army, including its 63rd Parachute Brigade, serving alongside the Bosnian Serbs in Bosnia.) In the last entry before he was killed the young soldier wrote, as conscripts do, of returning where he came from: 'Next time when I go back home I won't be coming back, because this is not my country, just mountains and hills. I would prefer to be killed at home in Serbia than to live here one thousand years.'

Of more military and technical interest was the official war diary of Major Pero Pavlovic. It was a page-numbered and supposedly secret document issued under the official stamp of the base in central Serbia to which he had been previously assigned. Pavlovic was a regular Yugoslav army officer ordered to Bosnia on 7 December 1993, while the Bosnian and Serbian Serbs were still allies. He entered Bosnia through Zvornik in civilian clothes, reported to army headquarters at Han Pijesak, and was assigned to Lukavica barracks, the forward base for Romanija Corps besieging Sarajevo. He was a professional soldier in the old JNA (Yugoslav National Army) mould, with neither doubts nor illusions. On the 14th of January 1994 he recorded the strengths and weaknesses of the 2nd Sarajevo Light Infantry to which he was attached. It had thirty-four officers where it should have had eighty and forty NCOs where it should have had seventy-seven. Its numbers were further reduced by casualties. In his entire brigade of 1,672 men, 271 had been lightly wounded, 120 seriously wounded and 164 killed. Every able-bodied man in the region was already mobilized, and many from outside. Pavlovic wrote: 'Any chance to draft more people is gone. The problem is influencing our chain of command and our readiness. The BiH (Bosnian) Army does not have these problems. And it's a very obvious suggestion who is going to win this war.'

The last entry was on the 5th October 1994, just before the Bosnian army offensive against Serb positions on Mount Bjelasnica. 'I don't know why he came to leave his bones here,' said Enver as he closed the diary with an air of satisfaction. 'He will definitely not be putting anything more down in his little notebook.' I was never in a war, even a civil war, in which each side had so little pity for the other's dead.

This was in the spring of 1995, and a sort of spring fever prevailed on both sides of the lines. The conciliators and peace-seekers, if there had ever been any, had fallen silent. It was a victory fever, a fierce belief in the war's winnability, and it affected important elements in the leaderships, both military and political. I found it astonishing. It went against all common sense and the hard grind of experience. It was in spite of all that they had suffered and sacrificed, and of what each side knew to its cost of the other's strength and resilience.

It seemed especially difficult to fathom on the Serb side – and the more so because access there was now closed off to us. I have a friend in UNPROFOR who studied the politics more than most, and acquired something of a reputation as an expert on the intentions of the Bosnian Serb leadership. He was seldom proved wrong. It was a reputation that he gained by predicting that they would do what they said they were going to do. Then they went ahead and did it. They were actually not that inscrutable. So when they spoke of their coming offensive and the swift victory which it would bring them, it may have been an expression of bravado, but the bravado was sincere and they believed it. They pointed out that since June 1992 they had been waging a defensive war (except for limited offensives in Gorazde and Bihac in 1994, both of which were actually counter-attacks). They had heavy weapons systems including surface missiles which they had hardly used, they probably had poison gas too, and according to one independent estimate only a third of their firepower had yet been brought to bear against their enemy. Now they threatened to use the rest and force the despised 'Turks' (the Muslims) to surrender.

It seemed a believable threat. The Serbs had a logic all their own and were impregnable to the arguments of others. They were not persuadable people. I recalled a conversation some months earlier in Pale with Jovan Zametica, Radovan Karadzic's donnish Anglo-Serb adviser, who had once been so undiplomatic with General Rose. I liked him in a personal and social way, though always wondering what a man like him was doing in a place like that. He for his part used his contacts with the foreign press as a sort of reality check, as well as a source of English language newspapers: for the government he served was putting up the shutters, and little light filtered in from the world outside.

We were talking on the balcony of the Hotel Panorama, overlooking the Presidency and the town below it, after the Serbs had rejected their last chance for peace, proposed by the Contact Group. 'John,' I asked – I anglicized his name to irritate him: there were mischief-makers among us who put it about that his first name was actually Omar – 'why have you done it? What on earth got into you that you voted for self-destruction?'

'We didn't,' he answered. 'But that is what the plan would have meant to us – the end of us as a people. And weren't you the one who wanted to bomb us anyway?'

'I never wanted to bomb you. I simply pointed out that there was a case for supporting the weak against the strong and the unarmed against the armed. Since you are forever telling me that it is the Serbs who are being victimized, you might even conclude that I am actually on your side.'

The argument was about my still-remembered *Panorama* programme. Zametica wasn't convinced, so I tried again: 'Look, as time goes by, and with all the world against you, the balance of forces is going to change. It is changing already. The Bosnian army will draw strength from its friends outside, the arms embargo will end, and your position will grow weaker. Can't you see that?'

'You don't understand,' he said, 'none of you understand. We have the strength to defend ourselves. And as to the rest, we don't care. *We really don't care.*'

Eventually of course they were forced to care. As the tides of battle duly turned against them, the Serbs themselves fled in tens of thousands in the largest single migration of these wars, and some of what had been done by them was done to them. Then they appealed for help to the United Nations – the same United Nations whose military observers they had chained and held hostage two months earlier. They noted bitterly that 13,000 of these refugees came from territories in Bosnia which would have been ceded to them under the Vance–Owen plan – the same plan which they had so blithely rejected two years earlier. Now it was all too late. The plan, the homes and the territories were all lost to them.

The already defiant Serbs were further outraged by the last American intermediary who came to see them. After a visit to Pale in February 1995 Richard Holbrooke, Assistant Secretary of State, was reported back to them as having said he would never go up the hill to Pale ever again and listen to any more claptrap from Radovan Karadzic. (The word he used was actually shorter, though the vowel sound was the same.) It was at this point precisely that the Serbs lost what little patience they had with the peace process. They pronounced it dead and sent Mr Akashi packing. 'The parties to the conflict,' he said, 'appear determined to plunge Bosnia into a new war with incalculable consequences.'

His warnings went unheeded. The ceasefire was melting with

the snow, pitched battles were being fought in northern and central Bosnia, mortar and sniper fire had returned to the capital with daily civilian casualties, the UN was warning in the darkest terms of the slide into full-scale war – and yet the outside world paid little attention. Because Bosnia seemed like old news, and even where it was not the cameras were being kept away from the front lines, it stayed out of the headlines, which was where the rest of Europe wanted it. This was the essence of fire-blanket diplomacy: that if the war's embers merely glowed they would trouble no one, and only if they burst into flames would they require some action. A European Community monitor (for some reason they never became European Union monitors, despite the role of Maastricht in precipitating the conflict) told me that when he sent his sombre predictions to Brussels he found no matching sense of urgency there. It was as if the European bureaucracy had lapsed into the same responsive habits as the American TV networks, and had the appetite for only one foreign crisis at a time. The present *crise du jour* was hardly peace-threatening, but at least it had novelty value: a fisheries dispute with the Canadians.

My own telephone in the BBC's office in the Sarajevo TV Centre was hardly ringing off the hook either. Both since and because of the information blockade I had been operating for some weeks, professionally speaking, at the far end of the back burner, and had filed very little. But I felt that I had talked to enough people and now knew enough to commit some television, not only about what was about to happen, but about what was already happening. There were soundbites aplenty, from the UN's spokesman, Alexander Ivanko, warning of war, from Radovan Karadzic threatening it, and from Haris Silajdzic outraged that the UN was yet again backing away from its mandate as attacks on the safe areas increased. The images from sniper's alley in Sarajevo were beginning to be reminiscent of the worst days of 1992, and the television services of both sides were serving up nightly doses of soldiervision from their respective front lines.

I primed my intervention for a Saturday, usually a quiet news day with large audiences and sufficient airtime. Foreign correspondents like Saturdays because they are mercifully free of the 'official news' of government pronouncements, and have space for dispatches from what we see as the real world beyond Dover beach. I negotiated – actually, I pleaded – with the duty editor, Eileen Fitt, for the two minutes that I felt were required to tell the story of the forthcoming war.

I don't know how it is with other professions, since I have never worked in anything but TV news, except once a long time ago when I counted pounds of frozen peas for Bird's Eye Foods in Lowestoft. But I do remember that there were some days when I felt more like counting the pounds of peas than other days. No doubt it is the same for bricklayers or accountants: some days are better than others for laying the bricks or shuffling the numbers. So it is with television news. And on the Saturday in question I felt particularly fired up to match the words to the pictures and do the business as well as it could be done. (The trick, incidentally, is to honour the pictures and yield primacy to them and let them do most of the talking, then to complement and even to caress them with a few words here and there.)

I composed the piece as I always do, pacing up and down trailing an extra long run of cable behind me and clutching an ancient 'lip mic' of the type pioneered by John Snagge for the University Boat Race. It is the only item of British equipment we carry and it works like magic. I am by nature extremely self-critical (not out of modesty but prudence: for in television if you don't check yourself there are plenty of others who will). But on this occasion I felt that I had it right, the words and the

247

pictures spoke to each other, I had finally prevailed against the information embargo, and the war report had something to say which had not been said before. The piece was duly satellited to London fifteen minutes before the early evening news. All they had to do was turn it around and push the button. I was for once quite satisfied. I had thrown the stone into the pond and waited for the ripple.

There was none. Nothing stirred. The piece was dropped to make way for a two-way live interview on some late-breaking and never-to-be-heard-of-again sensation in Washington. Or more accurately, it was not dropped but 'OOVed'. To be 'OOVed' is about the worst thing that can happen professionally to a war reporter in television – a bit like having teeth pulled without anaesthetic. OOV stands for 'out of vision'. The term describes the process by which a correspondent's report is eviscerated and cannibalized, then a few of the pictures are filleted out of it and voiced over by the newsreader in the studio. We fieldmen dread it. Something of the sort had happened to me once before, on the 5th of November 1972. (I have a long memory for these things.) In this case it had wasted three weeks' work.

For once I even envied the United Nations. Not only did they get to deliver their warnings, but I suspected their urbane spokesman, Alexander Ivanko, of purloining some of my clichés, about the ceasefire melting with the snow and the peacekeepers being left with no peace to keep. However, I could hardly complain. He got a hearing for them and I did not.

Cassandra, the prophetess of doom, was born before her time. She could have had a great career in television.

20

A DAY IN THE LIFE

May the 24th 1995. The Holiday Inn does not do wake-up calls, partly because its telephone service is temperamental and partly because it doesn't need to. The mortar crews start early on both sides, plus the machine-gunners, snipers and heavy artillery – the whole dawn chorus of Sarajevo at war. The bombardment starts at five and is set to last for a full nine hours – the heaviest since the most dangerous days of 1992.

Our team is smaller now than it was then, for reasons of safety as well as economy. It has only four members, three of them multi-skilled in keeping with the managerial doctrines of the times. Anamarija Muvrin is producer and interpreter and 'wicked witch' (her term) in charge of acquiring other people's videotapes. Nigel Bateson is cameraman extraordinary, with reserve skills as videotape editor, cook and paramedic. Carl Ward is videotape editor, soundman, archivist and back-up cameraman. Only the correspondent is too old a dog to learn new tricks. He limits himself to finding things out, making words, advising the others when they might care to get up in the morning, and setting them a start time which is known as 'wheels roll' to avoid misunderstanding. For this noble concern with punctuality they call him their sergeant-major.

Today the sergeant-major isn't needed. The team are already at battle stations. Anamarija is in the BBC radio office at the Holiday Inn, serving notice to a news desk that has grown weary of Bosnia that something is happening which they might wish to take note of. Carl with his camera is at his window zooming in on the ruins of the parliament office building, as its upper floors are splintered by Serb machine-gun fire. Nigel and I take to the streets – but cautiously, by the back way and under armour. We are keenly anxious to survive this war – perhaps I even more than he – and sometimes the big South African needs restraining. His courage could be damaging to his health.

Combat photography is hardly a sedentary profession, but it resembles the real estate business in this respect and this respect only, that there are just three things which matter: location, location and location. Camera position is everything – one which has a view of the action and a measure of cover too. We find the perfect vantage point: an abandoned sandbag emplacement at the south-west corner of what used to be the City Hall before the Serb artillery got at it. From here Nigel shoots two tapes full of what is known in the trade as 'bang bang' – long lens images of exploding shells rearranging the ridge line above us – and the soundbite of the day to go with them. This comes from John Jordan, the Rhode Island fireman twice wounded in action, who runs the front-line rescue service. He also once served in the US Marine Corps, and casts a professional eye over the mayhem around us. 'Medieval rules, First World War tactics, fifties technology,' he says, 'that's what this gig is. We're three years into it, and it's not like they don't have practice in stalemate here.' John sees the war in close-up more than most, and is in fact the only American anywhere near it. A full day of the most intensive combat since 1992 sounds like the city's climactic battle, yet at the end of it just three forward bunkers may have fallen to the Serbs. Sarajevo will be saved or taken inch by inch.

One of the secrets of survival journalism is not to linger in the line of fire, but to get out when you can with what you can. So before the Serbs start seeking out other targets we reverse at speed from our sandbag position, coordinating our retreat with the rest of the team through the VHF transceivers (known to us all as 'gizmos') which Nigel and Carl have bought at their own expense, and which also listen in on UN frequencies. We scoop up the others at the Holiday Inn, and race through sniper fire to our refuge and office at the television station. This concrete fortress competes with the hotel for the distinction of being the ugliest building in town, and the most frequently bombarded. The old Yugoslavs who built it were expecting to be attacked by all comers – either NATO or the Warsaw Pact, they could never quite work out which – but the all comers in the end were themselves. Within its massive shell-scarred walls we share an office with the American network ABC. This is where we commit television, and enjoy the little comforts of life which take on extra importance in a war zone.

One of these is breakfast – British army tea by courtesy of the Royal Welch Fusiliers, and fresh bread by courtesy of the most embattled bakery in the Balkans. (No chemicals penetrate the city's siege – except of course the phosphorus shells.) With toast in one hand and telephone in the other I try head office again, without success. Head office has other interests. 'Harold Wilson's dead.'

'I know and I'm sorry. But what has it got to do with me?'

'The programme's full of it: obituaries, tributes, analysis, live shots. You know how it goes. There's very little space for anything else.'

'Even World War Three?'

'Especially World War Three.' He thought I was kidding. Maybe I was, but only just. Getting these people's attention is an art in itself.

There is no time to argue the point, and only just enough to make it to the next of our daily rituals, the UN's press briefing.

This is held in a half-finished brick shed inside the PTT building, where once I strolled unchecked into General MacKenzie's office, to exchange information and pick up the news of the day from a personal friend. Now the thing has been formalized and we are body-searched like criminals by the French both coming and going. Even the Serbs at their most hostile road-blocks never dealt with us like these French. I wonder what they expect to find – seditious anti-UN literature, smuggled slivovitz, or the secret codes of an organization that isn't supposed to have them?

The good news is that the UN's briefers are perhaps the best they have ever had. Lieutenant-Colonel Gary Coward on the military side and Alexander Ivanko on the civilian side are open and candid and enjoy the confidence of the Bosnia commander, General Rupert Smith – which is just as well, since he is a reclusive soldier and all but invisible to most of us.

The bad news is that though the UN doesn't use codes it hardly needs to, for it does its business in barely decipherable jargon. 'Warring faction activity continued with 95 FIs reported and 10 X HMG bursts close to BRITBAT 2 OP' does not translate easily into plain English. What it means is that fighting between the two armies continued with ninety-five firing in-cidents reported and ten heavy machine-gun bursts close to an observation post of the second British batallion.

Gary gives the UN's version of this latest battle of Sarajevo without the usual scatter-shot of acronyms. The UN itself has been under attack at an observation post overlooking the front line, so it has a better view and better information than we have. It also appeals for restraint, as it always does. But supplies of restraint, as of so much else, are exhausted.

Instead, there's an escalation. On our return to the TV station we call in at our newsgatherers' cooperative, the Sarajevo Agency Pool, to find out who else has shot what. Michael Pohl of the news agency WTN has come back with an extraordinary image of some kind of a smoke bomb exploding near the hospital. Except that it is more than smoke: there is a chemical reaction churning away inside it. It looks like phosphorus.

Gary Coward is intercepted on his way past the TV building to give a second opinion. He has the qualifications. Though he's now in the Army Air Corps, he was once a gunner. We play him the tape in front of a camera – instant replay is as possible in news as in sports – and he confirms the use of phosphorus, a burning agent banned under the Geneva Conventions as a weapon of war in such circumstances. But Bosnia's war has been fought from the start against Geneva's rules, and little has changed but the scale of the violations. (A story is told of a prisoner in Novi Travnik being forced to cross the front lines with a bag of explosives strapped to his back, and then blown up when he reached the other side.)

By now we have our story but no market for it. We are close to deadline for the *One O'Clock News* and the last chance to make a bid for a slice of their airtime – a commodity so precious it appears to have been mortgaged at least twice over, or sold to a previous bidder. I should have learned to be a salesman before becoming a journalist, for I lack the skills of a huckster. But the use of phosphorus in a built-up area helps to make the case for me. The satellite is booked, and a report from Sarajevo is slotted in towards the end of the running order. It will not be off the top of the news for the next two weeks.

Lunch is taken during these negotiations, a lunch of bean soup made of ingredients imported from Split by armoured Land Rover in one of our supply runs. The cooks are local staff hired by our allies from ABC and known to their camera crews – with the political incorrectness of their kind – as the 'cooking babes'. I am generally critical of American TV news, when I note how little is produced by so many and at such great cost, but its logistics and infrastructure are enviable. The cooking babes are an integral part of the team; their bean soup fuels our television.

Now it is early afternoon, and there's another decision to make: whether to stay safe in the bunker of the TV station (the German networks are famous for this) or to return to the field of battle. We choose to return, more out of curiosity than bravado, leaving Carl and Anamarija behind. Reducing the numbers at risk is common sense, though is unknown territory we will take the interpreter with us. After three years of war Sarajevo – or the part of it that is still accessible – is far from unknown territory. Our afternoon stake-out is on 'Gipsy Hill', high ground behind the Holiday Inn with a commanding view of the action. That is its advantage. Its disadvantage is that it may not be entirely out of range of the Serbs in Grbavica. A UN patrol is up there alongside us, better armoured than we are, but present for much the same reasons. We are shooting the explosions, they are counting them. I have never enjoyed a better view of a war zone except perhaps once on the Golan Heights. But a nagging voice inside me wonders what is the use of any of it. Are we not all battlefield voyeurs of one sort or another, making a living out of other people's troubles? Even war profiteers? What have either of us done since the start of this conflict, they with their blue helmets and we with our cameras, that has brought peace a moment closer? And when the TV cameras are ranged three deep like birds of prey along sniper's alley, are not those who put them there expecting – *hoping* even – for the sharpshooters opposite to return to their deadly business?

Memo to Martin Bell from himself: you have been doing this for far too long, you are losing your senses of perspective and humour, you are suffering from war zone fatigue, it is time to take a break.

But not yet. We are not yet quite so far in the rolling news business that the tongue outruns the brain, but we are getting to it, and a day like this is a torrent of onrushing deadlines. Next there is the *Six O'Clock News* to be satisfied. The battle is only now subsiding, and there is so much material flowing into the TV station that the problem is not what to put in but what to leave out. And a characteristic soundbite from Haris Silajdzic: 'I wonder what the reaction will be if they throw some kind of a nuclear device here? I am sure even then the UN will find some reason not to do anything.'

At least the argument about airtime has been fought and won: the Harold Wilson tributes have been trimmed back to eleven minutes; the Bosnia story is propelled by phosphorus and rising up the running order. It is the phosphorus that sets the phones ringing. A safety-conscious BBC management is already inquiring about protective clothing and anti-phosphorus drills. I bless and curse them simultaneously. The next thing we know, they will be asking us to fill out a Hazard Assessment Form for the Bosnian war (which on a scale of one to ten would probably rate as a twelve). Besides, I have words to make and a deadline to meet.

The BBC's evening news ends at 7.30 p.m. Sarajevo time. On a normal day the same report can stand for the *Nine O'Clock News* (or be dropped from it) and the team can retire for the night to savour the limited pleasures of the Holiday Inn. This is not a normal day. Word has come from the Delegates Club, headquarters of the UN's Bosnia command, of an event about as rare as giraffes in Alaska. Lieutenant-General Rupert Smith, who replaced General Rose in January, is to make a public statement in front of the cameras. It is not that he is hostile to journalists – he is actually quite open to those who can find him – but he is certainly shy of their cameras, and those who stalk him need the patience of a wild-life photographer. He gives the impression that he would rather face a firing squad than a news conference.

There are things, however, which he has to do for himself and his spokesmen cannot do for him. One of these is to deliver an ultimatum to the Serbs that enough is enough and they have finally gone too far. The tanks and artillery that they have taken from the UN's weapons collection points must be returned, and their other heavy weapons removed from the total exclusion zone out of range of Sarajevo. General Mladic is not taking the UN commander's calls, so the threat is delivered by means of a crowded news conference. 'Failure to comply with either deadline will result in the offending party or parties being attacked from the air.'

General Smith is not the sort of commander who stays around to be questioned. He says what he has to say, gets up and walks out. His departure is the cue for a press stampede which shakes the floor of the prefabricated conference room. At such times the news business becomes a race with no prize for second place. Since the arrival of the BBC's World Service News we are in direct competition with CNN – and not at all impressed by their self-promotion as 'The World's News Leader' – and we challenge them day by day and deadline for deadline. The next is but minutes away, but on the way out of the compound we have to pause; a deadline is a deadline but a battle at night can be a thing of terrible beauty. It is resuming along the ridge line to the south. The city is lit by stars and parachute flares, just as it was when the war began. With every flare the machine-gunners open up along front lines which have hardly moved in all that time. But it is a wilderness now. The flare-lit landscape is scarred and shattered – ruins where there had been houses, and stumps where there had been trees.

That is just the obvious and visible damage. And what of those of us who were present then and are still present now? How can we ourselves have come through this unscathed?

Once more the voice of doubt will have to wait. Only ten

minutes remain before satellite time, in which to edit the general's ultimatum into the news of the battle which prompted it. By now Bosnia – the foreign crisis that won't go away – has definitely reclaimed London's attention. What they didn't want to know about in the morning they can't get enough of at night. The Wilson tributes slide down the running order and Bosnia takes their place.

The downside of this is the inevitable demand for a live shot. At the end of the news the man-on-the-spot, dishevelled and unshaven and war zone weary (but refusing on principle to wear make-up in the real world) must stand in a corridor of the TV station and take questions to which he has difficulty framing the answers. Principally, will the threatened air strikes happen and how will the Serbs react to them? The obvious answers are yes and with hostility. But predictions of doom and gloom seem somehow ill-mannered, as if we don't have enough of it without them. If TV news is ever reinvented, it could well dismiss the speculative live shot as a fad of the nineties, when showtime prevailed over substance.

By now it is ten-thirty and the last deadline has passed. We do not trawl the streets at night and never have since the war began. Instead we race for the safety of the Holiday Inn and its restaurant, which has been moved underground into what was once the nightclub. It is empty and candlelit (the battle of the day has provoked a power cut), but at least there is a menu now, which there never used to be. Among the familiar dishes, chicken and hamburger, it offers Grilled Dragon Weaver.

After all these years I will take the risks where I find them. It has not been a safe day or an easy one, but we have successfully dodged the bombs and the bullets, and the old routines which worked for us before – part fieldcraft and part superstition – have done the business again. I am not yet ready for innovation. The Grilled Dragon Weaver must wait.

21

SHOWDOWN

Kurt Schork, the Bosnia meister of Reuters – and 'chief reptile' to his critics inside the UN – had a glint in his eye which announced that he had made a discovery. It was that in the American retail trade there exists a category of workers described as 'appeasement technicians', who pacify the owners of faulty appliances until the real repairman arrives. It was only a matter of time before the phrase would appear in one of Kurt's dispatches, most probably in a reference to Yasushi Akashi, special representative of the Secretary-General and the UN's sovereign conciliator. The buzz in the UN bazaars was that the newly appointed force commander in Zagreb, General Bernard Janvier, was also a candidate for the title. Or perhaps Kurt would characterize the entire UN force, all 23,000 of them, as an army of appeasement technicians.

It was May 1995. The United Nations, which had done so much and saved so many through the thirty-seven months of the war, was now becalmed and rudderless and had lost its map. Its Protection Force wasn't protecting, its safe areas weren't safe. The Serbs were not only roaming the heavy weapons exclusion zones at will with their tanks and artillery, but firing them from the UN's own collection points. The UN wasn't so much doing as being: it was parked. One of its disillusioned officials concluded that it had chosen the WIN option: WIN, he explained, stood for Weak, Ineffective and Negative. The problem

258

was not so much in Sarajevo as in Zagreb and New York. 'We have to defend a policy,' said the UN's spokesman Alexander Ivanko, 'which no one can coherently explain to us.'

The last flawed and failed ceasefire was over, and his earlier warnings of a slide into total war seemed more than amply justified. Sarajevo returned on some days to the pitched battles of 1992, and on others to the grinding attritional warfare of 1914. Bosnia's war was history in the remaking. The volumes of shellfire for hours on end were of First World War intensity. Each side tried to undermine the other on the city's most embattled no man's land, the Jewish cemetery. The government forces were first to drive a mine shaft towards the Serbs, who answered with one of their own, which they blew up first. The resulting explosion shook the city, disturbing the dead as well as the living. (Sarajevo much more than New York was the city that never slept.) The defending Muslims came up with a truly Balkan explanation for the timing of the attack: it coincided with the Eurovision Song Contest, and was said to be a Serb protest against Bosnia's participation.

With so much commotion happening and impending, I was expecting to find the Holiday Inn as crowded as it had been when the Bosnian war was still a novelty and the world's photo-journalists flocked to it; for there are fashions in war zones too. Instead, the atrium of the planet's ultimate war hotel was empty and silent, like a defunct and dusty museum after closing time.

Not for the first time, I began to question my own news judgement. It may be that I was wrong and Alex Ivanko was wrong and against all the evidence a creeping peace would descend on Sarajevo, which would mercifully then disappear from the news agenda. Or it may be that we were right but no one cared. Or – more probably – that it was the seventy-second day of the O. J. Simpson trial, which had made a mockery of all news values. Many of the regulars of the war's first three years had tired of it, or their news editors had. Some had despaired of it.

My friends and former rivals from ITN and Sky News had redefined their notions of news – or their marketing moguls had done it for them – in such a way that they had not been seen in Bosnia for months. As ITN had once been most serious competitors (and with more verve than we had, which was always their strength), I took the trouble to find out what they were doing instead, and where they were doing it, in this climactic week. Their principal reports from abroad were about child prostitution in the Philippines and baby-stealing in Greece. Since Penny Marshall's scoop on the Serbian prison camps in August 1992 they had stopped competing with us in Bosnia. Their slide into tabloid television left me unimpressed. I wished them back on the high road where they belong.

Sarajevo had also been deserted at this time by the friends of Bosnia who had thronged to it in the second and third years of the war. These were well-wishers from many countries who had volunteered their services, often at great risk and cost to themselves, on a variety of projects from rebuilding the orphanage to saving the specimens in the city's front-line museum (for which a large quantity of pure alcohol had been promised, but mysteriously disappeared in transit). The friends of Bosnia stayed away not out of choice but necessity. The airlift was down and the only access road was under cannon fire. The city itself wore an air of abandonment. Its streets were empty and its markets closed, though Tuzla's weren't, and a general alert was sounded Bosnia-wide. The last ceasefire was over, and the UN was about to make a final attempt to exert its eroded authority.

This was the moment of General Smith's high-risk gamble. He had inherited the Bosnia command, a poisoned chalice in sky-blue UN colours, from General Rose four months earlier. But the team he had inherited to deal with it had lost, or was about to lose, its very few members with whom the Serbs were prepared to do business. These included Victor Andreyev, the veteran head of Civil Affairs, and Mike Stanley and Nick Costello, who were advisers as well as interpreters. For British army officers which they also were, they possessed a truly remarkable knowledge of Serbo-Croatian and an ability to translate the people as well as the language.

The UN needed them. It was adrift at the time of the change of command, and had been adrift at least since the Bihac fiasco the previous November. So General Smith acted. His demand to the Serbs that they remove or return their heavy weapons was not only an ultimatum to them, but a signal to UN Headquarters in New York that UNPROFOR's position was untenable, and it was time to get on or get out. 'The situation we are now in,' said Alexander Ivanko with Slavic understatement, 'illuminates the problems facing the mission for a long time.'

The ultimatum to the Serbs expired at midday on May the 25th. It passed without a tank or an artillery piece being returned to UN control. The sky above Sarajevo was criss-crossed with the contrails of war planes. It looked more like a sky-writing display than the prelude to only the fifth resort to force in NATO history (the other four had also been Bosnia-related). In mid-afternoon the air show ended. A mushroom cloud of thick black smoke arose above the valley in the direction of Pale. Two NATO aircraft had bombed its ammunition depot, a more ambitious target than any chosen by General Rose in 1994. The UN and NATO awaited the Serbs' response.

Typically it was not delivered to either of them, but to unarmed and innocent people in the streets of Tuzla. Bosnia's second city was not as shattered as its capital, being out of sniper if not artillery range, and it was not as well prepared for the war's barbarism. Ten mortar and heavy artillery rounds fell on a section of Tuzla where the warm spring evening had drawn young people to the streets and cafés as if the war were a world away. Sixty-nine were killed immediately, and more would die of their wounds in the days ahead. It was the worst single bombing of the war – more destructive even than Sarajevo's first market place massacre which had aroused the world's conscience and led at least to an easing of Bosnia's agony for a while.

I half expected the same to happen this time, for the images were as vivid and terrible – hard to use, but harder still not to – as those of the market place massacre, and the crime was as unconscionable. But I should have known better. The shelling of Tuzla had zero political impact – for reasons which spoke volumes about the peculiar chemistry between television and warfare.

It was followed the next morning by a second air strike on the same ammunition depot as the first. There was still no formal response from the Serbs except to break off all contact with UNPROFOR. But three hours later, glancing up at the screen where we monitored the output of their television service, I saw something unprecedented even in the annals of this war: a Canadian officer chained to a post, a Czech officer handcuffed to the steel door of an ammunition bunker, and a Polish officer held prisoner at a radar station. The Bosnian Serb army, which prided itself on its correctness as a military force, was reduced to using UN military observers as human shields. In Bosnia as in Iraq, hostage taking was part of the new world disorder.

The Canadian, Captain Patrick Rechner, was used by his captors to pass messages to UN headquarters: 'Just to confirm, what we are waiting from General Smith is confirmation that bombing will stop. If the bombing starts again I have been instructed to tell you that we will die for the sake of NATO.'

Then one of the Serbs broke in, in clipped and educated English: 'This is BSA soldier. Three UN observers are now in the site of the warehouse. Any more bombing, they will be the first to go. Understood?'

It was understood all too clearly. The first effect of the Serbs' hostage taking was to drive their mass murder of civilians in Tuzla so far from public view that it hardly featured as a footnote to that day's news. (I tried to resist this in my own report, but the cause was lost: the hostage taking was new, the shelling wasn't.) The second effect, as soon as the images were seen in the national capitals, was to paralyse action and confuse decision-making in the troop-contributing nations, and in the UN collectively. The Western democracies do not deal well with hostage crises.

The United Nations operation in Bosnia came to a total halt. For the second time in six months the UN urged its enforcement agency, NATO, not only to go away but to stay away. NATO aircraft stopped bombing and stopped flying. The weapons collection points ceased to function, even those few where a handful of French legionnaires, outnumbered and surrounded, courageously resisted being taken hostage. Six French light tanks fell into Serb hands, and three of them would be used in the days ahead to bombard the Muslims. The Serbs, in their own version of proportionality, decided that they didn't have enough British hostages, so they seized twenty-two Royal Welch Fusiliers from observations posts near Gorazde. The UN was no longer able even to work to its original mandate and *raison d'être* of escorting humanitarian aid. The convoys were halted; and when they resumed it was with an escort not of UNPROFOR but of the Bosnian Serb police.

But defeat was one thing, capitulation another. The UN announced that on principle it would not negotiate with hostage takers, and then proceeded to do so. For the first week such negotiations as there were were left to private citizens seeking the release of their countrymen, as they had every right to do. General MacKenzie was one of these. Now retired from the Canadian army, he used his influence quite properly with the Serbs on behalf of Patrick Rechner who had once been his

ADC. But the Serbs wanted more. They wished to have official delegations beating a path to Pale once more.

So it happened that the United Nations reversed itself. General Janvier, the force commander in Zagreb, became its designated appeasement technician. He held two secret meetings with the Bosnian Serb commander, General Mladic, one in Zvornik and the other in Pale, in which the release of the hostages was agreed in return for an undertaking of no more air strikes. (Whatever else was agreed – together with the cringing stance of the UN command at its highest level – emboldened General Mladic to move on to the seizure of Srebrenica only six weeks later. The way was opened to a war crime of great magnitude.) Among General Janvier's staff no one spoke out against this desertion of principle except his chief of staff and his acting spokesman, who were both British. The French, with ten times as many hostages as the British, were much more willing to compromise. General Smith, the British field commander in Bosnia, was not consulted in advance, but was invited to attend the secret meetings. He refused. He considered resignation, but was persuaded that to resign would be not only to rock the boat but to capsize it. As a man of honour he believed that the UN should stand by its promise not to do deals with hostage takers, but as a British army officer he was trained in a tradition of soldiering on in adversity.

The Serbs' bloodless victory over the United Nations was much more convincing than anything they were achieving against Bosnian government forces on the battlefield. It was safer to seize a hostage than to storm a trench line. By a single terrorist action they had seen off the mighty power of the Atlantic Alliance, they had played on the endemic weakness of the UN, and they had changed the climate of opinion on its many home fronts. The British tabloids thundered that it was time to 'Bring Our Boys Home'. More reflective editorialists reworked Bismarck's line about the Balkan wars not being worth the bones of a Pomeranian grenadier. And the subtext to countless interviews with the hostage families was that their loved ones had no business to be in Bosnia anyway. Now it was time for the UN to leave, and for the Bosnians themselves to fight it out to the last drop of each other's blood.

The one apparently resolute action taken at this time could be interpreted in the same direction. This was the decision by Britain and France to form a Rapid Reaction Force of some 10,000 men, to be mobilized within a month. Its two brigades, equipped as much for war-fighting as for peacekeeping, would finally protect the Protection Force. But it was noted – especially by the Bosnian government – that their artillery, helicopters and combat engineers could equally be used as an extraction force. There were some fourteen different withdrawal plans to choose between, ranging from a negotiated departure to an explosive fighting retreat. The one element these plans had in common was that they took account of the Bosnians – and specifically the Bosnian Muslims in the eastern enclaves – only in so far as they might try to block the withdrawal of the UN troops. For the rest, they were as forgotten as the victims of the Tuzla massacre, whose funerals took place at four in the morning, the least unsafe time of day.

The UN had reached a point, in the fourth year of its Bosnian commitment, at which it was working full time to feed itself, to protect itself and to negotiate the release of its hostages. That was all it was doing. It had become a logical absurdity, like the notice that a farmer put in his field saying 'Do not throw stones at this notice'.

The people who felt the effects of its delinquency most keenly were those whom it had come to feed and protect. The Serbs, who also felt betrayed by the UN, declared all their agreements with it null and void. They were expecting an attempted Muslim break-out from the capital, which in fact occurred.

They therefore tightened the siege. Water, gas and electricity were cut off as in the hardest days of 1992. Not a single relief convoy entered for more than a month. The victims on the government side of the lines – Serbs and Croats as well as Muslims – complained of being held in the world's largest concentration camp. The newspaper *Oslobodenje* reflected the dark humour of the times: 'What is the difference between Sarajevo and Auschwitz?'

'Auschwitz had gas. And showers.'

A friend from the war's early months, Kanita Focak, made the point more gently. She lived in part of an old caravanserai where her husband had been killed by shrapnel three years earlier, and she slept every night with her six-year-old son in a bomb shelter under the stairs. She hated no one – certainly not the Serbs – but was dismayed by the world's indifference. 'This is a prison,' she said. 'For more than three years we have been living in a prison. I feel like a Jew in the Second World War. And we have done nothing wrong. We are not guilty of anything, except that we are not Serbs.'

Her reproaches troubled me and I took them personally, which was not at all how she intended them. We in the press, to whom the Bosnian war was more than just another war, were not by now neutral in it even if we ever had been. We were on the side of the victims – and not only the Muslim victims, for Serbs at the time were fleeing from their villages in thousands. We were peacekeepers' accomplices, wishing the UN more success than it ever achieved, blaming it when it flinched from its mandate, and yet sharing responsibility for its failures.

The most humiliating of these was the collapse of its pretence of safe areas, signalled by the fall of Srebrenica and Zepa in July 1995. The Serbs had learned from previous experience, in Gorazde and Bihac, that the UN's response to a determined military offensive would be a verbal protest backed by a token air strike. That would be all. Its priority then would be the rescue of its own troops rather than the fate of the tens of thousands of civilians they were supposed to be protecting. So it happened that in Srebrenica the UN finally crossed the line that separates inaction from dishonour. The women and children were herded into pens under the guns of the triumphant Serbs, the men of military age were led away for 'questioning' as suspected war criminals, and the Dutch UN troops were reduced to urging the victims not to panic. Herb Okun, who with Cyrus Vance was UNPROFOR's architect, described it as one of the blackest days in the UN's history.

The most troubling element in all of this was not the UN's predictable loss of nerve but the sense of a sliding scale of values, the application of a double standard about which lives were worth protecting and which were not. Though UNPRO-FOR's commanders attempted some casuistry on this point, its very name implied that it was there to protect people. On many occasions it had protected people. Yet now, in these days of showdown, the eastern enclaves were falling and a Rapid Reaction Force was being mustered to protect only the protectors and leave the people to each other's mercies in a war without end. The strong would survive, the weak would not.

This was already happening. Even as the last of the UN's hostages were being released, the Serbs unloosed a new bombard-ment on Sarajevo. Thirty-three people were killed, many of them children, and 140 wounded by mortars and artillery – and by the war's newest weapon, a 500-pound aircraft bomb pro-pelled by rockets, the most destructive and indiscriminate yet. The world took little note of this, as if it were just more of the same.

The unstated principle seemed to be that British and French and Dutch lives mattered more – much more – than Bosnian lives. That probably reflected majority opinion in the troop-contributing nations. And it was what visiting government ministers meant in the course of their lightning tours of Bosnia, when they declared that their primary concern was the safety of British troops – in which case perhaps those troops should never have been in Bosnia at all, but playing war games out of harm's way on the ranges of Salisbury Plain.

Soldiers don't sign on to be safe. They sign on to serve, often in dangerous places. And peacekeeping is a hazardous enterprise, as they know better than anyone. They accept that. It is a business of risking lives to save lives, and they accept that too. In this case a dozen were lost and thousands saved. And who is to say that the sacrifice was in vain? Certainly not the soldiers themselves. One of them who had been assigned to the safe area of Gorazde, wrote to me afterwards of the impression it had made on him: 'Personally I would go back to Bosnia given the slightest opportunity, and I know that most men in the Battalion feel the same way.'

The moral mathematics is complex and variable, and adds up differently the closer one gets to the suffering. The soldiers and journalists get closer than most. For my own part, I have come through my time in Bosnia with a conviction that is deeply felt, but so hard to communicate that I return again to the words of Elie Wiesel: it is not because I cannot explain that you won't understand, but because you won't understand that I cannot explain. If, in a hospital in central Bosnia, you have seen a six-month-old girl with her leg blown off by a mortar bomb, it is of no consequence morally or practically whether she is Bosnian or British or Brazilian. Or for that matter whether she is Muslim or Croat or Serb. She is a six-month-old girl with her leg blown off, who needs more help and protection than she ever received. Common sense and common humanity demand that we do not abandon her.

22

DARKEST BEFORE DAWN

On the day of departure for my next assignment to the Bosnian war – it would have tempted fate too far to call it my last – I received a letter from an old soldier who had served with the 1st Commando Brigade during the advance into Germany in 1945. His reminiscences, especially of the river crossings under fire, were rather more vivid and particular than the official histories; they reflected the concerns of the ordinary soldier in warfare, which have little to do with the quest for medals and glory, and a great deal to do with surviving his orders as well as obeying them, and with pausing to brew up tea in strategic places.

My friend offered two pieces of conflicting advice from across the years. The first was to keep my head down and remember that I had only one of them. The second was the wartime motto of the army (and later navy) commandos: 'Bash on regardless'. I reflected that it was because I had been bashing on regardless with my head kept down for so long that I felt so many more aches and pains than when I first set foot in Bosnia in November 1991. Or it may have been the years of wearing forty pounds of body armour. The *Daily Mail* said I looked tired. The *Daily Mail* was right.

The old soldier's advice was well timed. This was May 1995, the second month of the fourth year of the war, and access to Sarajevo had never been more dangerous. The two land routes we used to take, one from Belgrade and the other from central

Bosnia, had long been closed by the Serbs. The air bridge had been down for five weeks since they announced they could no longer guarantee the safety of the flights, which was the Balkan way of threatening to shoot them down. That left only the road over Mount Igman, which was once a logging track but now the Bosnians' sole supply route. Its disadvantage was that for the last two miles it was under Serb cannon, machine-gun and mortar fire, and all in their line of sight. Our armoured Land Rover, successor to 'Miss Piggy', was proof against small-arms fire, but the Serbs' twenty-millimetre cannon could wipe it off the road.

The journey in that day was not so well timed. We had hoped for fog, but drove down the side of the mountain in bright sunshine instead. If we could see the Serbs that clearly they could surely see us – and they were targeting everything that moved. We knew that because on our way down we met our friends from the French network TF1 coming up. Their windscreen was splintered and the side of their armoured Range Rover had been hit by a machine-gun round; they were rather shaken up, and heading home. The bad news was that the Serbs were active, the good news was that they were not yet using armour-piercing rounds.

Now it was our turn. To anyone planning to drive through a two-mile target zone my first advice is – don't. But if you really have to, here is a three-point survival guide. First, don't drive at the edge of safe speed and try to turn a logging track into a Grand Prix circuit. Second, expect to be shot at and even be mildly surprised if you're not. And third, choose your companions with care; for panic is as dangerous as what causes it, and even among friends it can spread like a fire through a dry forest.

In this as in so much else I was lucky, though of the range of camera meisters we had used at the start of the war very few were still willing or available to see it through. One had become a father and quite reasonably concluded that fatherhood and wars didn't mix. Another had taken the plunge into underwater documentaries. A third had fallen ill. And most tragically Tuna of course was no longer with us.

The redoubtable Nigel Bateson was still present though, his generally ogre-like appearance disguising a gentle character and a fierce dedication to his craft. As we set off towards the Serb guns he announced, amid the usual expletives, how much he loved his job. And then he added, as if for the record, 'I'm too young to die. I still have fish to catch and babies to make.' I was in the process of reassuring him that when this excursion was over there would still be plenty of time for both, and even perhaps to rearrange his priorities, when we heard a loud explosion very close and thought the Land Rover had been hit. It was not the time or place to investigate, but later we realized that whatever it was had passed just above or behind us. The Serbs' failed marksmanship was our salvation.

It was not to be counted on however. The next time, or the time after that, they could be shooting straighter. Not for the first time I wondered how much longer I wished to go on playing this Balkan roulette. Besides, I still had to tackle the journey out again; and within two days of our arrival Sarajevo erupted with the most ferocious fighting since 1992. It seemed a good time to set down some thoughts about the meaning of this war which had so deeply marked me, which had consumed three years of my time and taken more lives than I knew. These would not be conclusions, for the war itself was very far from concluded, but they would draw some kind of a line under the first three years of it. I did this in the form of answers to the questions most frequently asked.

The first of these questions was, Why Bosnia? Why not Rwanda or Somalia or Haiti, or any of the other ungovernable republics which surface for a season on the TV news, then as mysteriously disappear? But Bosnia was always with us, or almost always, and received more sustained attention than any other crisis or country in my experience. Even the war in Vietnam was not covered on quite this scale. The critics seized on this and wondered why. As early as the second month of the war, in May 1992, a columnist in the *People* was on my case:

Gunfire crackled, mortar shells thumped into distant hillsides and BBC Correspondent Martin Bell, in a remarkably unmarked white suit, kept popping up to tell us about the latest developments in Yugoslavia's civil war. Such reports have dominated the BBC television news for weeks . . . I cannot help thinking that the BBC news editors have got their priorities wrong. The TV footage may be dramatic but I don't think the average British viewer is too riveted by happenings in Bosnia.

In the same vein an aspiring TV mogul, seeking a licence for a popular new channel, defined his agenda by what his hoped-for viewers *wouldn't* be seeing. 'Bosnia it ain't,' he said. It therefore gave me great pleasure, when the first edition of these reflections was published, to be interviewed about them on his channel by a lady of conspicuous charm and intelligence. (I hope she never had to introduce the topless darts.) For half an hour at least, Bosnia it was . . .

So why Bosnia? In my own case I talk about it because I know about it. If I were the BBC's man in Tibet or Tanzania I might do the same for them, but somehow I doubt it. The fact that war and genocide on a large scale have returned to the continent of Europe within fifty years of the last war and the last genocide brings to the conflict in Bosnia an extra urgency and resonance. It is not, as some have misinterpreted it, a racist argument, that the victims in Bosnia are white and the victims in Rwanda are black. It is a neighbourhood argument, that this is happening in our own backyard. It threatens the security of all of us, and we ignore it at our peril.

The second question is rather harder to answer. It is, why do I do this for a living? And having done it for longer than is prudent and reasonable, why do I not give it up? I can see many arguments for an early retirement, and only one for carrying on, which is that I have to see this thing through. Only now, after four years of living dangerously, it may be time to walk away. War reporting is a daft way to earn a living, but it provides the survivors with a privileged view of history in the making as well as a chance to contribute to its first draft, which is the news. And the Bosnian war, if it was nothing else, was history in the making – or, as I have argued, the remaking. I believe that events in Bosnia, and the failure of the rest of Europe to address and influence them until so late in the day, had a greater effect on the continent and its institutions than the political decisions taken in any of its capitals. That so much was at stake was another reason to stay. I felt like adapting St Augustine: O Lord make me distant and indifferent, but not yet.

I am further asked, am I not by now a total pessimist about these war zones, and what they tell us of human nature and the human condition in general? The answer is no, not at all. For in war there is also heroism, and not only the bravery of soldiers. In Bosnia it brought out the best as well as the worst in people – the courage of individuals who stood out against the savagery of the times, of Muslims who helped their Serb neighbours and Serbs who helped Muslims. There were also the volunteer heroes from many countries who were willing to serve in dangerous places and who saved lives against all odds. It was one of the privileges of war reporting to get to meet such people, and to learn what not to take for granted. The Bosnian war fore-shadowed all our futures both in the way that it was fought and in the way (if there was one) that it was dealt with.

The argument began as a minor one about a little-known war in a peripheral republic. 'We don't have a dog in that fight,' said James Baker, the former American Secretary of State who urged the Yugoslavs to stay together and his own country to stay out of it. More than three years later it had become the foreign policy preoccupation of the industrial democracies. It had divided the Americans, who did have a dog in that fight, from the Europeans who – with the exception of Germany – did not. It damaged every international institution which touched it, from the European Community to the United Nations to NATO. It ruined the reputations of many and made the reputations of none, except perhaps that of General Mladic, before his front lines started to crumble, and finally that of Richard Holbrooke when the imperatives of the American electoral calendar made an intervention necessary. Its extraordinary impact had to do with both history and geography. It is was war fought in time during the post-cold-war power vacuum, and in place on an ancient continental fault line where a tremor became an earthquake.

So the debate about it was about more than Bosnia. It still *is* about more than Bosnia (for it did not end with the peace process). It is about the future of the United Nations – if, after Bosnia, it has a future. It is about the relations between the great powers – if, after Bosnia, there are still great powers. It is about the danger of a return to the anarchy of competing nation states. It is about the new world order, if there is one. It is about the risks we are willing to take in the cause of peace. It is about policy and principle, and whether we may insist on keeping a connection between them. And when an incoming Foreign Secretary quotes with approval Lord Palmerston's dictum that 'The furtherance of British interests should be the only object of a British Foreign Secretary', we may legitimately wonder, what ever happened to British principles? Don't we have them any more? And if we don't, what kind of people are we?

I am not a political animal and never have been, but I was drawn to one side of this debate by the kind of people I found there – people like Larry Hollingworth, Lew MacKenzie, Colm Doyle, Bob Stewart, Philippe Morillon, Mark Cook, Alastair Duncan, John Jordan the fireman, and all the drivers of the ODA who brought hope to desperate people in dangerous places. Elie Wiesel, because of what he said and where he said it, also belonged in that company.

On the other side there stood the 'nothing can be done' club. Its arguments were plausible and drew strength from the rising toll of casualties among the peacekeepers, and from the reluctance of Bosnia's leaders to seek peace among themselves. The case rested on a narrow definition of national interest. Its advocates urged that we retreat to our national fortresses – especially attractive if, as in Britain's case, the fortress comes equipped with a moat – and wait for the conflagration to burn itself out or pass us by. But it was in the interests of all our children – theirs as well as ours – that they should not prevail.

The reason is simple. While I was in the thick of it, and even later during a serious attempt to resolve it, the conflict in Bosnia has seemed to me the most *consequential* war for two generations. It threatened direr consequences even than the Vietnam war, which though it involved one superpower in combat against the client state of another was not only fought, but managed, under cold war rules. Each superpower understood the other's interests and limits. It may have been just a subjective and personal impression, but in the ditches of Vietnam I never got that sense of being an eyewitness to the onset of the Third World War that I felt so often in the trenches of Bosnia. The world was more predictable then, and safer.

The omens were the grimmer because the United Nations – now as then the last and best hope of us all – had failed the challenge before it. It was stuck fast in the Bosnian quagmire –

or morass or quicksand. All the analogies were glutinous and gloomy, suggesting no way on and no way out. Bosnia exposed the UN's infirmities – weaknesses of structure and of the collective will of its member states – more cruelly and over a longer period then even such contemporary crises as Rwanda or Somalia. And yet the record was not one of total failure. Even in disarray the UN saved lives, as Larry Hollingworth knew better than anyone since he was there from the start. 'Everything was *ad hoc*,' he said. 'We made it up as we went along. But I would say we saved a hundred thousand lives. There was no question of that.'

It may be that over time Bosnia will come to be seen as the UN's Dunkirk, a defeat and retreat from which lessons were learned which would lead it to manage this and other crises differently: to be patient about peacekeeping, realistic about peace enforcement, and never again to adopt conflicting mandates. It was the UN's own people – soldiers and civilians, the servants of peace – who felt its failures most acutely. One wrote to me, 'Unfortunately the more UN work I do, the less I believe in it.'

In July 1995 the UN's fortunes in Bosnia were at their lowest ebb. It was battered and beaten. It had dishonourably abandoned the unsafe areas of Zepa and Srebrenica. Its mobility was blocked by the militias of all three sides; a brigade of its Rapid Reaction Force languished miserably at Ploce on the Croatian coast. No air strikes had been risked since May. The war itself continued unabated. The only superpower left standing, the United States, had overflown the battlefields at great height and introduced its ground troops only once, to rescue an F16 pilot shot down by a SAM6 missile. It seemed a symbol of America's commitment – a fast and spectacular escape presented as a victory.

War reporting as a way of life offers different types and varieties of despair. One of these, if not an affectation, is a sort of protective cast of mind that helps to keep us going in the direst circumstances when common sense would have urged us to quit long ago. The charming Elly Biles, who shouldered a camera for Reuters Television in these darkest of days, expressed it better than anyone: 'I have felt so much better,' she said, 'since I gave up hope'.

But there was a deeper despair, beyond the reach of even Elly's humour, to which I succumbed at this time. It was compounded by a sense of failure. I would say to myself: Martin Bell, you are supposed to be a hot-shot reporter and to have a way with words, you are working in the most powerful medium known to man and using the most extraordinary images from the first war in Europe for half a century – and *none of it has had any effect at all*; you might as well have become a pinstriped diplomat for all the difference you made.

This was also the time when the first edition of these reflections had to go to the printer. So I ended it with some pessimism:

I had hoped to close this, my first and probably my only book, in the peace of my small house in London. Instead it is night-time in a war without end, and the supposedly fearless war reporter is flinching from the snipers' bullets as they whip past his window in the Holiday Inn. South of the hotel a stream of tracer cascades on to the ruins of Debelo Brdo, the most fought-over acre in the war. The thunder of artillery echoes from mountain to mountain. And in the north the Bosnian army is mounting an offensive on the high ground of Cemerska Planina. That translates literally as the Mountain of Extreme Grief. It seems somehow a suitable place for a battle in Bosnia, which after three years of war is an entire country of extreme grief – and extreme danger too.

The grief is shared by the Bosnians themselves. The danger threatens us all.

I had not supposed that things could get worse, but of course I should have known better. On 28 August five mortars were fired into the centre of Sarajevo in mid-morning, when it would be busiest. Four of them landed harmlessly. The fifth glanced off a roof and exploded in the main shopping street where it was most crowded with passers-by and cigarette sellers. Thirty-seven people were killed – the highest death toll in any one incident in the capital since February 1994. The television pictures were truly appalling, and under the rules of the good-taste guidelines very few of them could be shown on the BBC. (Though I did slip in, from the street cleaning that followed, a heart-stopping image of blood being washed down a storm drain; now, no doubt, there is a new rule about blood in storm drains.)

The question that arose then – the question that *always* arose in these cases – was what would the UN do about it? On past performance, I supposed, nothing at all. And there would be the usual reasons: the firing point could not be identified, the radar had failed to pick up the mortar's trajectory, and the peace process – even when there wasn't one – had to be protected.

But this time I was wrong, completely and conclusively wrong. This time it was to be different.

23

FAINTHEARTS CONFOUNDED

The man who made the difference was General Rupert Smith: UN Bosnia commander, congenital public relations recluse, Gulf War hero and connoisseur of desperate predicaments. He *had* to be a connoisseur of desperate predicaments. For now he was in one, as he had been almost without respite since inheriting the Sarajevo command the previous January. As a yachtsman, which he also was, he was partial to seafaring metaphors. He described it as 'beating to windward'.

General Smith surveyed his options, as his predecessor had, but was not beguiled by any fancy staff-work offering a variant of the status quo. The status quo was his problem, not his solution. It held 34,000 UN soldiers in harm's way to no purpose. It was what he had to escape from. He had no choice really but to withdraw or to escalate, to get out or to get on. Neither course would be popular with the governments contributing troops to his operation. But it was not the General's business to court the favour of governments, including his own. It was his business to set out the consequences of action – and, especially in the Bosnian case, of *inaction*. For it was prevarication over the years that had cost so many lives. The foot-dragging and hand-wringing had actually been lethal.

His opportunity came, as General Rose's had, with a market place massacre. There was a certain tragic symmetry to the two events. The mortars exploded nearly eighteen months apart but within a hundred yards of the same place. The difference, aside from the character and analysis of the two generals, was that over that period there had been a significant shift of power within the UN's command structure. Under the old dual-key arrangement between the UN and NATO, there could be no air strikes against targets in Bosnia unless both keys were turned, the UN's and NATO's. Either organization – and in practice it was always the UN – held the effective power of veto. The UN's key was in the hands of Yasushi Akashi, its Special Representative and at-all-costs conciliator. No wonder that the air strikes of 1994 had been too little, too late and directed at token targets – hitting the tent and not the tank, the runway not the aircraft. Following vociferous NATO (and chiefly American) complaints, the UN's key then passed to its Zagreb commander, General Bernard Janvier. That might not have made much difference, for he was a conciliator himself. He was much under Akashi's influence and of his mind-set.

But at the time of the market place bombing of 28 August, General Janvier was on leave. In his absence the authority for air strikes was devolved to the next senior UN commander, General Smith, in Sarajevo. He had the additional advantage of being on the spot. He waited only for the crater analysis and calculation of trajectories, which showed 'beyond reasonable doubt' that the mortars had been fired from Serb-held territory. He did not wait for General Janvier's return. And once the key had been turned, with NATO's enthusiastic endorsement, all the UN's fabled capacity for paralysis was unable to turn it back.

The result was spectacular and quite literally earth-shaking. It was the first time I had received my wake-up call in the Holiday Inn from the sound of friendly fire. The hotel quaked, not from the usual rattle of local mortar and machine-gun fire, but from the thunder of falling bombs on the rim of the mountains, where the Serbs had their command bunkers, their heavy weapons and reserves of armament. The NATO air strikes began at two in the morning. They lit the night sky with the flashes and flames of secondary explosions. Two hours later, in the first light of dawn, the French 155-millimetre guns joined in resoundingly from their positions on Mount Igman. It was the Rapid Reaction Force finally reacting, and the first use of artillery ever in UN peacekeeping. I remember thinking, I should be on the phone to London at once; I should be organizing satellites; I should be getting the world's attention for this. But for a while I switched myself off professionally. It was too overwhelming. I just stood and gaped, unbelieving. This was the option that for three and a half years the policy-makers had told us was inconceivable, the road they could not go down. Yet now they had taken it, irreversibly. The bullet-scarred windows of the old pub rattled. And through the jaded press corps in the battered hotel there spread a feeling new to all of us – a sense of awe and wonderment.

I also observed that this was my *second* fireworks show from hell in less than five years (the first had been in the Gulf War in 1991) – and that both had been initiated by the same man, General Rupert Smith. It was an unlikely coincidence, for he was as far from the image of the mad bomber as any man in uniform could be. He was, for a paratrooper, a peaceably minded and unusually reflective soldier. He was also equipped with a strong sense of right and wrong, which he tried to hide (as senior officers tend to, lest they be thought in some way 'unsound'; the army is indeed a most strange institution). Yet he called in more firepower, a higher exploding tonnage of shells and rockets, first in Iraq and then in Bosnia, than any British commander in the fifty years since the Second World War. He did it in both cases because he had to and there was no other option open. The legend of 'Bomber Smith', I believe, is unlikely to take hold.

The UN command had learned from past mistakes. The action taken at the end of August was less open to reprisals than the lighter bombardment attempted three months earlier – the one that led to military observers being chained to bridges and radar stations. On the morning of 31 August General Smith received a call from General Mladic, amid the ruins, angrily reminding him that there were still fifty British soldiers in the line of hostage-taking, the remnant of the Royal Welch Fusiliers not yet withdrawn from Gorazde. General Smith said nothing, because nothing was what it was politic to say. In fact, the Fusiliers' departure, previously agreed with the Serbs, had been accelerated. They were out of Gorazde and through Serb lines just hours before the air strikes. And the Serb commander let them pass, having received no orders to block them. (The moral of this is: never overestimate your enemy. He may be as stupid as you think he is.)

The bombardment was everything that NATO and the UN had threatened, and everything the earlier pin-prick raids had not been – wide, deep and disproportionate. Especially disproportionate. Laser-guided and scientifically accurate though it was, not all the targets turned out to be military. A livestock market in Doboj was hit, as was a mushroom farm that had the misfortune to look from the air like weapons depot. But these were among the least of the Serbs' problems.

In the second week of the bombardment their front lines crumbled. They blamed NATO for this because they needed a scapegoat, and in truth their command and control were badly damaged. But the real reason was a coincident blitzkrieg by the Croats on their western front – not the Bosnian Croats of the HVO, but main-force units from Croatia itself, armour and infantry rearmed and retrained (the deutschmark and the dollar both contributing), the new military power in the Balkans. The Serbs had lost their border outposts, Glamoc and Grahovo, two months earlier. Now a string of other towns fell in their once impregnable heartland: Donji Vakuf, Drvar, Kljuc, Sipovo, Mrkonjic Grad and Sanski Most. Also Jajce, which had never been theirs, but they had seized and ransacked anyway. Prijedor, the home town of ethnic cleansing, was threatened. Banja Luka itself was within rocket range of the victorious Croats – and plunged into darkness when the hydro-electric station at Bocac fell to them. For the third time in a year the roads were clogged with the tractor-driven flight of retreating Serbs. By mid-September more than a hundred thousand of them were on the move. ('Serbs them right,' crowed the *Sun*, unfeelingly.)

In the hour of the Serbs' defeat the strength of their citizens' army became its weakness. The women and children fled to escape the fighting, and the soldiers who were their husbands and fathers fled to protect them. When the tide of retreat reached the next village back, its people too would pack up their things and head east. So the whole front line rolled back unstoppably. The Serbs had neither mobile reserves nor second lines of defence. They had never needed them. They had never *expected* to need them. For were they not warriors and fighters-to-the-death, the heirs to a thousand years of heroism, and who had supposed for a moment that this would happen? (Actually I had, and had told them so in Pale and Jahorina in the days when we were still on speaking terms. But who would ever pay heed to a mere journalist?)

All that they were left with, which was small consolation, was the rhetoric of retreat and recrimination. This was supplied in ample quantities by Radovan Karadzic, who had become Commander-in-Chief (a self-promotion that his generals pointedly ignored), and who showed an almost Hitlerian belief in the power of words alone to hold the line. 'We have reached a key moment,' he declared in August after Glamoc and Grahovo had fallen. 'We cannot afford to lose one more municipality. The mistake is here with us in the high command . . . Maybe we went a bit too far with General Mladic: we have made a legend of him. The enemy has changed and we must change.' Then later in August, when Drvar was threatened: 'The town must be defended at all costs.' And in mid-October, after the rout at Sanski Most: 'There should be no retreat. The soldiers should only go forward. And we can liberate Sanski Most and certainly defend Prijedor.' But it was words, all words and nothing but words. The Serbs had become the victims of their own defiance.

The break in the stalemate was also the hinge on which other events could turn. A ceasefire was agreed and, after a faltering start, took hold. A serious negotiation began for the first time in two and a half years. The Americans arrived with a hard-driving diplomat, Richard Holbrooke, to bang heads together – chiefly those of their own clients in the Bosnian government who had a habit of backing away from concessions already made. Holbrooke reinvigorated the language of diplomacy. 'Mr President,' he said to Izetbegovic, 'you are shooting craps with your country's destiny.'

But there was something here that eluded and troubled me – some missing element that I couldn't pin down. It didn't help that because of the momentousness of these events I was withdrawn from the war zone and turned into a sort of pundit and instant historian, shackled to a desk in head office and set in front of a computer that meant about as much to me as an Egyptian hieroglyphic. The editorial conversations would go something like this:

'Martin, we would like you to do us the story of the war so far.'

'How long can you give me?'

'How about a minute and a half?'

'*A minute and a half?* You've got to be joking.'

'Then your usual minute and forty-two seconds.'

'I'll do it. But you do realize that there are one or two little details that I just might have to leave out?'

The upside of it was that I was also tasked to produce a longer chronicle of the war for *Newsnight*, which is the BBC's wildlife reserve for reflective journalism. It gave me the opportunity to visit Herb Okun in New York. Herb is a good friend and wise owl. It was he who, with Cyrus Vance, negotiated an end to the Croatian war in January 1992; who celebrated his sixtieth birthday by crossing a front line without either armour or escort; and who did more than anyone to prevent the spread of the Bosnian war to Macedonia. We talked at length about all these conflicts, actual and potential, and especially about the chances of a settlement in Bosnia. It was then that Herb supplied the missing link. 'It seems to me,' he said, 'that *the Serbs are being bombed into accepting their own peace plan.*'

He was right, of course. The plan on offer was much more nearly their plan than their adversaries'. The Serbs had wanted partition, and they got partition, albeit within the fiction of a single state. They had wanted autonomy, and they got autonomy – though the territorial division grieved them, especially the loss of their suburbs in Sarajevo. But so great had been their losses in the war's closing weeks that they would actually retrieve through negotiation more land than they handed over. And the plan in its final form, finessed and imposed in three weeks of bargaining at the Wright-Patterson Air Force Base in Dayton, Ohio, was *less* advantageous to the Muslims than the Vance–Owen plan, which the Americans themselves had dismissed nearly three years earlier. Of the eastern enclaves only Gorazde remained. Vance–Owen would have saved them both Zepa and Srebrenica, not to mention the tens of thousands of lives – between three and five thousand in Srebrenica alone – which had been lost in the subsequent fighting and executions. It was another case of inaction costing lives.

But Vance–Owen was not an American plan, and was rejected by the Americans for just that reason. Lord Owen recalls that at the critical meeting to explain it to the new administration, the Secretary of the State Warren Christopher was 'dismayingly equivocal' and 'appeared as if he had not had the time to read even a short factual information sheet on what was the essence of our plan'.★ The Muslims were encouraged to hold out for a better deal.

But the Dayton plan was as American as Dayton itself. Though it drew from the ideas of others, the Americans owned it – lock, stock and annexe. And they chose the bleak air base in Ohio both as a symbol of their reach and power and as a standing reproach to the Europeans, whose diplomats had toiled for years in their gilded chanceries and in all that time had produced on Bosnia precisely the square root of nothing – or nothing but broken agreements and violated ceasefires. 'What is it with the Europeans?' asked Holbrooke. 'Why can't they get their act together on anything?' There had to be a better way of doing it. So the Europeans were shouldered aside, the merest spectators at Dayton with the minimum courtesies. It was an American show and the testing ground for a diplomacy of New World directness, not subtle but skilful, which would make up in force for what it lacked in frills. The absence of frills was central to it. Heads of State, who at home would summon a motorcade for a visit to their hairdresser, were treated with all the special privileges of an American airman first class. High livers like Slobodan Milosevic, who derided the Americans as 'juice men' (that is, they drank no slivovitz), were reduced to eating their meals off trays in the canteen – and, which was worse, in the company of their adversaries. They had no escape and every incentive to reach an early agreement. It was cheaper and healthier than Geneva, and a great deal more effective.

★ *Balkan Odyssey*, by David Owen, London, Victor Gollancz, 1995.

Yasushi Akashi, the UN's Special Representative, reflected from afar on these shifts of power and diplomacy. He had the leisure to do so, for events had marginalized him completely and he had indeed been reassigned to duties in New York. Before he left I had a farewell lunch with him in a cavernous Zagreb restaurant, where he dissected the fish set in front of him with quite extraordinary surgical skill. So flawless a performance was it that I reflected – privately, of course – that perhaps he should have chosen to be a surgeon rather than a negotiator, or at least a negotiator in the Balkans, where the only currency was the kind of force that he was unwilling to use. He was a servant of peace who sought peace by persuasion; and it seemed tactless to rake over the coals of old controversies and blame him for losing opportunities he might have seized. Besides, I lack the instincts of an inquisitor. So we talked instead of the diplomacy. He said that he had always found Milosevic the easiest to deal with, because of his total control of those around him. The Europeans and Americans, in their diplomatic cultures and approaches, belonged to different planets. The Europeans had proved to be weak and divided. The Americans were, above all, purposeful. It was this purposefulness that drove the peace process forward and brought it to a conclusion against the odds, even though the map that went with it rewarded ethnic cleansing to an extent that the Vance–Owen plan never did. The treaty was signed in Paris on 14 December. It had a transforming impact.

UNPROFOR, the protection force that didn't protect, became IFOR, the implementation force that would *have* to implement the peace treaty or go the same discredited way as its predecessor. Because there was no time to lose and the transfer of authority occurred only six days after the signing there was also no time for IFOR's heavy weapons, its big guns and tanks, to move into place. So in its early days, the days that would make the difference between success and failure, the troops enforcing the new mandate were the troops who had been so frustrated under the old one. All the front-line soldiers were the same (for which they duly collected an extra medal). Much was made of the firepower they had and their willingness to use it, but essentially it was a game played with smoke and mirrors.

The grand master of smoke and mirrors was Richard Dannatt, the brigadier who commanded this small force and had to make it appear a much larger one, rather like a stage army. A platoon of infantry had to look like a battalion and a troop of artillery like a regiment. So it was that three light field guns were rushed around the landscape, sometimes towed and sometimes airlifted, amid much barking of commands and aligning of targets. The local militias, who generally moved at a more leisurely, horse-drawn pace, were much impressed by this. It gave a new meaning to the phrase 'the theatre of war'. The brigadier called it 'manoeuvre peacekeeping'.

The role of lead battalion in NATO's first-ever ground operation fell to the Royal Regiment of Fusiliers, who had chafed especially under the old restrictions. They had taken to calling themselves the First Fusiliers, to distinguish themselves from the other RRF, the Rapid Reaction Force (and also, I suspect, from other fusiliers). They celebrated the change in the best way they knew, which was to hold a parade. They cleared the snow to make just enough space for two companies, a padre, a guard of honour and two flagpoles in the shoe factory which was their base in the town of Bugojno. To mark their release from UN duty, the pipes and drums played the theme from *The Great Escape*. Their commanding officer, the charismatic Lieutenant-Colonel Trevor Minter, stood Patton-like before them and told them in the bluntest terms that their new mission was nothing like their old one; they were back to serious soldiering. He ended: 'Let no man stand in our way.' The drums rolled, the faded UN flag was lowered and the crisp, clear colours of the Union Jack were hoisted. (There was still no IFOR flag.) The men replaced their UN berets with the Fusiliers' red and white hackle. 'Now I feel like a soldier again,' muttered one of them under his breath, adding the usual expletive. They were armed not exactly as they had been for peacekeeping, for they had brought their mortars and anti-tank weapons out of storage. But it was the hackle that made the difference.

'What beautiful feathers,' said Anamarija our ever-present producer and interpreter.

'Those aren't feathers,' replied the sergeant-major with sergeant-majorly hauteur. 'That's a hackle.'

'Why is the end of it red?' she asked.

'It was dipped in the blood of the French, in the battle of St Lucia.'

The Fusiliers were new to the idea of multinational soldiering; and though IFOR was supposed to be a composite force, the other nations in these early days were nowhere to be seen. For its first operation the hackles were replaced by combat helmets, and the armoured column approached the front line flying thickets of Union Jacks. Croats and Serbs were dug in half a mile from each other fifteen miles south of Banja Luka, in a canyon so deep in the middle of nowhere that they didn't have a name for it. So the Fusiliers gave it one. They called it Black Dog. And they secured the Black Dog crossing in less than five minutes. The Croats offered no resistance as their bunkers were swept away, and the Serbs greeted the British with smiles and hand-shakes like long-lost friends, as if to say, what took you so long, where have you been all this time while we waited for you? An armoured column of the Light Dragoons (motto: charm and guile, according to their commander Major Robert Polley) then came barrelling through and met the same fate. They were ambushed in the next village north with slivovitz. In terms of compliance,

IFOR achieved more in its first hours than the UN did in years. They did it, quite simply, with the threat of force. And because the force was believable, no man *did* stand in their way.

But it was the strangest military operation that I had ever seen. Normally a small number of officers at headquarters commands a large number of troops on the ground. As a former Other Rank, I was once one of those commanded, so I knew these things. But IFOR stood the pyramid on its head. For its first operation, the Black Dog crossing, a corps commanded a division which commanded a brigade which commanded a battalion which commanded a company – just one company, 'X' Company of the Royal Regiment of Fusiliers, which was actually doing the business. From that point on it became 'NATO's Lead Company'. A sign proclaimed this at the Black Dog Café, the ruined house which was its home for a while. Jock Stacey, 'X' Company's sergeant-major, was as happy as any man could be who lived in a ruin. 'Now we've got the green on,' he said, pointing with some pride at his combat helmet, 'we can act more like professional soldiers, we can be more robust and hopefully get on with our job. We don't need to crawl about any more.'

'D' Day, 20 December, was doubly peculiar. Not only did it field a remarkably high proportion of commanders to other ranks (I met two generals that day but only one major, 'X' Company's Chris Claridge), but it also lacked Americans. It spectacularly lacked Americans. This was, after all, an American plan being implemented. The multinational force was supposed to be storming across front lines all over Bosnia, including the northern sector round Tuzla, the American divisional headquarters. But there weren't any Americans present to do the storming. They had been delayed by fog and floods – fog which stopped them landing at the airfield, and floods which hampered their engineers building a pontoon bridge across the Sava River.

All that the Americans had plenty of was journalists – more journalists, actually, than soldiers. The TV networks threw money at the story of the Americans' arrival as if it were the Second Coming, the Superbowl and the New Hampshire Primary all rolled into one. They threw money at it long before it happened. Bosnia had no other reality for them. They imported six tons of communications equipment so that Tuzla could talk all the time to New York, whether or not it had anything to say. This telephone exchange was at the same time so sophisticated and so ignorant – much like the networks themselves, come to think of it – that *it actually thought it was in New York*; it had a 212 area code. They built stages and platforms and commentary booths at the gates of the air base, so that their million-dollar performers could report on location, live and continuously, about . . . well, about the fog and the floods principally, because the dozen troops who had arrived had gone into hiding. I was fascinated. Everything that I most dislike about the business I am in was camped in one shouting, seething, self-regarding compost at the entrance to the air base – the hype and hysteria, the tyranny of rolling news, the deference to a distant newsroom, the live-shot lunacy, the inane exchanges with an anchorman called Mort. (Christiane Amanpour of CNN, you are personally exempted from all of this tirade.) The electronic circus that came to town was reputed to have cost six million dollars. It left me wondering, what else might Tuzla – poor, sulphurous, war-battered Tuzla – have done with that six million dollars?

Our own operation was cheaper and less flamboyant. It was based near the British divisional headquarters, in one of the few undamaged houses in Gornji Vakuf. We felt like Gypsy Television. This was our eighth Bosnian home in three and a half years. It was as comfortable as the house in Vitez, the one with the goats and the incoming sniper fire, and it felt a great deal safer – at least until an avalanche fell on to the satellite dish and put it out of business for a while. From Gornji Vakuf we reported IFOR's successes and setbacks. The successes were obvious, as its authority and numbers grew and it was joined by its heavy weapons – the same tanks that had seen service in the Gulf, and many of the same soldiers too, played in by the same pipe major. Soldiers are like fashions: if you stay around long enough, the same ones will come back. My old friends in the Queen's Royal Hussars had somehow survived an amalgamation and retained their Irish identity.

The setbacks were the bitter harvest of the reckless sowing of mines. The front lines held thousands of minefields and millions of mines. These could not be signed away at the stroke of a pen in Paris. No maps existed of some of the minefields and the records of others were lost in the memories of soldiers who had since been killed. So the casualties continued well after the fighting was over. In the early days of the deployment three Light Dragoons were killed when their armoured reconnaissance vehicle was blown off the road by a mine. IFOR persisted. It took risks because it had to: and UNPROFOR's talent for hiding in bunkers was not an option open to it. Sergeant Michael Garcia of the Royal Engineers was supervising the clearance of a forest mine-field by the HVO when he was slightly wounded, and one of the Croats badly wounded, by an unseen mine the HVO had laid. Next day he was back on duty in the same minefield as if it were the most natural thing in the world. I asked him, why? His answer was, why not? Peace has its heroes just as much as war.

Other difficulties arose from the grey and ambiguous margins of the mandate – the search for the evidence of war crimes. IFOR had the freedom of movement that the UN had always lacked, all parts of Bosnia were open to it, but how could it stand neutrally between the Serbs and the government forces and yet go after the Serbs who were principally charged? And what sort of help should it give to the War Crimes Tribunal? Though I had myself agreed to give evidence to the Tribunal – and in fact did so; it might as well have been used by the defence as by the prosecution – I had a feeling that the search for justice might conflict with the search for peace. Bosnia could have one or the other, but not both. (And was not the Dayton map itself an enshrinement of injustice, to the Muslims of Eastern Bosnia?)

Aside from these difficulties IFOR was everything that UN-PROFOR had not been: an effective and balanced force that operated equally on both sides of the lines. During a tour of its operations by a visiting general I spotted in his accompanying court of upwardly mobile staff officers an old friend from UNPROFOR days. He had in fact held a senior position in the UN's Bosnia command and had defended the bunker-based caution then in fashion. The question was inevitable.

'Couldn't this have been done years before?'

'Yes,' he said, 'I think it could have been.'

It was a question that I also had to face during my brief and unwelcome spell as a studio pundit. I had spent enough years dodging bullets; it would have been easy enough to have dodged this one with the usual evasions of the TV reporter at bay: that it was hard to know, that only time would tell, and other dull wordage to the same effect. But if the Bosnian war had taught me anything, it was *not to prevaricate*.

'Couldn't this have been done before?'

'Yes,' I echoed, 'I think it could have been.'

EPILOGUE

So a sort of peace prevailed, or at least a respite from war: not a cure, but a time of remission. Sarajevo, apart from its ruins and wreckage, transformed itself without conviction into a passable imitation of other cities. Traffic jams and officious policemen returned to the streets; the quintessentially peacetime concept of a *parking offence* was restored after a four-year absence; the Holiday Inn cashed in on its fame by hoisting its prices to a point where it was charging more for less than any hotel on earth; reporters who had shunned it during the fighting flocked to it in tailored combat jackets and preening themselves on their courage; the steel shutters and sniper-blinding containers disappeared from sniper's alley; the victims of the siege could finally walk the city without fear.

So much to the good. The principal, and probably lasting, change was the return under the Dayton agreement of the five Serb-held suburbs to Bosnian government control. This reunited the capital; and the Americans, who were much in the proclamation business, proclaimed it as their achievement. Perhaps it was, but it was bought at a great cost. What they failed to note in their triumphalism was that Sarajevo was the united capital of a partitioned country; the dream of a multi-ethnic Bosnia was gone; the Muslimization of the city and its government provoked the resignation of its respected mayor, Tarik Kupusovic, who lamented 'Sarajevo's suicide'; the Serbs fled in droves rather than live together with their former enemies, burning and looting as they left; in all their suburbs there was hardly a door frame left standing.

Grbavica, where the Serbs were closest to the heart of the city, was the last to be transferred. It was there, in the shell of his darkened and bullet-scarred home, that I shared a farewell coffee with Drazenko Djukanovic. Drazenko was a friend from earlier in the war. (I outraged some colleagues by having Serb friends, but was unrepentant about it.) He was a journalist who edited the local newspaper whenever ink and newsprint could be found for it. He was also one of the suburb's front-line commanders, twice wounded in its defence. (The mere notion of the Serbs' *defence* astonished the in-rushing journalists. 'Was this where the Serbs laid siege to the city?' one asked in a voice that simmered with excitement. 'Yes indeed,' I answered, '*and* it was where the Serbs defended themselves.')

Drazenko savoured the last cup of coffee that he would drink in his home town. He talked of the war and whether it was over, which he doubted. He seemed more shaken now than when he was hobbling about his trench lines on a stick.

'For me,' he said, 'this is the worst moment, even worse than when I was wounded by the Muslim snipers. How can I feel this peace when I must lose my town?'

He did not have the option of staying, since as a commander he would certainly have been considered a war criminal: the concept of honour among enemies was alien to all sides in the Bosnian war. The Serbs had not been defeated, in his view, but betrayed. They had won the war and lost the peace. This had been their fate for 600 years. Now they had done it again.

But there was no question of breaking the Dayton agreement. The Serbs, the most defiant of the peoples of Bosnia towards UNPROFOR, were now the most compliant towards IFOR.

Again it was the lesson that force prevailed. Just as it was the force of the Serbs that prevailed against the Muslims at the start of the war, and the force of the Croats that prevailed against the Serbs at the end of the war, so now it was the force of IFOR that commanded compliance – the tanks and artillery and enough staff officers to run a land war in Europe. These officers, mostly British, were based in the Hotel Serbia in Ilidza – the same hotel where we had set up our edit machines in April 1992, where I had harangued the estimable Colm Doyle, and from where we had been finally driven out by mortar fire. It was the place where I had started in the war and it seemed a good place to finish. But now this elegant spa hotel was hardly recognizable. Set about with barbed wire in the mud and slush of winter, it had all the cheerlessness of a NATO corps headquarters, which it was, and twice as many officers as it needed.

So many of them were assigned there with so little to do that they were eventually reduced to issuing an operational order about 'Action to be Taken in the Event of an Earthquake'. *And this in Bosnia*, where the only earth tremors that I had noticed were from the explosion of 500-pound aircraft bombs. IFOR's soldiers were gravely warned to look out for the signs and omens: birds circling at a great height, dogs behaving strangely and snakes coming out of the ground. This was done in all seriousness. I knew in that instant that I could never even think of becoming a fiction writer: with the world as it is and people as they are, so weird and extraordinary, no invented stories could hold a candle to the real ones.

IFOR's soldiers on the ground, with the exception of its bridge-building and mine-clearing engineers, were equally under-stretched. There were many other tasks that they could have been doing, but so great was the American concern and obsession with 'mission creep' that these were turned aside without much of a hearing. The ground forces commander, General Mike

Walker (a Royal Anglian, I noted, to his credit), held in reserve an all-purpose 'at our peril' speech which he dusted off and delivered on these occasions.

'At our peril,' he declared, 'does IFOR get involved in police work. At our peril do we join in the search for war criminals or the evidence of war crimes. At our peril do we deploy our soldiers to guard the sites of mass graves, probable or suspected.' He had in his office a map with 193 such sites marked on it.

And yet ... this was also the time when the unguarded ground of the killing fields began to give up its secrets. It was more than six months after the fall of Srebrenica and the disappearance there of between 3,000 and 5,000 men of military age (that is, between sixteen and sixty, though some were missing who were younger and some older). Much was feared about their fate, but very little was known. Now at last the ground unfroze and the evidence came to light. Investigators from the International Criminal Tribunal at the Hague, working with only distant IFOR protection, probed a dozen sites of executions and ambushes around the former enclave. A number of eyewitnesses came forward, including Mevludin Oric who astonishingly survived under a pile of corpses after a mass execution. And two of the executioners themselves, Drazen Erdemovic and Radoslav Kremanovic, volunteered to tell their story in Belgrade after a falling-out with a superior officer in the Bosnian Serb army. They told of their part in a firing squad which worked all day on or about 16 July 1995 to kill 1,000 Muslim prisoners, systematically and in cold blood, at Banjevo Farm north of Zvornik. Many who did not die immediately pleaded with their executioners for the mercy of being put out of their pain. One soldier alone finished off 700 of the victims with a handgun shot to the head.

To me this testimony read like the text of a nightmare, the written equivalent of some of the television footage that we had censored out from the bombings of Sarajevo. It was hard to read – and harder still to reflect on – that such things had not only been done, but been done in a country where 34,000 United Nations troops were still on a mission to protect the people, and in a part of that country to which their mandate most specifically applied. It was as if we had learned nothing and forgotten everything since the start of the conflict. The executions around Srebrenica were the biggest single atrocity of the war, and the greatest war crime committed in Europe since 1945. As the War Crimes Tribunal described them, 'These were truly scenes from hell, written on the darkest pages of human history.'

Moreover, and as the United Nations must have known, the killings were predictable if not inevitable. Whatever the written agreements that were reached, it was always unlikely that the Serbs would exchange or release these thousands of prisoners. They held the Muslims of Srebrenica collectively responsible for a series of killings in the area, culminating in the massacre of fifty Serbs near Bratunac on 7 January 1993, the Orthodox Christmas Day. (It was the footage of this which I had included in my *Panorama* programme and which had so much provoked the ire of Mr Simon Jenkins in *The Times*.) The Serbs then waited two and a half years for revenge: there was no place in Bosnia and no point in the war where the Geneva Conventions were less likely to be observed. Anyone familiar with Eastern Bosnia would know this.

I am in controversial territory here. But it seemed to me then, and still does, that the trail of culpability for Srebrenica leads – as with the earlier genocide in Europe – not only to those who made it happen but also to those who *let it happen*. (Remember Elie Wiesel's point about indifference: 'Indifference is a sin and a punishment.') And it connects directly with the wider issues that I have raised, and which are not much publicly debated, of what risks and casualties we are willing to take in the cause of peace, and whether our foreign policy should be based only on a calculation of national interest. (I have even heard it argued that what happened in Yugoslavia was of no real consequence to us because we never exported much there except tourists.)

On a strict calculation of national interest Srebrenica was none of our business. It did not touch our security, our prosperity or any of the usual political and electoral nerve-endings. It was not the business of any of the countries of the European Union except Holland; and it was the national interest of the Dutch to extricate their soldiers as quickly as possible and at whatever cost, which is what they did. But if you put history into fast rewind, and follow this argument back over fifty years, you will see its destination with chilling clarity. Was Buchenwald none of our business? Was Belsen none of our business? Were Auschwitz and Birkenau none of our business? The case collapses under the weight of history, and of its own invidiousness.

I do not normally write like this. I do not normally *feel* like this. I realized that I was getting angry and it was time to leave. Over the Bosnian years I had felt a whole range of emotions – fear, horror, dismay, sadness, even sometimes hope and exhilaration – but never before such anger; and anger doesn't consort with useful journalism. Indignation is different. Indignation can help a journalist kick down the doors behind which the truth lies hidden. But anger ensnares him. Anger blinds the mind and skews the judgement.

There were other and coincident reasons for leaving Bosnia behind. For five years I had reported nothing but wars; but during this period I had earned the dubious distinction of being the BBC reporter most shot at, and it was time to hand this over to someone younger. I was well on the wrong side of fifty-five. The joints creaked under the weight of the body armour, so heavy that even the soldiers were astonished by it; the life-saving turn of speed across open ground was not as fast as it used to be; and the fifteen-mile hike with backpack through enemy lines (even if it was wise, which I always doubted) would have tested my endurance to the limit.

Twice before in my life I had vowed to soldier no more. The first time was when I was twenty and leaving the Suffolk Regiment. The second time was when I was fifty-two and leaving the Gulf. This time I promised to make no promises, even to myself. I wished only to diversify – perhaps the trench lines from time to time, because that was what I was known for, but I sought other challenges too. I wrote a piece for *The Times* which was little more than a thousand-word job application, even angling for a place on the BBC's team to cover the next election. I argued that since elections were regularly conducted in the metaphors of warfare – the very idea of a *campaign* is strictly military – why not go all the way and hire a real war reporter to do the business? The clash of soundbites and skirmishing of spin-doctors would offer the excitement of combat with none of the danger.

This proposal was met with the silence that it doubtless deserved. I realized then that a journalist could be typecast just as much as an actor. Expectations prevailed. Chronicling the conflicts and commotions of the world would continue to be what I did for a living, because it was all that I had ever done that anyone had noticed. (No one ever said, weren't you the one who reported on Princess Diana in Canada entirely in rhyming couplets?) So the alternative to the war zones would be . . . more war zones.

My plans for a lingering farewell to Bosnia were brought to an abrupt and tragic end by the death of the American Commerce Secretary, Ron Brown, in an air crash near Dubrovnik in Croatia. We left at midnight in a great hurry, driving south and west through broken villages and the fiercest of Balkan storms. The roads and rivers, as so often in Bosnia, seemed confused

about which was which. I concentrated on distinguishing between them, but with an inner eye on the times I had been
through and on the friends I had left behind: Tuna who had
been killed by the Serbs, Brian Hulls who had just died of
cancer, and many others who had no memorial. I thought also
of those wonderful old soldiers of the Suffolk Regiment, of the
peace in Europe which they had fought for and which had
prevailed until these wars, and of how we should have to
continue to fight for it in one way or another – or at least not to
take it for granted; for if we take it for granted we shall surely
lose it. I knew that the wars had changed me, I hoped for the
better, but could never really be sure.

On returning home some days later I found a bottle of
champagne waiting for me and a message with it. The message
said: 'Another war over. Here's to the next one.' And then they
measured me up for a new flak jacket.

READ MORE IN PENGUIN

In every corner of the world, on every subject under the sun, Penguin represents quality and variety – the very best in publishing today.

For complete information about books available from Penguin – including Puffins, Penguin Classics and Arkana – and how to order them, write to us at the appropriate address below. Please note that for copyright reasons the selection of books varies from country to country.

In the United Kingdom: Please write to *Dept. EP, Penguin Books Ltd, Bath Road, Harmondsworth, West Drayton, Middlesex UB7 ODA*

In the United States: Please write to *Consumer Sales, Penguin USA, P.O. Box 999, Dept. 17109, Bergenfield, New Jersey 07621-0120.* VISA and MasterCard holders call 1-800-253-6476 to order Penguin titles

In Canada: Please write to *Penguin Books Canada Ltd, 10 Alcorn Avenue, Suite 300, Toronto, Ontario M4V 3B2*

In Australia: Please write to *Penguin Books Australia Ltd, P.O. Box 257, Ringwood, Victoria 3134*

In New Zealand: Please write to *Penguin Books (NZ) Ltd, Private Bag 102902, North Shore Mail Centre, Auckland 10*

In India: Please write to *Penguin Books India Pvt Ltd, 706 Eros Apartments, 56 Nehru Place, New Delhi 110 019*

In the Netherlands: Please write to *Penguin Books Netherlands bv, Postbus 3507, NL-1001 AH Amsterdam*

In Germany: Please write to *Penguin Books Deutschland GmbH, Metzlerstrasse 26, 60594 Frankfurt am Main*

In Spain: Please write to *Penguin Books S. A., Bravo Murillo 19, 1° B, 28015 Madrid*

In Italy: Please write to *Penguin Italia s.r.l., Via Felice Casati 20, I–20124 Milano*

In France: Please write to *Penguin France S. A., 17 rue Lejeune, F–31000 Toulouse*

In Japan: Please write to *Penguin Books Japan, Ishikiribashi Building, 2–5–4, Suido, Bunkyo-ku, Tokyo 112*

In Greece: Please write to *Penguin Hellas Ltd, Dimocritou 3, GR–106 71 Athens*

In South Africa: Please write to *Longman Penguin Southern Africa (Pty) Ltd, Private Bag X08, Bertsham 2013*

READ MORE IN PENGUIN

HISTORY

The Making of Europe   Robert Bartlett

'Bartlett does more than anyone before him to bring out the way in which medieval Europe was shaped by [a] great wave of internal conquest, colonization and evangelization. He also stresses its consequences for the future history of the world' – *Guardian*

The Somme Battlefields   Martin and Mary Middlebrook

This evocative, original book provides a definitive guide to the cemeteries, memorials and battlefields from the age of Crécy and Agincourt to the great Allied sweep which drove the Germans back in 1944, concentrating above all on the scenes of ferocious fighting in 1916 and 1918.

Ancient Slavery and Modern Ideology   M. I. Finley

Few topics in the study of classical civilization could be more central – and more controversial – than slavery. In this magnificent book, M. I. Finley cuts through the thickets of modern ideology to get at the essential facts. 'A major creative achievement in historical interpretation' – *The Times Higher Education Supplement*

The Penguin History of Greece   A. R. Burn

Readable, erudite, enthusiastic and balanced, this one-volume history of Hellas sweeps the reader along from the days of Mycenae and the splendours of Athens to the conquests of Alexander and the final dark decades.

The Laurel and the Ivy   Robert Kee

'Parnell continues to haunt the Irish historical imagination a century after his death ... Robert Kee's patient and delicate probing enables him to reconstruct the workings of that elusive mind as persuasively, or at least as plausibly, as seems possible ... This splendid biography, which is as readable as it is rigorous, greatly enhances our understanding of both Parnell, and of the Ireland of his time' – *The Times Literary Supplement*

READ MORE IN PENGUIN

HISTORY

Citizens Simon Schama

The award-winning chronicle of the French Revolution. 'The most marvellous book I have read about the French Revolution in the last fifty years' – Richard Cobb in *The Times*

To the Finland Station Edmund Wilson

In this authoritative work Edmund Wilson, considered by many to be America's greatest twentieth-century critic, turns his attention to Europe's revolutionary traditions, tracing the roots of nationalism, socialism and Marxism as these movements spread across the Continent creating unrest, revolt and widespread social change.

The Tyranny of History W. J. F. Jenner

A fifth of the world's population lives within the boundaries of China, a vast empire barely under the control of the repressive ruling Communist regime. Beneath the economic boom China is in a state of crisis that goes far deeper than the problems of its current leaders to a value system that is rooted in the autocratic traditions of China's past.

The English Bible and the Seventeenth-Century Revolution
Christopher Hill

'What caused the English civil war? What brought Charles I to the scaffold?' Answer to both questions: the Bible. To sustain this provocative thesis, Christopher Hill's new book maps English intellectual history from the Reformation to 1660, showing how scripture dominated every department of thought from sexual relations to political theory ... 'His erudition is staggering' – *Sunday Times*

Private Lives, Public Spirit: Britain 1870–1914 Jose Harris

'Provides the most convincing – and demanding – synthesis yet available of these crowded and tumultuous years' – *Observer* Books of the Year. 'Remarkable ... it locates the origins of far-reaching social change as far back as the 1880s [and] goes on to challenge most of the popular assumptions made about the Victorian and Edwardian periods' – *Literary Review*

READ MORE IN PENGUIN

A CHOICE OF NON-FICTION

Time Out Film Guide   Edited by John Pym

The definitive, up-to-the-minute directory of every aspect of world cinema from classics and silent epics to reissues and the latest releases.

Flames in the Field   Rita Kramer

During July 1944, four women agents met their deaths at Struthof-Natzweiler concentration camp at the hands of the SS. They were members of the Special Operations Executive, sent to Nazi-occupied France in 1943. *Flames in the Field* reveals that the odds against their survival were weighted even more heavily than they could possibly have contemplated, for their network was penetrated by double agents and security was dangerously lax.

Colored People   Henry Louis Gates Jr.

'A wittily drawn portrait of a semi-rural American community, in the years when racial segregation was first coming under legal challenge ... In the most beautiful English ... he recreates a past to which, in every imaginable sense, there is no going back' – *Mail on Sunday*

Naturalist   Edward O. Wilson

'His extraordinary drive, encyclopaedic knowledge and insatiable curiosity shine through on virtually every page' – *Sunday Telegraph*. 'There are wonderful accounts of his adventures with snakes, a gigantic ray, butterflies, flies and, of course, ants ... a fascinating insight into a great mind' – *Guardian*

Roots Schmoots   Howard Jacobson

'This is no exercise in sentimental journeys. Jacobson writes with a rare wit and the book sparkles with his gritty humour ... he displays a deliciously caustic edge in his analysis of what is wrong, and right, with modern Jewry' – *Mail on Sunday*

READ MORE IN PENGUIN

A CHOICE OF NON-FICTION

Mornings in the Dark   Edited by David Parkinson
The Graham Greene Film Reader

Prompted by 'a sense of fun' and 'that dangerous third Martini' at a party in June 1935, Graham Greene volunteered himself as the *Spectator* film critic. 'His film reviews are among the most trenchant, witty and memorable one is ever likely to read' – *Sunday Times*

Real Lives, Half Lives   Jeremy Hall

The world has been 'radioactive' for a hundred years – providing countless benefits to medicine and science – but there is a downside to the human mastery of nuclear physics. *Real Lives, Half Lives* uncovers the bizarre and secret stories of people who have been exposed, in one way or another, to radioactivity across the world.

Hidden Lives   Margaret Forster

'A memoir of Forster's grandmother and mother which reflects on the changes in women's lives – about sex, family, work – across three generations. It is a moving, evocative account, passionate in its belief in progress, punchy as a detective novel in its story of Forster's search for her grandmother's illegitimate daughter. It also shows how biography can challenge our basic assumptions about which lives have been significant and why' – *Financial Times*

Eating Children   Jill Tweedie

'Jill Tweedie re-creates in fascinating detail the scenes and conditions that shaped her, scarred her, broke her up or put her back together ... a remarkable story' – *Vogue*. 'A beautiful and courageous book' – Maya Angelou

The Lost Heart of Asia   Colin Thubron

'Thubron's journey takes him through a spectacular, talismanic geography of desert and mountain ... a whole glittering, terrible and romantic history lies abandoned along with thoughts of more prosperous times' – *The Times*

READ MORE IN PENGUIN

A CHOICE OF NON-FICTION

African Nights Kuki Gallmann

Through a tapestry of interwoven true episodes, Kuki Gallmann here evokes the magic that touches all African life. The adventure of a moonlit picnic on a vanishing island; her son's entrancement with chameleons and the mystical visit of a king cobra to his grave; the mysterious compassion of an elephant herd – each event conveys her delight and wonder at the whole fabric of creation.

Far Flung Floyd Keith Floyd

Keith Floyd's culinary odyssey takes him to the far-flung East and the exotic flavours of Malaysia, Hong Kong, Vietnam and Thailand. The irrepressible Floyd as usual spices his recipes with witty stories, wry observation and a generous pinch of gastronomic wisdom.

The Reading Solution Paul Kropp with Wendy Cooling

The Reading Solution makes excellent suggestions for books – both fiction and non-fiction – for readers of all ages that will stimulate a love of reading. Listing hugely enjoyable books from history and humour to thrillers and poetry selections, *The Reading Solution* provides all the help you need to ensure that your child becomes – and stays – a willing, enthusiastic reader.

Lucie Duff Gordon Katherine Frank
A Passage to Egypt

'Lucie Duff Gordon's life is a rich field for a biographer, and Katherine Frank does her justice ... what stays in the mind is a portrait of an exceptional woman, funny, wry, occasionally flamboyant, always generous-spirited, and firmly rooted in the social history of her day' – *The Times Literary Supplement*

The Missing of the Somme Geoff Dyer

'A gentle, patient, loving book. It is about mourning and memory, about how the Great War has been represented – and our sense of it shaped and defined – by different artistic media ... its textures are the very rhythms of memory and consciousness' – *Guardian*

READ MORE IN PENGUIN

A CHOICE OF NON-FICTION

The Pillars of Hercules Paul Theroux

At the gateway to the Mediterranean lie the two Pillars of Hercules. Beginning his journey in Gibraltar, Paul Theroux travels the long way round – through the ravaged developments of the Costa del Sol, into Corsica and Sicily and beyond – to Morocco's southern pillar. 'A terrific book, full of fun as well as anxiety, of vivid characters and curious experiences' – *The Times*

Where the Girls Are Susan J. Douglas

In this brilliantly researched and hugely entertaining examination of women and popular culture, Susan J. Douglas demonstrates the ways in which music, TV, books, advertising, news and film have affected women of her generation. Essential reading for cultural critics, feminists and everyone else who has ever ironed their hair or worn a miniskirt.

Journals: 1954–1958 Allen Ginsberg

These pages open with Ginsberg at the age of twenty-eight, penniless, travelling alone and unknown in California. Yet, by July 1958 he was returning from Paris to New York as the poet who, with Jack Kerouac, led and inspired the Beats . . .

The New Spaniards John Hooper

Spain has become a land of extraordinary paradoxes in which traditional attitudes and contemporary preoccupations exist side by side. The country attracts millions of visitors – yet few see beyond the hotels and resorts of its coastline. John Hooper's fascinating study brings to life the many faces of Spain in the 1990s.

A Tuscan Childhood Kinta Beevor

Kinta Beevor was five when she fell in love with her parents' castle facing the Carrara mountains. 'The descriptions of the harvesting and preparation of food and wine by the locals could not be bettered . . . alive with vivid characters' – *Observer*

READ MORE IN PENGUIN

A CHOICE OF NON-FICTION

Fisher's Face   Jan Morris

Admiral of the Fleet Lord 'Jacky' Fisher (1841–1920) was one of the greatest naval reformers in history. 'An intimate recreation of the man in all his extraordinary complexity, his mercurial humours, his ferocious energy and bloodthirstiness, his childlike innocence, his Machiavellian charm' – *Daily Mail*

Mrs Jordan's Profession   Claire Tomalin

The story of Dora Jordan and her relationship with the Duke of Clarence, later King William IV. 'Meticulous biography at its creative best' – *Observer*. 'A fascinating and affecting story, one in which the mutually attractive, mutually suspicious, equally glittering worlds of court and theatre meet, and one which vividly illustrates the social codes of pre-Victorian Britain' – *Sunday Times*

John Major: From Brixton to Downing Street   Penny Junor

Within a year of a record-breaking general election victory, John Major became the most unpopular Prime Minister ever. With his party deeply divided and his government lurching from crisis to crisis, few thought he could survive. This absorbing biography uses interviews with family, friends, foes, Cabinet colleagues and the Prime Minister himself to uncover the real John Major.

The Bondage of Fear   Fergal Keane

'An important source for anyone trying to understand how South Africa achieved its transfer of power' – *Independent*. 'A first-class journalistic account ... likely to be the most memorable account of this terrible, uplifting time' – *Literary Review*

The Oxbridge Conspiracy   Walter Ellis

'A brave book that needed to be written ... Oxbridge imparts to our élite values which, in their anti-commerce, anti-technology, anti-market snobbery, make them unfit to run a modern economy. It is the Oxbridge élite which has presided over the decline of this nation' – *Financial Times*

READ MORE IN PENGUIN

A CHOICE OF NON-FICTION

Thesiger Michael Asher

'Compiled from lengthy interviews with the man himself, meticulous pilgrimages over the same ground, and conversations with his surviving travelling companions, the book both celebrates Thesiger and incorporates what you might call the case against' – *Guardian*

Nelson: A Personal History Christopher Hibbert

'Impeccably researched and written with Christopher Hibbert's habitual elegance of style, this is a fine biography of a figure genuinely larger than life' – *Sunday Telegraph*

The History of the Ginger Man J. P. Donleavy

Combining literary history with autobiography, this is the dramatic story of J. P. Donleavy's struggle to create and publish his contemporary classic *The Ginger Man*. 'An endearingly revealing book ... vintage Donleavy' – *Observer*

Ireland and the Irish John Ardagh

'He has conducted dozens of interviews in all the provinces of the island, with schoolmasters, poets, nuns, bishops, businessmen, farmers large and small, and anyone else, it seems, in any walk of life, who might have anything to say' – *The Times*. 'This scholarly, balanced and compassionate book ought to be read by every British politician – every British citizen, for that matter' – Jan Morris

South of Haunted Dreams Eddy L. Harris

In the southern United States, there is an imaginary line – the Mason-Dixon line – that once marked the boundary of the almost unimaginable institution of slavery. Lost behind it is the history of almost every black American. 'Harris went out looking for the face and mind of white racism. What he found wasn't what he expected – at least, not exactly. Harris finds his own very real, and contradictory, history on the highways of the American South' – *Washington Post Book World*

READ MORE IN PENGUIN

BIOGRAPHY AND AUTOBIOGRAPHY

Freedom from Fear Aung San Suu Kyi

Aung San Suu Kyi, human-rights activist and leader of Burma's National League for Democracy, was detained in 1989 by SLORC, the ruling military junta. In July 1995 she was liberated from six years' house arrest. *Freedom From Fear* contains speeches, letters and interviews, as well as forewords by Archbishop Desmond Tutu and Václav Havel and gives a voice to Burma's 'woman of destiny'.

Memories of a Catholic Girlhood Mary McCarthy

'Many a time in the course of doing these memoirs,' Mary McCarthy says, 'I have wished that I were writing fiction.' 'Superb . . . so heartbreaking that in comparison Jane Eyre seems to have got off lightly' – *Spectator*

A Short Walk from Harrods Dirk Bogarde

In this volume of memoirs, Dirk Bogarde pays tribute to the corner of Provence that was his home for over two decades, and to Forwood, his manager and friend of fifty years, whose long and wretched illness brought an end to a paradise. 'A brave and moving book' – *Daily Telegraph*

When Shrimps Learn to Whistle Denis Healey

The Time of My Life was widely acclaimed as a masterpiece. Taking up the most powerful political themes that emerge from it Denis Healey now gives us this stimulating companion volume. 'Forty-three years of ruminations . . . by the greatest foreign secretary we never had' – *New Statesman & Society*

Eating Children Jill Tweedie

Jill Tweedie's second memoir, *Frightening People*, incomplete due to her tragically early death in 1993, is published here for the first time. 'Magnificent . . . with wit, without a shred of self-pity, she tells the story of an unhappy middle-class suburban child with a monstrously cruel father, and a hopeless mother' – *Guardian*